Policy Implications of Research in Education

Scope of the Series

In education, as in other fields, there are often significant gaps between research knowledge and current policy and practice. While there are many reasons for this gap, one that stands out is that policy-makers and practitioners may simply not know about important research findings because these findings are not published in forums aimed at them.

Policy Implications of Research in Education aims to clearly and comprehensively present the implications for education policy and practice drawn from important lines of current education research in a manner that is accessible and useful for policy-makers, educational authorities and practitioners.

More information about this series at http://www.springer.com/series/11212

Susan Ledger • Lesley Vidovich • Tom O'Donoghue

Global to Local Curriculum Policy Processes

The Enactment of the International Baccalaureate in Remote International Schools

 Springer

Susan Ledger
School of Education
Murdoch University
Perth, Australia

Lesley Vidovich
Tom O'Donoghue
Graduate School of Education
The University of Western Australia
Crawley, Australia

ISBN 978-3-319-08761-0   ISBN 978-3-319-08762-7 (eBook)
DOI 10.1007/978-3-319-08762-7
Springer Cham Heidelberg New York Dordrecht London

Library of Congress Control Number: 2014947101

Printed on acid-free paper

Springer is part of Springer Science+Business Media (www.springer.com)

Contents

Chapter 1
Introduction

1.1 The Issue

Given the exponential growth of international schools caused by an ever changing globalized world and a mobile workforce, international curriculum policy is becoming more complex. A realisation of this situation leads on to recognising the need for a range of policy analysis studies in the field. The study reported in this book was conceptualized in the light of such recognition. It was concerned with exploring the dynamics of curriculum policy processes involved in the adoption, production and enactment of one of the programmes accredited by the International Baccalaureate Organization (IBO). The programme in question is the International Baccalaureate Primary Years Programme (IBPYP), one of the four programmes that go to make up the increasingly popular suite of programmes offered by the IBO.

It was recognized from the outset that the study could have been conducted across a wide variety of settings. It was decided, however, that one of the most productive ways to explore such a relatively unexplored field would be by focusing on one of the most 'unusual' settings in which the situation is manifested. Accordingly, when the opportunity presented itself to study the adoption, production and enactment of the IBPYO at three remote international schools in Indonesia, it was readily embraced.

The study was also inspired by our curiosity about how the phenomena of 'international schools' and 'remote schools' complement, or compete with, each other. In particular, we were motivated to undertake it as a result of our experiences in teaching and delivering professional development in a wide range of international settings, coupled with the role of the first-named author as an IBPYP coordinator in an international school. In summary, we wanted to gain a better understanding of the educational policies informing curriculum policy in both 'international schools' and 'remote schools', and the interconnectivity that might exist between them.

© Springer International Publishing Switzerland 2014
S. Ledger et al., *Global to Local Curriculum Policy Processes*,
Policy Implications of Research in Education 4, DOI 10.1007/978-3-319-08762-7_1

Much has been written about international schools (see Bates 2011b; Hayden and Thompson 2011; Levy 2007; Rizvi 2007; Skelton 2007; Snowball 2007; Sylvester 2007). However, there is only a small corpus of studies that analyse curriculum policy for such schools (Bagnall 2008; Cambridge 2011; Wylie 2011). Even less has been written about curriculum policy relating to international schools in Indonesia (Heyward 2002; Heyward et al. 2011), while there appear to be no studies whatsoever that have analysed international school policy and associated micropolitics in remote settings in Indonesia. The research project reported in this book sought to address the latter deficits, and to understand the complexities involved within a framework that would take cognisance of the relationships between global, regional, national and local levels of education policy processes. In doing so, it contributes to the current body of research on international education, remote education, and policy processes. The location of the study at the intersection of these three fields of research makes it unique.

The literature reviewed for the study which is at the heart of this book is detailed in a later chapter. Within that chapter, particular attention is given to explicating relevant concepts. However, a brief definition of a number of them is offered at this point as initial signposts for the reader. The definition of an 'international school' used in the study is one of a school that offers a curriculum that differs from that of the host country and identifies itself as 'being international'. An 'international teacher' is one who is employed within a school that identifies itself as being 'international' (Hayden 2007). The International Baccalaureate Primary Years Programme (IBPYP) refers to the particular programme developed by the IBO for students in the primary years and which is outlined in terms of its ideology, underlying beliefs, mission, values, paedagogy, and required resources (Hill 2007). 'Internationalization' relates to "the worldwide discussions, processes, and institutions affecting local educational practices and policies" (Spring 2009, p. 1) across state, national and international borders. Finally, 'globalization' is defined as an "outcome of various structural processes that manifest in different ways" and "produce entrenched and enduring patterns of worldwide interconnectedness" (Rizvi and Lingard 2010, p. 24).

The remainder of this chapter presents an overview of the book. It is divided into three main sections. The first section outlines the conceptualization of policy and policy analysis that underpins the study. The second section focuses on the particular matter of curriculum and curriculum policy. The third section details the research approach adopted for the study. It considers how the study was conceptualized and designed, the nature of the research questions, the nature of associated informing theories, and the nature of the research methods employed.

1.2 Policy and Policy Analysis

The position on policy adopted in this book is informed by Ball's (1994a, p. 10) seminal definition that it "is both text and action, words and deeds. It is what is enacted as well as what is intended". Our position is also informed by Rizvi and

Lingard's (2010, p. 14) view that policy "is multi-dimensional and multi-layered and occurs at multiple sites". Also, in terms of 'policy analysis', what we report is consistent with Ozga's (2001) and Ham and Hill's (1993) notion of an analysis 'of' policy, rather than with the notion of an analysis 'for' policy.

The conceptualization of policy has moved from linear to cyclic and from product to process. The historical changes and changing views related to the analysis of policy processes represent the dynamic nature of policy itself (Allen 2002). Recent approaches explore policy processes through anthropological, archaeological and ecological perspectives (Scheurich 2000; Wedel and Feldman 2005; Winter 2012). It has been argued that the policy studies field is artificially constructed, full of complexities, dynamic in nature, imbued with values and competing interests, and ultimately difficult to define (Elmore and Sykes 1992). Taylor (2003, p. 25) encapsulated such a view when she argued that policy processes are "complex, interactive and multi-layered". Similarly, in relation to education policy, Ball (1990, 2006) referred to the 'messy realities' of policy complexities, whilst Vidovich (2002, 2007) commented on the 'multiplicities and interrelatedness' of policy processes. Education policy has also been described as a "human creation that is closer to art than science" (Jallade et al. 2001) and as being subjective in nature and interpretation. Boyd (1999, p. 227) argues further, claiming that anyone trying to make sense of policy research in education is "likely to be struck by the numerous contradictions and paradoxes that perplex the field".

1.2.1 Methods Used to Analyze Policy

Just as the concept of policy has evolved over time, so too have the methods used to analyse policy. The re-conceptualization of policy has moved from policy as a product to policy as a process and, more recently, to policy viewed through a social imaginary lens (Rizvi and Lingard 2006). Models of educational policy have tried to include methods of documenting the processes involved in developing policy, or policy-making, across the trajectory (Bowe et al. 1992). Also, frameworks have been developed to identify and explain the gap between policy formulation and policy realization (Ball 1994a; Rizvi and Lingard 2010; Vidovich 2007, 2013). These conceptualizations and models can all help in uncovering the complexity of the policy process.

In the mid-1960s, Dahllof (1969) introduced the frame-factor theory, arguing that it is necessary to take the processes that lead to a certain policy result in education into consideration in any analysis. Dahllof also found that these processes were governed and restricted by certain frames, including time at the disposal of policy actors, available textbooks, and rule and goal systems. Although the frame factor theory was rooted in the positivist tradition, it carried the seed for a paradigm shift because it undermined long-standing explanations of educational policy and the enactment of policy, pointing towards new possibilities. Also, by the mid-1980s, the role of teachers in policy processes came to be considered more important than in previous decades.

In the early 1990s, the adoption of critical sociological theories of education led to a questioning of how the policy frames were constituted, and re-conceptualists mounted a strong attack on the dominant positivist paradigm. The re-conceptualists presumed that the content and practice of schooling reproduced hegemonic ideology and existing social order. During this time, policy in education was regarded as not only being the result of political compromises, but also as being influenced by power and special interests of particular stakeholders, including teachers. The assumption behind this view was the need to identify the power differential between key stakeholders in policy construction and enactment.

The exercise of power by key stakeholders was noted within Ball's (1990) policy analysis framework and was further developed by Vidovich (2007) and Rizvi and Lingard (2010). Also, Foucault's concept of power began to inform the work of education policy analysts from the 1990s, particularly forged by the work of Ball (1994a, b). This approach was significant in emphasizing the 'messiness' of policy processes in schools.

Zajda (2005) has outlined the emergence of three major paradigm shifts in the field over the past three decades. The first shift was from the linear approach to educational planning and policy reforms, to step planning models and human capital theory of the 1960–1970s. This meant that policy direction and reform moved to a more holistic approach. The second major paradigm shift, from positivism to anti-positivism research, was in the 1970s and 1980s. This Mitter (1997) described as involving the postmodernist revolt. The third policy paradigm shift was described as a "re-statement of egalitarian inspired imperative and equality for all" (Zajda 2005, pp. 1–2).

Currently, a trend toward a more eclectic approach to policy and policy analysis is developing. It includes elements from previous paradigms, such as the frame factor theories (1960–1970s), process model theories (1980s–1990s) and the egalitarian imperatives of the 'global citizen', or 'internationally-minded student' approaches (1990–2010). This trend highlights the interrelatedness and complexities of education policy-making, and there is a use of globalization's 'small world' notion as a metaphor to emphasise global interconnectivity. It also includes Green's (2009) suggestion that 'time and place matter' in policy construction and enactment. Overall, this new approach to policy encompasses multiplicity and 'hybridity' (Rizvi and Lingard 2010; Vidovich 2007; Zhao 2010), rather than homogeneity and normalization. It reflects the proliferation of difference accompanying globalization (Pinar 2003) and the multifaceted nature of policy as a field of study.

1.2.2   Policy Trajectory Studies

The concept of a 'policy trajectory' informed the study outlined later in this book as it captures the multi-levelled nature of policy in a globalized world (Ball 1994a, 2006; Rizvi and Lingard 2010; Vidovich 2007). This is to subscribe to Ball's (1994a, p. 10) notion that "policies are always incomplete in so far as they relate to, or map onto, the 'wild profusion of local practice'". The situation is also complicated currently by the renewed focus on exploring policy as practice at the local (micro) level that 'removes policy from its pedestal' (Ozga 2001; Vidovich 2007) and recognizes the importance of 'local place' (Green 2008). Also, a more critical perspective on the policy process can emerge when policy development and enactment are contextualized in global, national and local terms (Marginson and Rhoades 2002), as well as in both space and time.

The notion of contextualizing the policy process and policy makers in education at a given 'place and space' emerged in the 1990s (Fitz 1994; Ozga 2001) and has been developed more recently, with policy makers and local settings being considered as being at the heart of policy processes. In other words, the structure of an organization and the personnel involved in the policy environment are deemed to be important in any policy analysis. It means that one needs to recognize that, at the local level, enacting education policy falls directly into the hands of school teachers and principals and is driven by the priorities, constraints and climate set by these policy players and the environment that surrounds them. It also means that, no matter what technologies, resources, or supports are provided, education policy only becomes a reality when teachers enact it (Ornstein and Hunkins 2004).

It is also important to recognize that, no matter how well designed and executed, policy can never be value free. This is because competing values and interests embedded in educational policy are "value laden and debatable and many aspects have far reaching implications for the distribution of opportunity, social justice, and the shape and character of future society" (Boyd 1999, p. 239). On this, Currie (2004) likens policy to the concept of globalization, in that both cannot be considered neutral terms. Rather, they are embedded with political and economic ideologies. The competing values and interests endemic in educational policy-making inform policy initiation, production and enactment (Bates 2011a; Rizvi and Lingard 2010; Vidovich 2007).

A consideration of the ambiguous and contested nature of education policy goes some way toward explaining the frequency of contradictions in the area. Contemporary trends in policy research have acknowledged the significant role of technology in the globalization and internationalization of policy (Walsh 2007). Thus, policy definitions and conceptualizations have changed over time. One conclusion that could be drawn is that no matter what form policies take, they are ultimately "designed to ensure consistency in the application of authorized norms and values across various groups and communities; they are designed to build consent, and may also have an educative purpose" (Rizvi and Lingard 2010, pp. 8–9).

Ball's (1994a, 2006) conceptualization of the policy trajectory as a framework for analysis, already referred to, is one of the most all-encompassing available as it recognizes the multi-layered and value-laden nature of policy. He separates the contexts heuristically into the contexts of influences, policy text production, practices, outcomes and political strategies, to capture the embedded biases and contextual differences inherent within policy processes. Other conceptualizations of policy as a policy trajectory (Rizvi and Lingard 2010; Vidovich 2007) build on

Ball's notion of contexts (although collapsing political strategies into outcomes), and capture the multi-level aspect of the policy process across global, national and local levels.

1.3   Curriculum and Curriculum Policy

Policy drives curriculum and curriculum reflects, interprets and informs policy; the two have a symbiotic relationship full of complexity and connections. Rosenholtz (1989, p. 175) recognized this close connection and drew the conclusion that "whatever impact educational policy has on school success is significantly affected by the quality of linkages between policy, the curriculum, and the intended beneficiaries of policy – the teachers and students". As 'beneficiaries', teachers carry the message of curriculum to students and school communities. This makes them powerful players in the curriculum policy process (Yates and Grumet 2011). In an ever-changing world, curriculum is being continually reconfigured, critiqued and defined.

Traditionally curriculum has been locally, or nationally, organized. In recent times, however, it has become heavily permeated by global movements and issues, and has been influenced by international bodies and by practices in various countries (Yates and Grummet 2011). Accordingly, it is appropriate that brief attention be paid to various perspectives on curriculum and curriculum policy, connections between curriculum policy and globalization, and the marketization of curriculum policy.

1.3.1   Perspectives on Curriculum and Curriculum Policy

Curriculum, like policy, is a social field of study. On this, Grundy (1987) has highlighted its social construction. Also, since the 1960s, the 'cultural construction' of curriculum policy has changed. Initially, a general argument was that curriculum consists of the actual learning opportunities provided at a given time and place. Later, Pinar (2004) conceptualized curriculum as a lived experience involving the quality of relationships within the school and the values embodied in the way the school operates, in addition to lesson content and extracurricular activities. Schubert's (2008) conceptualization of curriculum goes further, capturing the breadth and scope of curriculum in the twenty-first century by separating it into eight areas: the intended curriculum, the taught curriculum, the experienced curriculum, the embodied curriculum, the hidden curriculum, the tested curriculum, the null curriculum, and the outside curriculum. Most recently, Cambridge (2011, p. 142) has highlighted the role of education in the reproduction of societal culture, where "the construction of a curriculum requires the selection, sequencing and pacing of content". This view highlights the subjectivity involved in curriculum design. Other definitions also exist, like those of Yates and Grumet (2011) who suggest that curriculum should be about participation in the world and the identification of 'what matters' in the world. In addition, these theorists acknowledge that deciding what is important for the next generation is always going to be hotly contested and subjective.

Notwithstanding considerations so far, the search for a single definition of curriculum is probably futile in a globalized world. Instead of defining curriculum, Grundy (1987) searched for a meta-foundation for the structuring of curriculum. She based her research on Habermas' (1972) theory of knowledge-constitutive interests and used it to provide a coherent theoretical foundation for the work of curriculum deliberation and practice. Carr and Kemmis (1986) went on to provide insights into the application of this theory.

Robitaille (1993) identified three components of curriculum, namely, the designed, the taught, and the learned. Taking a different approach, Boyer (1994) re-conceptualized curriculum into core commonalities and universal experiences that transcend a discipline- based curriculum. Components of both Robitaille's (1993) curriculum design and Boyer's (1994, 1996) commonalities can be seen in the curriculum structure of the IBPYP developed in 1996, the International Primary Curriculum established in 2000, and contemporary national curricula in the UK and Australia. Yates and Grumet (2011, p. 247), echoing the globalized trends in these curricula, challenge us to "construct curricula that acknowledge tension and ambiguity, and encourage young people to see themselves and each other as persons capable of thinking and acting in this complicated place and time".

The various perspectives on curriculum considered above are inherently linked to curriculum policy. On this, Yates (2011) considers curriculum policy as being embodied in policy texts and overarching curriculum policy frameworks. At the same time, it is important to keep in mind that curriculum policy is often influenced by local, national and global forces and agendas, and is translated by policy actors at each level.

1.3.2 Globalization and Curriculum Policy

The ease of global policy transference and adaption, coupled with the flow of curriculum policy structure and design, is representative of the interconnectivity and transnational nature of curriculum policy. This has been termed 'policy borrowing or learning' and can occur across borders and jurisdictions (Levin 1998; Phillips and Ochs 2004; Rizvi and Lingard 2010). On this, the world of international education, including that of the IBPYP, is a good example of how curriculum policy ideals and design are influenced by globalization forces. Hayden and Thompson (2011, p. 31) refer to Thompson's (1998) categorization of curricula for international schools as *exportation* (the marketing abroad of existing national curricula and examinations), *adaption* (where existing national curricula are adapted to the international context), *integration* (where 'best practices' from a range of successful curricula are brought together into one new curriculum), and *creation* (where a new programme is developed from first principles). Many international school curriculum policies, or schools attempting to internationalize their curriculum policies, can be located within one, or some, of these categories.

The nature of local curriculum policy relies primarily on the beliefs and value systems of individual administrators and teachers, and how they make meaning of curriculum and paedagogy at their level. Marsh (2009, p. 23) has commented on this process as follows: "when we choose to teach in a certain way in a classroom we are following some kind of personal theory or model . . . it may be implicit rather than explicit but it is still evident". Here it is also instructive to keep in mind the view that teachers' perspectives and their tacit knowledge are both culturally and individually constructed, and guide the way they interpret and enact curriculum (Polanyi 1967). This tacit knowledge is experientially based and is guided by what they have learned from others through their perceptions of success and their perspective on 'what is good'.

During the last decade the concept in many countries of 'what is good' for students has been translated into the characteristics of a 'global citizen', or 'internationally-minded student' (Hayden 2006; Hill 2007; Marshall 2011; Walker 2007). Recently, it has also come to be associated with the notion of 'global competencies' (Bates 2011a; Zhao 2010). In this regard, it is useful to consider that, in Bagnall's (2011) detailed account of the history of the IB, the IBO is seen as having become a provider of 'global cultural capital'. Terms like this also appear in a range of international education policy documents and form part of the lexicon related to international schools and the push to 'internationalize' education.

If constructing a global citizen is the focus of curriculum policy design, it can be argued that we are moving toward global homogeneity. Clarence's (2011, p. 58) review of Rizvi and Lingard's (2010) *Globalizing Education Policy* text highlights this perspective. Also, there is a view that the homogenizing effect on education policy through increased policy borrowing blurs global boundaries, and over time has been reconfiguring the roles and authority structures of nation-states. Paris (2003, p. 235) analysed the IB programmes using this frame, suggesting that they are "a homogenization of educational ideas which subsumes cultural and national diversity".

Many countries are attempting to 'internationalize' their education systems by including global perspectives in the development of their new curricula. Australia's national curriculum is one example of this:

> Increasingly in a world where knowledge itself is constantly growing and evolving, students need to develop a set of skills, behaviours and dispositions, or general capabilities that apply across discipline content and equip them to be lifelong learners able to operate with confidence in a complex, information-rich, globalised world. (www.australiancurriculum. edu.au/Curriculum)

National curricula around the globe reveal similar intent. For example, a statement on the underlying values in Finnish curriculum policy refers to "the instruction that helps to support the formation of the pupil's own identity, and his or her part in Finnish society and a globalizing world" (www.oph.fi/corecurricula).

Similarly, the 2012 *South African National Curriculum Statement* (www.education. gov.za.CAPS), states that "the curriculum promotes knowledge in local contexts, while being sensitive to global imperatives" (General Aims, 1.3A).

1.3.3   Marketization of Curriculum Policy

In a 'borderless' changing world of accelerated migration, where global marketiza- tion, modernization and commodification of education exists, there are implications for curriculum policy. The global push for international education, international ideals and global competencies are having an impact on curriculum policy design and delivery at local, state and national levels. An example includes the purchasing of globally branded school curricula and internationally branded texts.

Lingard (2003) argues that some texts that are not officially part of policies could be used as de-facto policies in a context of increasing site-based management. The intermeshing of texts and curriculum is a development commonly found in both national and international school systems to transfer international values, ideas and information to local settings. Here one is reminded of the abundance of curriculum textbooks and packaged kits with a global, international, or values, focus that are regularly found in schools, or on display at international teacher conferences.

Schools themselves are also adopting already established and internationally recognized curricula to supplement, or support, their efforts to internationalize their curriculum policies (Cambridge 2010). This movement is a possible outcome of neo-liberal competitive ideology. On this, the international school movement can be seen as a reflection of Vongalis' (2004) belief that the intensity of global competition in a knowledge economy has moved international education toward market-based learning and national contexts. Bagnall (2010) argues that within this context the IBO has become a provider of global cultural capital. The significance of this development is such that Hayden and Thompson (2011) anticipate that a formal system of regulating international schools will emerge, and will be accompanied by the establishment of a 'league table' influenced by the current evidence-based and 'audit culture' world of education.

1.4   The Research Approach

The study which is reported in this book, it will be recalled, was concerned with exploring the dynamics of curriculum policy processes involved in the adoption, production and enactment of the IBO's IBPYP in three remote international schools in Indonesia. It was conceptualized as a policy analysis study, located centrally within the intersection of the two bodies of literature considered in the previous two sections of this chapter, namely, the literature on policy and policy analysis, and the literature on curriculum and curriculum policy. As the next two chapters indicate, it is also a study that sits at the intersection of the current body of research on international education, remote education, and policy processes.

The aim of the study was explored through a set of research questions based on the conceptualization of policy as a 'trajectory' (Ball 1994a, 2006; Rizvi and Lingard 2010; Vidovich 2007). Although Ball's 'policy trajectory' consists of five contexts (contexts of influences, policy text production, practices, outcomes and political strategies), for the study his final two contexts, that of outcomes and policy strategies, were encapsulated as one and referred to collectively as policy 'outcomes'. This is consistent with Rizvi and Lingard's (2010) use of the term 'outcomes' to encompass Ball's final two contexts as they both deal with power and inequity. It is also consistent with Vidovich's (2007) policy trajectory approach, derived from Ball's (1994a, 2006) model, and incorporating consideration of both the macro constraints (wider policy agendas) and the micro agency of policy actors within individual educational institutions.

In the light of the foregoing, the following research questions were generated to guide the empirical component of the project: (1) What were the key influences that had an impact on the initiation of curriculum policy reform at the case study schools? (2) What were the key features of the curriculum policy texts in the case study schools and how were they produced? (3) What policy practices were evident in the case study schools? (4) What were the outcomes and implications of curriculum policy reform for the case study schools, international education and remote education? The assumption was that the pursuit of these questions in the three case study schools would assist in capturing the complexities and interrelatedness of the different contexts of the IBPYP curriculum policy processes. They are also questions that were informed by interpretivist social theory. We took this stance as we espouse the 'theoretical eclecticism' of Ozga (2001) and Cibulka (1994), and have been influenced by Peters and Humes (2003, p. 109), who argue that "greater theoretical sophistication and creativity involves more than one theory alone".

The ability to understand the human and social reality of educators in the field of international education pointed to the value of adopting an interpretivist paradigm. On this, O'Donoghue (2007) has stated that interpretivist research applies to those pursuing an interest in understanding the meaning behind something. Fundamentally, meaning is a socially constructed notion. Also, as O'Donoghue (2007, p. 9) has suggested, it means that researchers must "emphasize social interaction as the basis for knowledge" and take cognizance of the centrality of the teacher and group dynamics in curriculum policy processes. In similar vein, it can be argued that the social world surrounding policy has an impact on the multiple worlds and multiple identities in which teachers engage. In the case of our study, these worlds included the world of the IBO, the world of international schools, the local world of remote contexts, and teachers' personal worlds.

In an ever-changing world, new and multiple lenses are required to assist in the analysis of data and to keep abreast of the effects of technological, economic and social changes. Thus, we also adopted a critical theory approach, especially in our analysis of data in relation to both the three individual school case studies, in cross-case analysis and along the policy trajectory, from macro (global) to micro (school) levels. This approach can facilitate the interrogation of power structures with respect to curriculum policy processes and within different contexts. It looks beyond rhetoric and examines patterns of inequality and the results of real-life struggles (Pitman and Vidovich 2012). In doing so, it provides a tool that can "show us our world and ourselves through new and valuable lenses … and can strengthen our ability to think logically, creatively and provide a good deal of insight" (Tyson 2006, p. 3).

Regarding data collection, a combination of methods was used. Key IBPYP documents produced by the IBO, and also at the school level, were collected, and individual and group interviews were conducted. This combination brought both breadth and depth to the study; a recognized strength of research of this nature (Travers 2009). It also permitted us to analyse individual perspectives, capture the 'voices' of participants, allow for group interaction to take place, analyse policy documents, and investigate the wide range of contextual influences.

As the study progressed, data collection, analysis and theory were deemed to be intimately intertwined and iterative (Ezzy 2002). The mechanics of data analysis of contextual descriptions, documents and interviews, were addressed through the use of two complementary approaches. This first of these is Miles and Huberman's (1994) interactive model for exploring qualitative data. The second is Lichtman's (2010) 'three Cs' of analysis, where one moves from coded data, to categorizing, and to the identification of concepts. Combining both approaches engaged us in what O'Toole and Beckett (2010) call a form of 'distilling data'.

Following the analysis of each case, a cross-case analysis was conducted. Overall, the intention of the study was not to generalize the research findings to other IBPYP international schools, or to other remote schools. Rather, it was to arrive at meta-level themes that could provide 'food for thought' and assist others in the generation of theory related to the intersection of curriculum policy, international education and remote education.

1.5 Outline of the Chapters

The book consists of nine chapters. Chapter 2 contextualizes the research. It positions the researchers and introduces the International Baccalaureate, the Indonesian setting, and the remote schooling contexts in which the study was conducted. Chapter 3 is organized into two main sections. It begins by fore-grounding the ever-changing macro level phenomenon of globalization. The second section details the changing face of international education and international schools and teachers, as well as the ideological constructs they espouse such as notions of 'international mindedness'. Chapter 4 provides a detailed account of the research approach adopted in the study which is at the heart of the book and which is reported in the next three chapters. Chapters 5, 6 and 7 present the findings of the study in relation to the three remote international case-study schools in Indonesia. Each chapter deals with one case and is presented in two major sections. The first section in each chapter profiles the case study setting and describes the geographic, demographic, economic, political, paedagogical, technological and socio-cultural environments (Hill 2007; Roberts 2003; Wylie 2006). The second section outlines the findings in relation to the school in question. These are presented in terms of the contexts of curriculum policy processes already detailed, namely, the contexts of influences, policy text production, practices, and outcomes. Chapter 8 presents a cross-case analysis of the results. The final chapter, Chap. 9, is in four sections. The first section returns to the research questions and presents a total of 15 propositions generated from the findings. The second section identifies the key 'policy threads' revealed through the meta-analysis across the entire policy trajectory. The third section reflects on the research process undertaken and draws conclusions regarding implications for policy and practice. The fourth section discusses possibilities for future research.

References

Allen, M. (2002). Cultural borderlands: Cultural dissonance in the international school. *International Schools Journal, 20*(2), 42–53.

Bagnall, N. F. (2008). Case studies of four international schools. In N. F. Bagnall (Ed.), *International schools as agents for change* (pp. 109–125). New York: Nova Science.

Bagnall, N. F. (2010). *Education without borders: Forty years of the international baccalaureate, 1970–2010*. Berlin: VDM Publishing House Ltd.

Bagnall, N. F. (2011). Know thyself: Research, comparative culture and identity in comparative research. In L. Markauskaite, P. Freebody, & J. Irwin (Eds.), *Methodological choice and design: Scholarship, policy and practice in social and educational research* (pp. 203–208). Dordrecht: Springer.

Ball, S. J. (1990). *Politics and policy making in education: Explorations in policy sociology*. London/New York: Taylor & Francis.

Ball, S. J. (1994a). *Education reform: A critical and post-structural approach*. Buckingham: Open University Press.

Ball, S. J. (1994b). Some reflections on policy theory: A brief response to Hatcher and Troyna. *Journal of Education Policy, 9*(2), 171–182.

Ball, S. J. (2006). *Education policy and social class: The selected works of Stephen J. Ball*. Abingdon: Routledge.

Bates, R. (Ed.). (2011a). *Schooling internationally: Globalisation, internationalisation and the future for international schools*. Abingdon: Routledge.

Bates, R. (2011b, July). *Learning to teach internationally: What international teachers need to know*. Paper presented at the Australian teacher education association annual conference, Melbourne.

Bowe, R., Ball, S. J., & Gold, A. (1992). *Reforming education and changing schools: Case studies in policy sociology*. Abingdon: Routledge.

Boyd, W. L. (1999). Paradoxes of educational policy and productivity. *Educational Policy, 13*(2), 227–250.

Boyer, E. L. (1994, March). Creating the new American college. *Chronicle of Higher Education*, 8–48.

Boyer, E. L. (1996). The commitment to character: A basic priority for every school. *Update on Law-Related Education, 20*(1), 4–8.

Cambridge, J. (2010). Review of 'The Production of Educational Knowledge in the Global Era' by J. Resnik. *Journal of Research in International Education, 9*(1), 98–100.

Cambridge, J. (2011). International curriculum. In R. Bates (Ed.), *Schooling internationally: Globalisation, internationalisation and the future for the international schools* (pp. 121–147). Abingdon: Routledge.

Carr, W., & Kemmis, S. (1986). *Becoming critical: Education, knowledge and action.* Waurn Ponds: Deakin University.

Cibulka, J. G. (1994). Policy analysis and the study of the politics of education. *Journal of Education Policy, 9*(5), 105–125.

Clarence, H. (2011). *Review of global education policy.* http://www.developmenteducationreview. com/issue13-focus1. Accessed 3 Sept 2011.

Currie, J. (2004). The neo-liberal paradigm and higher education: A critique. In J. K. Odin & P. T. Manicas (Eds.), *Globalization and higher education* (pp. 42–68). Hawaii: University of Hawaii Press.

Dahllof, U. (1969). The need for models in curriculum planning. *European Education, 1*(1), 12–19.

Elmore, R., & Sykes, G. (1992). Curriculum policy. In P. W. Jackson (Ed.), *Handbook of research on curriculum* (pp. 185–215). New York: Macmillan.

Ezzy, D. (2002). *Qualitative analysis: Practice and innovation.* London: Routledge.

Fitz, J. (1994). Implementation research and education policy: Practice and prospects. *British Journal of Educational Studies, 42*(1), 53–69.

Green, B. (2008). *Spaces and places: The NSW rural (teacher) education project.* Wagga Wagga: Centre for Information Studies.

Green, B. (Ed.). (2009). *Understanding and researching professional practice.* Rotterdam: Sense Publishers.

Grundy, S. (1987). *Curriculum: Product or praxis?* Abingdon: Routledge Falmer.

Habermas, J. (1972). *Knowledge and human interests* (J. J. Shapiro, Trans.). Boston: Beacon Press.

Ham, C., & Hill, M. J. (1993). *The policy process in the modern capitalist state.* London: Harvester Wheatsheaf.

Hayden, M. (2006). *Introduction to international education.* London: Sage Publications Ltd.

Hayden, M. (2007). Professional development of educators: The international education context. In M. Hayden, J. Thompson, & J. Levy (Eds.), *The Sage handbook of research in international education* (pp. 223–232). London: Sage Publications Ltd.

Hayden, M. C., & Thompson, J. (2011). Teachers for the international school of the future. In R. Bates (Ed.), *Schooling internationally: Globalisation, internationalisation and the future for international schools* (pp. 83–100). Abingdon: Routledge.

Heyward, M. (2002). From international to intercultural: Redefining the international school for a globalized world. *Journal of Research in International Education, 1*(1), 9–32.

Heyward, M., Cannon, R. A., & Sarjono, J. (2011). *Implementing school-based management in Indonesia.* Jacarta: RTI Press.

Hill, I. (2007). International education as developed by the International Baccalaureate Organization. In J. Thompson, M. Hayden, & J. Levy (Eds.), *The SAGE handbook of research in international education* (pp. 25–38). London: Sage.

Jallade, L., Radi, M., & Cuenin, S. (2001). *National education policies and programmes and international cooperation: What role for UNESCO?* Paris: United Nations Educational, Scientific and Cultural Organization.

Levin, M. (1998). *Teach me!: Kids will learn when oppression is the lesson.* New York: Monthly Review Press.

Levy, J. (2007). Pre-service teacher preparation for international settings. In M. Hayden, J. Thompson, & J. Levy (Eds.), *The Sage handbook of research in international education* (pp. 213–222). Thousand Oaks: Sage Publications Ltd.

Lichtman, M. (2010). *Understanding and evaluating qualitative educational research.* Los Angeles: Sage Publications Ltd.

Lingard, B. (2003). Teachers and school reform: Working with pedagogies and productive assessment. *Melbourne Studies in Education, 44*(2), 1–18.

Marginson, S., & Rhoades, G. (2002). Beyond national states, markets, and systems of higher education: A glonacal agency heuristic. *Higher Education, 43*(3), 281–309.

Marsh, C. J. (2009). *Key concepts for understanding curriculum.* Abingdon: Routledge.

Marshall, H. (2011). Instrumentalism, ideals and imaginaries: Theorising the contested space of global citizenship education in schools. *Globalisation, Societies and Education, 9*(3–4), 411–426.

Miles, M. B., & Huberman, A. M. (1994). *Qualitative data analysis: An expanded sourcebook.* Thousand Oaks: Sage Publications Ltd.

Mitter, W. (1997). Challenges to comparative education: Between retrospect and expectation. *International Review of Education, 43*(5), 401–412.

O'Donoghue, T. A. (2007). *Planning your qualitative research project: An introduction to interpretivist research in education.* Abingdon: Routledge.

Ornstein, A. C., & Hunkins, F. P. (2004). *Curriculum foundations, principles, and issues* (4th ed.). Boston: Allyn & Bacon.

O'Toole, J., & Beckett, D. (2010). *Educational research: Creative thinking and doing.* South Melbourne: Oxford University Press.

Ozga, J. (2001). Policy research in educational settings: Contested terrain. *Journal of Education Policy, 16*(1), 85–87.

Paris, P. G. (2003). The International Baccalaureate: A case study on why students choose to do the IB. *International Education Journal, 4*(3), 232–243.

Peters, M. A., & Humes, W. (2003). Editorial. Education in the knowledge economy. *Policy Futures in Education, 1*(1), 1.

Phillips, D., & Ochs, K. (2004). Researching policy borrowing: Some methodological challenges in comparative education. *British Educational Research Journal, 30*(6), 773–784.

Pinar, W. (Ed.). (2003). *International handbook of curriculum research.* Mahwah: Taylor & Francis.

Pinar, W. (2004). *What is curriculum theory?* Mahwah: Lawrence Erlbaum Associates, Inc.

Pitman, T., & Vidovich, L. (2012). Recognition of prior learning (RPL) policy in Australian higher education: The dynamics of position taking. *Journal of Educational Policy, 27*(1), 761–774.

Polanyi, M. (1967). Sense-giving and sense-reading. *Philosophy, 42*(162), 301–325.

Rizvi, F. (2007). Internationalization of curriculum: A critical perspective. In M. Hayden, J. Thompson, & J. Levy (Eds.), *The Sage handbook of research in international education* (pp. 390–403). Thousand Oaks: Sage Publications Ltd.

Rizvi, F., & Lingard, B. (2006). Globalization and the changing nature of the OECD's education work. In H. Lauder, P. Brown, J. A. Dillagough, & A. H. Halsey (Eds.), *Education, globalization and social change* (pp. 247–260). Oxford: Oxford University Press.

Rizvi, F., & Lingard, B. (2010). *Globalizing education policy.* London: Taylor & Francis.

Roberts, B. (2003). What should international education be? From emergent theory to practice. *International Schools Journal, 22*(2), 69–79.

Robitaille, D. F. (1993). *Curriculum frameworks for mathematics and science* (TIMSS monograph no. 1). Vancouver: Pacific Educational Press, Faculty of Education, University of British Columbia.

Rosenholtz, S. J. (1989). *Teachers' workplace: The social organization of schools.* White Plains: Longman.

Scheurich, J. J. (2000). An archaeology of 'plain talk'. *Qualitative Inquiry, 6*(3), 337–348.

Schubert, W. (2008). Curriculum inquiry. In F. Connelly & H. M. Phillion (Eds.), *Handbook of curriculum and instruction* (pp. 399–419). Thousand Oaks: Sage Publications Ltd.

Skelton, M. (2007). International-mindedness and the brain: The difficulties of 'becoming'. In M. Hayden, J. Thompson, & J. Levy (Eds.), *The Sage handbook of research in international education* (pp. 379–389). London: Sage Publications Ltd.

Snowball, L. (2007). Becoming more internationally minded: International teacher certification and professional development. In M. Hayden, J. Thompson, & J. Levy (Eds.), *The Sage handbook of research in international education* (pp. 247–255). London: Sage Publications Ltd.

Spring, J. (2009). *Globalization of education: An introduction.* New York: Taylor & Francis.

Sylvester, R. (2007). Historical resources for research in international education. In M. Hayden, J. Thompson, & J. Levy (Eds.), *The Sage handbook of research in international education* (pp. 185–195). London: Sage Publications Ltd.

Taylor, M. (2003). *Public policy in the community.* Houndmills: Palgrave Macmillan.

Thompson, J. J. (1998). Towards a model for international education. In M. Hayden & J. Thompson (Eds.), *International education: Principles and practice* (pp. 276–290). London: Kogan Page.

Travers, M. (2009). New methods, old problems: A sceptical view of innovation in qualitative research. *Qualitative Research, 9*(2), 161–179.

Tyson, L. (2006). *Critical theory today: A user-friendly guide* (2nd ed.). New York: Routledge.

Vidovich, L. (2002). *Expanding the toolbox for policy analysis: Some conceptual and practical approaches.* Hong Kong: Comparative Education Policy Research Unit, Department of Public and Social Administration, City University of Hong Kong.

Vidovich, L. (2007). Removing policy from its pedestal: Some theoretical framings and practical possibilities. *Educational Review, 59*(3), 285–298.

Vidovich, L. (2013). Policy research in higher education: Theories and methods for globalising times? In J. Huisman & M. Tight (Eds.), *Theory and method in higher education research* (pp. 21–40). London: Emerald Press.

Vongalis, A. (2004). Global education policy directives: Impact on teachers from the north and south. *International Education Journal, 5*(4), 488–501.

Walker, G. (2007). Challenges from a new world. In M. Hayden, J. Thompson, & J. Levy (Eds.), *The Sage handbook of research in international education* (pp. 404–411). London: Sage Publications Ltd.

Walsh, A. (2007). An exploration of Biggs' constructive alignment in the context of work-based learning. *Assessment and Evaluation in Higher Education, 32*(1), 79–87.

Wedel, J., & Feldman, G. (2005). Why an anthropology of public policy? *Anthropology Today, 21*(1), 1–12.

Winter, C. (2012). School curriculum, globalisation and the constitution of policy problems and solutions. *Journal of Education Policy, 27*(3), 295–314.

Wylie, J. (2006). Cultural geographies in practice: Smoothlands: fragments/landscapes/fragments. *Cultural Geographies, 13*(3), 458–465.

Wylie, M. (2011). Global networking and the world of international education. In R. Bates (Ed.), *Schooling internationally: Globalisation, internationalisation and the future for international schools* (pp. 21–38). Abingdon: Routledge.

Yates. (2011, September). *Curriculum as a public policy enterprise: Australian state differences and the past forty years of curriculum reforms.* Paper presented at the British Educational Research Association Annual Conference, London.

Yates, L., & Grumet, M. (2011). *Curriculum in today's world: Configuring knowledge, identities, work and politics. World yearbook of education 2011.* Abingdon: Routledge.

Zajda, J. I. (2005). *International handbook on globalisation, education and policy research: Global pedagogies and policies.* Dordrecht: Springer.

Zhao, Y. (2010). Preparing globally competent teachers: A new imperative for teacher education. *Journal of Teacher Education, 61*(5), 422–431.

Chapter 2
The Context

2.1 Introduction

This chapter is concerned with the context within which the policy analysis study on the introduction of the International Baccalaureate (the IB) at three international schools in remote communities in Indonesia, was located. Specifically, it focuses on three contexts: the International Baccalaureate (IB), the Indonesian context, and remote schooling. Section 2.2 provides the background to the IB and positions it within the field of international education. It details its history, key features, structure, mission and global growth, including the educational ideologies that influenced the emergence of the International Baccalaureate Primary Years Programme (IBPYP). Section 2.3 provides an outline of education in the Indonesian context, including its history and structure, as well as relevant government department policies related to international schools. Section 2.4 introduces the field of remote schooling and issues related to living and working in remote locations.

2.2 The International Baccalaureate

The IB, including the IBPYP, can be viewed as being positioned within the field of international education (Dolby and Rahman 2008). However, the term 'international education' is ambiguous, difficult to define, and misleading, particularly in a borderless world that, in the view of Bonk (2009), has opened up educational opportunities for anyone to learn anything from anyone at anytime. It has been constructed from a multitude of "conceptual anomalies, exuberant expectations and philosophical perspectives and perceptions" (Bunnell 2007, p. 349). Along with related constructs of

© Springer International Publishing Switzerland 2014
S. Ledger et al., *Global to Local Curriculum Policy Processes*,
Policy Implications of Research in Education 4, DOI 10.1007/978-3-319-08762-7_2

'international schools', 'international curriculum' and 'international-mindedness', however, it continues to be in search of an agreed identity. The approach adopted here is not one that attempts to find agreed definitions of these terms. Rather, it is an attempt to unravel the layers of each, particularly in regard to the IBPYP.

The burgeoning market commodity that is 'international education' caters for the ever-increasing number of internationally mobile workers and their families. The changing face of these workers, in turn, is having an impact on international schools. One example of this impact is the emergence of a new breed of schools aligned with large multi-national companies in areas such as mining, industry and finance (Hayden and Thompson 2011).

Choice in the international educational market has also grown (Bagnall 2008). The inclusion of the International Primary Curriculum (International Primary Curriculum 2010) and International Middle Years Curriculum (International Middle Years Curriculum 2010) has added to the list of recognized international curricula providers that include the European Council of International Schools, the Cambridge International, the Yew Chung International School Curriculum, the Council of International Schools, the Round Square Schools, the International Bureau of Education, and Global Education Management Systems. Hayden and Thompson (2011) present a comprehensive list of these and other organizations, and illustrate their influences on the growing number of international, national, religious and commercially-based international schools that represent the diverse 'international education' marketplace.

The emergence of international education as a multi-million dollar industry also needs to be considered (Bunnell 2011). It is made up of "a burgeoning peripheral industry of service providers for the increasing number of international schools and their associated school communities" (Ellwood 2004, p. 5). These include publishing companies, professional development providers and human resource organizations. The publishers produce curriculum texts directly linked to each curriculum or assessment tool for international schools; the professional development provision relates to values education, global issues and technological competencies; and the large human resource organizations manage the recruitment of those teachers on the 'international school circuit'.

Technological advances have played a key role in enabling core features of international curriculum design, curriculum texts and professional development offerings to circulate around the globe at a phenomenal speed. The global social network and operational processes provided by international organizations such as the IBPYP help to facilitate the transference of knowledge and understanding of their particular curriculum policy. At the same time, it is vital to keep in mind that no matter what technologies, resources or support are provided, curriculum policy only becomes a reality when teachers enact it (Ornstein and Hunkins 2004).

2.2.1   History and Philosophy of the International Baccalaureate

The body of international organizations and curriculum providers that exist today within the field of international education is diverse. One of the oldest of the organizations involved is the IBO, which started out with a single programme for internationally mobile students preparing for university. Now it offers four programmes for students aged from 3 to 19 years. The original International Baccalaureate Diploma Programme (IBDP) for high school-aged students matriculating after completing their final 2 years of school provided, as it still does, an internationally recognized university entrance qualification. The Middle Years Programme (IBMYP) was introduced in 1994 for students in grades 6–10. The IBPYP, followed in 1997 and was designed for students aged from 3 to 12 years. Finally, the International Baccalaureate Career-related certificate (IBCC) was introduced in 2012 for students 16–19 years of age. The four IB programmes (the IBPYP, the IBMYP, the IBDP and the IBCC) are presented as an 'IB International Continuum' (IBO 2009). All share a common mission to develop 'internationally minded' students (IBO 2012).

Looking at matters more broadly, international schools for much of the period since World War II, have primarily accommodated children of foreign diplomats and the mobile middle classes. More recently, however, with the increased ease of travel and the emergence of transnational workplaces, the international schooling sector has developed into a conglomerate of schools with a multiplicity of definitions and contexts. Regarding the IB, Bunnell (2011) presents an overview of its evolution historically. Its birth and infancy period (1969–1983) was one of exploration, trial and expansion. During this time, the programme grew from being offered in one IB school to being offered in 130 schools. The 'youthful' period (1984–1999) was a time of expansion for the IB as it grew from 130 to 800 programmes and moved into a consolidation mode. This was the era when it shifted from having an international schools approach to involvement with national schooling and to being adopted by a wider variety of schools, many of them being non-elite. Within its adulthood period (since 1999) the IB grew exponentially; between 2000 and 2013 the number of IB schools went from 1,000 to 3,600.

The IBDP is the oldest programme in the IB curriculum suite. Bagnall (2010) provides a comprehensive history of its evolution from 1970 to 2010. In the early years it was a pre-university curriculum with a common set of external examinations for students in schools throughout the world seeking to return to their home countries with a recognized curriculum. An elitist perception of the programme developed during this time because of the socio-economic background of the students involved in it. Although the first IB schools were predominantly private international schools they included a small number of private national institutions and schools belonging to state education departments. However, over time this changed, such that over half of all authorized IB World Schools in 2012 were state-run schools (IBO 2012).

The IBPYP is an outcome of the International Schools Curriculum Project. Since its inception in 1997, until 2006, it grew "between 10 and 25 % each year" (Hayden 2006, p. 135) in particular regions. Also, between 2005 and 2010 the number of IBPYP schools trebled from just over 200 to 600 (IBO 2012). By 2012, it had increased to 945 schools in over 140 countries. At a regional level, the number of Asia Pacific IBPYP schools grew from 52 in 2005, to 270 in 2012.

The large uptake of IB programmes in schools throughout the world, including in South East Asia, has generated much debate. There is concern that international ideologies minimize national perspectives and transnational conflicts (Brown and Lauder 2011). Some interpret the uniformity of the IB ideology, curriculum and governance as a normative exercise that promotes homogeneity (Quist 2005), while others consider the IBPYP to be a unifying force for curriculum reform (Hill 2007). Nonetheless, the IB has emerged as a globally recognized educational brand in the world of international education.

In 2006, in what Bunnell (2011) labels the adulthood phase of the IB, substantial changes to its organizational infrastructure were made in preparation for anticipated expansion. The appointment of a leading businessman, Jeffrey Beard, as Director, was seen as a strategic policy decision for the organization. It resulted in the adoption of a corporate style of management and the development of systemic changes to the organization in order to cater for predicted growth.

2.2.2   The IBO's Organizational Structures and Processes

The IBO is a non-profit organization that receives funding in the form of annual fees from its schools. Additional income is drawn from such fee-based services as professional development, publications and student assessment. Donors offer additional financial support to the IBO and at times governments provide funding to support special projects and initiatives. An overview of the IBO's financial figures based on its annual report of 2010 showed an annual income of 105 million US dollars, representing an increase of nearly 40 million dollars since 2006. The IBO's operational costs were separated into five areas: staff costs of 54 million dollars, examination fees of 24 million dollars, workshops and conferences at 8.8 million dollars, authorization and evaluation fees at 2.2 million dollars, publications at 400,000 dollars and a an 'other' category worth 10 million dollars.

In 2011, the IBO launched its 2020 vision for the organization. It simplified legal and tax structures, created a new council advisory role and changed its governance structure. The organization is led by a Board of Governors and an ombudsman role has been appointed to support the organization's commitment to being service-oriented (IBO 2011b). Each department within the IBO develops goals and financial forecasts for 3 years at a time. The forecasts address the aims embedded in the organization's strategic plan. The corporate approach to the IBO's management structures reflects the global push toward the commodification of education. This is a situation where organizations, including international schools, are required to balance the demands and tensions of a 'double bottom line' involving education and economics.

The IBO's Board of Governors (15–25 elected members) is drawn from a list of people nominated by the Heads Council and Regional Councils (IBO 2011a). There are only three ex-officio positions in the organization, which are filled by the Director General, the Chair of the Examining Board, and the Chair of the Heads Council. The IBO's organizational structure described in the 2011 strategic plan encourages diversity of gender, culture and geography.

The IBO Board has six permanent committees. They deal with access and advancement, audit, compensation, education, finance, and governance. Three of these represent compliance and governance (audit, compensation and governance), two deal with policy (education and finance) and the sixth one relates to creating a vision and direction for the other committees. This macro level structure is where global policies are produced and enacted. The regional offices and schools are where the policies are interpreted and enacted.

The IBO has a range of offices around the world that serve different purposes. They cater for 140 countries where IB schools are operating. The Director General is based in Geneva (Switzerland) and the Curriculum and Assessment Centre is in Cardiff (UK). The research unit was based at the University of Bath in the (UK) but following the renewed focus on research highlighted at the IB Asia Pacific Conference in Singapore in 2012, the head of research was relocated to the USA. The IBO has regional offices, or representatives, in Beijing, Buenos Aires, Cardiff, Geneva, Mumbai, New York, Singapore, Sydney, Tokyo and Vancouver. In 2010, the organization established three 'global IB centres' in the regions. The first opened in Bethesda (Maryland, USA) in 2010 as the Americas Global IB Centre and the second opened in The Hague (Netherlands) in 2011 as the 'Europe, Africa and Middle East Global Centre'. The 'Asia-Pacific Global Centre' in Singapore caters for the Asia Pacific and the South-East Asian region. It has been operating for over 10 years. The positioning of these global centres in the USA, Europe and Singapore reflect its areas of growth.

The IBO is an organization that values its reputation for quality, high standards and paedagogical leadership. The original mission statement, developed in 1969, still states:

> The International Baccalaureate aims to develop inquiring, knowledgeable and caring young people who help to create a better and more peaceful world through intercultural understanding and respect. To this end the organisation works with schools, governments and international organisations to develop challenging programmes of international education and rigorous assessment. These programmes encourage students across the world to become active, compassionate and lifelong learners who understand that other people with their differences can also be right. (IBO 2012)

This is supported by a set of core values, outlined as follows:

IB is motivated by a mission to create a better world through education
IB values partnerships to achieve its goals by working together
IB values quality and its reputation for high standards
IB values participation that actively involves its stakeholders
IB values international-mindedness by embracing diversity
IB values paedagogical leadership by innovating in educational practice. (IBO 2009)

The mission statement and the statement of core values have triggered continual debate and discussion regarding the IBO's perceived 'altruistic' and 'western viewpoint' on social reform in education. The IBPYP aims to promote 'international-mindedness' in students and educators through what is called the IB Learner Profile (IBO 2003b). This consists of a set of ten attributes, or ideals, that the IBO believes will inspire, motivate and focus the work of schools and teachers, and unite them in a common purpose (IBO 2011c). The conceptualization of the 'Learner Profile' emerged during the original policy production phase of the IBPYP in 1997, and was known initially as the 'Student Profile'. The change of name to 'Learner Profile' in the early 2000s saw it embedded as the central core of all IBO programs. The ten attributes of the profile suggest that students should be inquirers, be knowledgeable, be thinkers, be communicators, be principled, be open-minded, be caring, be risk-takers, be balanced, and be reflective. These attributes are embedded in the IB mission statement and are considered central to the development of internationally-minded students and teachers, although much debate has surrounded their meaning.

2.2.3   *The Authorization Process*

IB schools are required to work successfully through a sequence of events if they are to become IB authorized. First, they register interest with the IBO's regional centre and conduct a feasibility study. This involves analysing philosophy, curriculum, organization and resources at the school level in order to see if it has the capacity to address the IB *Programme Standards and Practices* (IBO 2003a, 2011c). Once accepted as a candidate school, the authorization process commences with the support of the regional IB officers. Schools work through this 'candidature phase' over a few years. It involves a 'training period', in which schools enact the *Programme Standards and Practices*. School policies, processes, organization and resources are designed and delivered to reflect the mandated practices. The school is expected to appoint an IB coordinator, commit to professional development training and provide time for collaborative planning with staff during the candidature. An on-site visit by an IB pre-authorization team takes place, involving an intensive reflective regime. The *Programme Standards and Practices* (IBO 2011c) are non-negotiable and must be adhered to if the school is to be successful in gaining its authorization. At the same time, as long as a school can justify that it is moving towards addressing the IB Standards, some flexibility is available.

At the end of the candidature stage, the 'authorization team' evaluates the school's capacity to deliver the programme. The IBO's regional office reviews both the report from the authorization team and documentation produced by the school. If the school successfully addresses the requirements it attains the status of an IB authorized school. From that point onwards, it is required to be re-authorized every 3 years. This includes completing a self-study questionnaire and evaluation report, coupled with a school community report that sets future goals.

Throughout the authorization process the IBO offers a range of support to schools, principals, IB coordinators and staff. It provides access to a website known as the 'Online Curriculum Centre' and provides a variety of publications, along with opportunities for involvement in the curriculum review processes. The IBO's regional office provides workshops and organizes conferences, and also offers support. Recent technological initiatives that are used include the 'Digital Space Initiative' (now referred to as the 'Virtual Learning Community'), the 'IB Blogasphere', which is a new web portal for the online professional learning service, 'Epals Online Learning Community', and the 'Opening Classroom Doors' initiative which provides video clips of schools 'enacting' such components of the IBPYP as collaborative planning sessions. Independent regional networks have also been developed to link IBPYP teachers to colleagues in other IBPYP schools in their region. While these networks differ in their provision of support, they provide access to district professional development and collegial support, and provide a voice for the region. Also, while they are not fully endorsed by the IBO in that they are not hosted on the IB website, they are recognized as a valuable support.

The authorization process is well documented and supported by the IBO. Key IB documents guide the process for all programmes and specific texts support the authorization process for each programme. Key players offer support during the candidature stage of authorization. These are the officers at the regional level, the authorization team at the national level, and the IB coordinator at the local school level.

2.2.4   *International Baccalaureate Primary Years Programme (IBPYP)*

The IBPYP caters for children from 3 to 12 years of age. It is a trans-disciplinary programme designed to foster the development of the whole child. Its curriculum framework is structured in a trans-disciplinary way around a written curriculum, taught curriculum and assessed curriculum. Paedagogically it embraces construc-tivism through a concept-based, inquiry approach to learning. The curriculum framework consists of five essential elements: concepts, knowledge, skills, attitudes and action. The knowledge component is developed through students engaging in inquiry into the following six trans-disciplinary themes of global significance: who we are, where we are in place and time, how we express ourselves, how the world works, how we organise ourselves, and sharing the planet. The structure of the IB trans-disciplinary themes reflects Boyer's (1994, p. 18) construction of curriculum as "core commonalities"', rather than as a "subject areas"' approach.

The IB *Continuum of International Education* (IBO 2009) was developed to promote cohesion across all IB programmes. It highlights the 'Mission Statement', the 'Learner Profile' and the 'Standards and Practices' as core elements in each of them. It also highlights the key features of the programmes by presenting them as seven continua: the structural continuum, the learning to learn continuum, the special education needs continuum, the academic honesty continuum, the assessment continuum, the consolidation of learning continuum, and the action continuum. Each continuum articulates the scope and sequence of IB policy.

The IBPYP continua represent the paedagogy and ideology behind the IBPYP. For example, the 'learning to learn continuum' is about constructing meaning. It is aimed at developing meta-cognitive knowledge about learners and how they learn best for self-improvement. The 'language-learning continuum' highlights the importance of mother tongue development for students and promotes the learning of an additional language from the age of 7. The 'special education needs continuum' encourages the development of inclusive programmes and engagement in early intervention in pupils' learning. The 'academic honesty continuum' was designed to facilitate the development of the academic capacities of students through the IB Learner Profile and of essential elements of the PYP. The 'assessment continuum' is focused on internal assessment, feedback and goal setting. It features a 'consolidation of learning' element identified as a presentation by each student at the culmination of his or her learning in each programme; PYP students complete an 'exhibition', MYP students develop a 'personal project', and DP students write an 'extended essay'. Finally, the 'action continuum' outlines the scope of how children can enact their learning, moving from voluntary demonstration to community service. The action cycle of 'reflect, choose and act' is introduced and encouraged throughout the PYP.

The IBPYP provides scope and sequences for all subject areas within the five trans-disciplinary themes. It outlines the specific content for Language, Mathematics, Social Studies, Science and Technology, Personal and Social Education (PSE), Physical Education, Visual Arts, Music, and Drama. The associated scope and sequence documents are structured in the same way for each subject area. The overall expectations are provided at the beginning of each section and content is outlined. The remaining sections are divided into four parts. Part One 'What do you want students to learn?' includes specific expectations, or central ideas, where sample questions are provided. Part Two, 'How best will students learn?' includes good-practice teaching activities. Part Three, 'How will we know what students have learned?' includes a range of assessment activities, both formative and summative. Part Four outlines the subject link to the 'programme of inquiry'. This is where the document explains how the curricular expectations for social studies, science, technology and PSE are to be expressed using the content of a 'unit of inquiry'.

2.3 Education in Indonesia

This section provides an overview of education in Indonesia, including its history, its structure, government policy, the emergence of international schools, and the adoption by schools of the IBPYP. With over 50 million students and 2.6 million teachers in more than 250,000 schools, Indonesia has the third largest education system in the South East Asian region and the fourth largest in the world, behind China, India and the USA. The country has many different indigenous cultures and language groups. Of the 214 million people who live in the country, 76 million are school-aged children. Many live in remote areas that have high incidences of poverty, high costs of schooling and limited access to high quality education. In 2011, over 110,000 expatriates held working visas in Indonesia and many of their children attended international schools.

Two ministries are responsible for managing the education system in Indonesia. The pattern is that 84 % of schools are managed under the Ministry of National Education and the remaining 16 % are under the Ministry of Religious Affairs. International schools and private schools fall under the jurisdiction of one or other of these departments, depending on whether the school is a state school, or a religious school. Twenty-seven schools in Indonesia offer the IBPYP. Over half of these are private schools, including four that are religion-based.

2.3.1 History of Education in Indonesia

Public education was virtually non-existent in Indonesia until the colonial government established a system of village schools in 1906 (Kristiansen and Pratikno 2006). By 1913, with an estimated population of 40 million, public schools numbered approximately 3,500, while there was a similar number of private and religious schools. Only a very few locals from Javanese elite groups were permitted to study in the schools of the Dutch colonialists. By 1930, the Dutch had introduced formal education to nearly every province of the Dutch East Indies. Nevertheless, less than 6 % of the population was literate in 1945.

After Independence in 1949, Indonesia developed a national education plan to support the 1945 constitution. This policy stipulated that every citizen had the right to obtain an education and that the government had the responsibility to provide one national educational system. Financial constraints limited government efforts at the time. Many schools that arose during this era were predominantly private and run by religious groups.

The expansion of public primary schooling emerged when increasing national oil revenues started to feed into government budgets from 1973 (Kristiansen and Pratikno 2006). Large amounts of money channelled through a Presidential Instruction Grant, were used to construct thousands of schools throughout the country. The number of primary schools increased from 65,000 in 1973 to 130,000 in 1984 and the number of enrolled children doubled to 26 million. Following a government decree in 1974, school boards known as 'BP3s', were established in most schools. These were used extensively to legitimize the imposing of levies charged on parents (Moegiadi and Jiyono 1991). In 1989, the government committed to providing 9 years of schooling, rather than 6. Nine-year compulsory education was officially introduced in 1994, with the target of providing for 95 % of the nation's students by 2004. However, only 90 out of 440 districts reached the official target. During this time 3.2 million children aged between 13 and 15 were not enrolled in compulsory education.

Private schools have maintained a dominant role in the educational system in Indonesia. Before the 2005 decentralization reform, 17 % of students at elementary school level were enrolled in private schools, while in junior and senior high schools the figures were 40 % and 50 % respectively (EdStats 2006). Private schools at the elementary school level are normally characterized by their lower operational costs and lower academic quality (Van Schaik 2009), even though the government provides substantial subsidies. Also, private school graduates generally gain much lower scores in public examinations than do those in public schools.

Finally, while the number of private elite schools in Indonesia traditionally has been small, the indications by 2006 were that the numbers were increasing (Kristianssen and Pratikno 2006). The majority of schools adopting the IBPYP curriculum are part of an elite private school movement. In 2012 there were 27 authorized IBPYP schools in Indonesia and 15 candidate schools (IBO 2011a).

2.3.2   The Structure of the School System in Indonesia

With the exception of structures for early childhood education, the Indonesian system still mirrors the three-tiered elementary, primary and high school model put in place by the Dutch and common in many other countries. Indonesian children do not generally have access to formal education before the age of 5, kindergarten is not compulsory, and of the 49,000 kindergartens in the nation, 99.35 % are privately operated. In contrast, 93 % of all elementary schools in Indonesia are government operated. Although primary school fees in the public sector were officially abolished in 1977, as were secondary school fees in 1994, most schools in Indonesia still do charge fees.

Six years at elementary school is compulsory, except in the case of those at some schools that offer an accelerated learning programme. Here students who perform well can finish in 5 years rather than 6. Middle schooling is also compulsory and is considered part of elementary education. Students attend middle school for 3 years from the age of 13 to 15. After graduation, students may move on to high school, or cease formal education.

High school is not compulsory and is offered to students who are 15 years of age, or older. They can attend one of two streams: general high school where students are prepared for tertiary education, or vocational high school where they are prepared for the workforce. The number of high schools within the country is significantly less than the number of elementary and middle schools. Also, fees are charged. At the higher education level Indonesia has 145 state universities and 450 private universities (AusAid 2011).

2.3.3 Government Education Policy in Indonesia

The Indonesian national philosophy is that of 'Pancasila'. It embodies five principles: the belief in one God; a just and civilized humanity; Indonesian unity; democracy; and social justice for all the peoples of Indonesia. The nationalist leader, Sukarno, first presented Pancasila in 1945. It is still embedded in all Indonesian government policies, including those related to education.

Education has become central to the Indonesian Government's development agenda. Total government spending on the sector is increasing, but the percentage of such spending relative to what is spent on other areas is falling. In the mid-1980s, 17–18 % of central government expenditure was on education. In 1997, this was reduced to 14 %, and by 2003 it was down to 5 %. By now, the National Education Law (No. 20/2003) and the Constitution Amendment III had been passed. They emphasized that all Indonesian citizens had the right to education and the Government had an obligation to finance basic education without charging fees. It was mandated that the Government should allocate 20 % of its expenditure to education. As a result, spending on education doubled between 2004 and 2006 (Kristianssen and Pratikno 2006). By 2007, it was more than for any other sector, reaching an equivalent of US$14 billion, or more than 16 % of total government expenditure. As a share of gross domestic product (3.4 %) expenditure is now comparable to that in countries at a similar stage of development.

The Indonesian Ministry of Education's strategic plan for 2005–2009 aimed to increase access to education, improve education quality, and provide better governance of the education sector. A large investment of funds in education targeted the goals in the strategic plan. During this time the Teacher Law (No. 14/2005) was passed. This law introduced important changes to the employment conditions and requirements for the certification of teachers. The main aim was to improve the quality of education and raise the profile of teacher preparation. What is noticeable is that there is no strategic approach for targeting rural and remote schooling in Indonesia, while the corpus of research into rural and remote education in the nation is limited (Wahyudi 2004).

2.3.4 International Schools in Indonesia, Including Those Offering the IBPYP

In the early 1900s, only a few wealthy Javanese groups were allowed access to the Dutch schools in Indonesia, where the Dutch curriculum was taught.

Following Independence, and especially during the boom era of the 1970s to the 1980s, international schools flourished in the country. The rise of English-speaking international schools with links to US curricula, the British General Certificate of Secondary Education (GCSE), and the IB programmes, constituted the first wave of international schooling in the country. These international schools and their curricular options provided elite Indonesians with access to an English-speaking education without having to go abroad.

All schools in Indonesia, including international schools, are required to comply with the demands of the Ministry of National Education, or the Ministry of Religious Affairs, as well as those of government legislation related to immigration. In 2006, over 40 international schools were spread throughout the country, of which eight were IB schools. In 2011, the number of international schools in the country stood at 67, of which 27 were IBPYP schools (IBO 2011a).

The largest category of international schools in Indonesia, which makes up 30 % of the group, consists of schools that offer an overseas curriculum specifically for a foreign cohort. They cater for students from Australia, Netherlands, France, Pakistan, Korea, Taipei, Japan, India, Britain, Singapore, Canada and the USA. Each of these schools has to meet requirements laid down by Indonesian government legislation, as well as meet local educational demands. Nearly 13 % of them are religious-based. Christian schools are found largely in the east of the country. Islamic schools are generally found in Java and in regions to the north and west.

'Company schools' sponsored by large mining organizations also make up a small cohort of international schools emerging throughout Indonesia. These schools are often located in remote regional areas close to mine sites. Caltex, Texmaco, Freeport-McMoran, Phelps Dodge and Newmont are key mining companies found within the nation and each operates company-owned schools on site. The smallest group of international schools are those small private schools based on non-state alternative curriculum methods. These include Montessori and Reggio Emelia schools, as well as such schools as the Green School Bali which supports 'sustainable education' and the Technology International School in Jakarta, with its individualized ICT programme.

The first IB international school in Indonesia (IBDP) was authorized in 1978. In 2011, the number of international schools offering fully authorized IBPYP programmes was 27, and there were 15 candidate schools (IBO 2011a). Many of the IBPYP schools are located in large cities, or regional centres, but some are springing up in more remote locations aligned with large multi-national mining companies. Three remote international schools are presented in the case studies detailed later in this book. Two of them are small company-based mining schools and the other is a small independent international school. Geographically they are all located in rural areas that are also considered remote due to difficulty of access and isolation. Indeed, one of the schools is only accessible by helicopter, or by bus convoy, when there is civil unrest in the region, even though it is located only 30 km from an airport.

2.4 Rural and Remote Education

It is unhelpful to work with the assumption that rural, remote, or isolated schools can be understood through using a singular, simplistic term, or definition. Rather, the complexity of each term and definition needs to be clearly articulated. Rural in Indonesia is quite different from rural in Australia, or rural in China. Rural centres in Indonesia can be found less than 2 km from city fringes and some remote centres are so isolated that the only way of gaining access is by foot, or helicopter. Therefore, before labelling areas as being rural, remote or isolated, it is important to look at the context in which the area is located globally, nationally and locally (Sharplin 2009).

Green (2009) is one authority who warns of the problem of over-generalizing about rural contexts. Nevertheless, for the purpose of this discussion, remote and rural are interpreted in geographical terms as being isolated from a major centre. In light of this, the first sub-section below presents an overview of rural and remote schooling. Two more sub-sections, one that considers life and work in remote school communities, and the other that considers life and work in remote international school communities, follow.

2.4.1 Overview of Rural and Remote Schooling

Rural and remote communities are faced with issues of diversity and difference caused by forces of globalization and internationalization involving a large mobile workforce (Tonts 2011). Relating to this context, literature in the field of rural and remote schooling highlights several themes. These include attraction and retention of teachers, pre-service preparation, quality of teachers, leadership, educational continuity, access to ICT, and professional development (Halsey 2012; Miles et al. 2004; Reid et al. 2009; Trinidad et al. 2010; White et al. 2008).

Various scholars have attempted to define rurality and remoteness (Cloke and Little 1997; Wakerman 2004) and a range of categorizations, typologies and indexes have been offered to help guide policy. These, however, are often contested, a matter that adds ambiguity to the task. In social terms, rurality can mean being isolated from family, friends, colleagues and, at times, the local community. It can also embrace the geography, demography and economic landscape that can have an impact on the local context. Such interconnectivity is referred to by Reid et al. (2009) as 'rural social place'. On this, Green (2008) suggests that contextual considerations should be taken into account in all aspects and instances of policy and paedagogy, particularly with regard to remote schooling.

The local community and surrounding environment are key factors that influence the enactment of policy in rural and remote schools (Halsey 2006, 2012; Green 2008; Sharplin 2009). Hayden (2006, p. 147) identified three external influences on schools as being the "local community, the global community and quality assurance methods". Recognition of these influences, in addition to Green's call for them to be included in policy studies, has opened up discussion about what constitutes a local community and how a school staff connects, or disconnects, with it. On this, Halsey (2012) highlights the importance of schools linking with the local community in rural and remote settings. But these links can range between strong and tenuous, and they can have an impact on schools in a range of ways. The links also occur, and are significant, in international school settings, as the next two sub-sections indicate.

2.4.2   Life and Work in Remote School Communities

Many issues surround living and working in rural, or remote, settings including the importance of developing relationships between a school and its local community (Halsey 2012). Other relevant issues relate to a sense of belonging and place, isolation and how to connect to the 'outside' world, managing people, and attracting and retaining staff. Each of these issues is explored below.

The first issue relates to developing relationships within the community as such relations can strongly influence how schools construct and actualize policy. Making connections between a school and the local community – whether it be an international, metropolitan or remote school – can be fraught with complexities and, at times, conflict. However, what remains constant for people living in rural and remote centres is the notion that schools are central meeting places for the community. In fact, in many cases, schools are often the largest organization in a town, or area. Therefore, respect on the part of the school and local community for each other, and the involvement of both with each other, need to be forthcoming.

The second major issue involved in living and working in remote settings relates to a sense of belonging and a sense of place. Green (2008) alerts us to the significance of a school as a 'place' and its relationships to 'other places' and social practices that surround it. A major role of schools in rural and remote areas is to provide safe places for all stakeholders, particularly if the area is one of civil unrest, upheaval, or conflict. At the same time, the reality for many transient teachers venturing into remote schools is that their place of teaching does not equate to home, or act as a safe place. On the contrary, living in a remote, or rural, community can represent a type of 'un-homing', particularly for those who grew up in cities (McConaghy and Bloomfield 2004).

It is also the case that many placements, remote or international, are usually considered a temporary interlude for 'nomadic subjects' (Delueze and Guittari 1987) such as international teachers. For them, the notion of 'place' has emerged as a form of identification. Thus, an individual's personal theory of 'place and belonging' may be a significant influence on how he, or she, enacts the policy. Therefore, the crucial impact of 'place' and 'community' needs to be better understood, although Green (2008) reminds us that there is little understanding of place and space with regard to either policy, or paedagogy. It is, however, becoming an issue of great interest in sociology and other disciplines.

The third major issue relating to living in rural and remote locations concerns connections with the 'outside world'. Such globalization forces as the increasing ease of communication and travel have played a significant role in removing the 'tyranny of distance and isolation' often associated with rural and remote living. One associated paradox is that students can be in close contact with communities thousands of miles away, yet be isolated from the community to which they are geographically close (Bunnell 2006a, b). Global technological advances that have the capacity to connect, and yet also disconnect, students, teachers and schools from their local community have played a major part in creating the situation.

The consequence of increased globalization is two-fold for remote communities. On a positive note, the ease of communication and technological access can connect the remote centre to the global community. On the other hand, there is the possibility of a disconnection with the local community taking place. In other words, technological advances can contribute to creating the double-edged sword of globalization forces that have the capacity to connect and disconnect individuals, systems and nations. In the words of Porter and Vidovich (2000, p. 449), globalization is a concept that is "both a sought after dream and a dreaded devil".

A fourth issue regarding teaching and schooling in remote locations relates to managing people. A certain type of teacher is attracted to remote school settings. He, or she, often share common experiences. Also, they often share similar attributes and similar reasons for wanting to teach in such locations (Reid et al. 2009). The way teachers of this type relate to each other can have an impact on school operations and culture. In small schools, anonymity can be lost and some people can find it hard to delineate between personal and professional issues (Caffyn 2011). For those in leadership roles in such schools, the situation can result in fractionalization, debate and discord.

2.4.3   Life and Work in Remote International School Communities

The development of international schools in remote locations is a recent phenomenon. It has accompanied the emergence of a mobile workforce related to resource and economic development. Furthermore, such forces of globalization as technology have spread international education opportunities to remote settings around the globe (Glass 2010). Thus, international schools in remote locations are a special category within the international school grouping.

The particular field of research on remote international schools intersects with other fields of study, especially that field on relationships within a school, between a school and community, and between a school and the 'outside' world (global, national, regional, and local). On this, the key players in each context can determine how relationships develop. In addressing the matter, Berting (2010) argues that identifying traits of families and teachers can enable schools to set up structures to take account of differences and promote harmony between them. Also, Allen (2002b) holds that promoting the idea of difference rather than community can result in a sense of isolation.

International schools often operate as elite enclaves, or what Pearce (1994) labels 'cultural bubbles'. Allen (2002a) imagines the scenario to be like atolls in a coral sea. These atolls are particularly evident within the context of developing countries, or rural and remote areas. The economic and cultural differences between those within these enclaves and the 'others' outside can be extreme. At times people hide behind "security or language issues for their lack of connection" with local host communities (Hayden 2006, p. 148). This brings to mind the 'enclave' construct identified by Cambridge and Thompson (2004, p. 165). This relates to a situation where families are "isolating their children's educational environment from exposure to local culture". A contrasting view suggests that the external community fear that its own culture may be contaminated by the Anglo-American culture which the international school is perceived to bring with it. Such isolation of both communities is likely found where there is a perceived 'culture clash' between the school and the local community (Hayden 2006).

The superficiality of how some local and school communities interact was highlighted by McKenzie (1998, p. 250), who found that many teachers had little or "any genuine or sustained contact with their ambient society". More recently, Hayden (2006) has suggested that international schools need to raise the awareness, and develop a much deeper understanding of, the similarities between the local context and culture and their own situation, rather than persist with the more traditional 'us and them' perception of difference and superficial contact. Overall, the debate is moving from one centred on differences and similarities between school and local communities, to a focus on acceptance and a more symbiotic relationship between the two.

While developing a profile of international schools, Berting (2010) designed a quadrant model to help identify an international school population. Each quadrant (Q) is based on recognizing traits of international teachers and families:

Q1: Local families unilingual and have little international experience who choose to go to
     international schools to gain English experience and reflect their social status;
Q2: International families from English speaking countries on their first international
     posting often unilingual and never embrace the local language or culture;
Q3: Cosmopolitan and local families with extensive international experience and who may
     be multi-lingual and are often bridge builders between communities; and
Q4: The cosmopolitan international family that have adapted to local community, are often
     multilingual, active participants in the school and local community and understand the
     intrinsic value of international education. (Berting 2010, pp. 32–33)

Recognizing the composition of the family and teachers involved in international school communities outlined in Berting's (2010) quadrants provides schools with important information that can help to promote and develop relationships between community and schools, whether they are located in rural, remote or urban settings.

Rural, remote and international school communities are part of a global educational community strongly connected by networks of educational organizations and social networking facilities. Globalization forces such as technological advances have facilitated these connections. Some international educational organizations offer rural and remote teachers access to online support, newsletters, online professional development and informal social networks. These large organizations include the European Council of Schools, the United World Colleges, the International Schools Services, Global Education Management Systems and International Baccalaureate schools. Other associations that offer similar online support as well as professional and social networks for international schools include the Association of American Schools in Central America, The Federation of British International Schools in South and East Asia, the Swiss Group of International Schools, the Association of International Schools in Africa, the Association for the Advancement of International Education and the Academy for International School Heads.

To summarise, the issues surrounding rural and remote education and schools in a diversity of settings are complex. They relate to a sense of belonging and place, isolation and connecting with the 'outside' world, leadership and managing people, and concerns about attracting and retaining teachers. There are clearly advantages and disadvantages for teachers living and working in remote settings. Also, teachers in these localized contexts are increasingly influenced by global and social factors surrounding them. At the local level the micro-politics within teaching cohorts can reflect the biases and self-interests of individuals and groups. Social, economic and cultural factors can be magnified, and micro-politics can be very personalized and powerful (Caffyn 2011). The associated strategy offered by Zhao (2010) is that there should be an emphasis on developing knowledge 'about' others, perspectives 'on' others, attitudes 'towards' others and ability to interact 'with' others to help enhance interpersonal relationships. The global competencies which would be developed as a result, he holds, have the capacity to benefit teaching cohorts in remote and remote international schools.

2.5 Conclusion

This chapter has detailed the context of the study at the core of later chapters in this book, by explaining the three contexts in which it is located, namely, the IB and the IBPYP, the Indonesian educational context, and issues surrounding rural and remote education. The exponential growth of IBPYP schools, coupled with the changing face of the teacher and student populations in international schools, has brought about much discussion and debate. This chapter has revealed the many anomalies and contradictions that exist in regard to international and rural and remote education, as well as commonalities between them.

Within Indonesia, the IBPYP is growing alongside other emerging international curricula. The Ministry of Education in Indonesia recognizes this development, and is responding by changing policies related to international schools as well as internationalizing its national schooling.

With predictions of future growth trends, the IB can expect to have 10,000 authorized schools across the world by 2020. In 2011, 3,400 IB schools located in 143 schools catered for over one million students (IBO 2011a). The 27 IBPYP-authorized international schools in Indonesia constitute a small proportion of this global phenomenon. However, with the increase in mining and economic activity, and the increasing number of mobile middle class families expected to be living in Indonesia in the near future, these numbers seem destined to increase.

The next chapter, Chap. 3, now locates the exposition to date within the context of the relevant academic literature. In particular, it explores the phenomena of globalization and internationalization, the conceptualization of the policy process, and the conceptualization of international education and schools. The complex and contested nature of these constructs is examined through the lens of global change.

References

Allen, K. (2002a). Atolls, seas of culture and global nets. In M. C. Hayden, J. J. Thompson, & G. Walker (Eds.), *International education in practice: Dimensions for national and international schools* (pp. 112–135). London: Kogan Page.

Allen, M. (2002b). Cultural borderlands: Cultural dissonance in the international school. *International Schools Journal, 20*(2), 42–53.

AusAID. (2011). *Australian aid*. http://www.ausaid.gov.au/Pages/home.aspx. Accessed 1 Dec 2012.

Bagnall, N. F. (2008). *International schools as agents for change*. New York: Nova Science Publishers, Inc.

Bagnall, N. F. (2010). *Education without borders: Forty years of the International Baccalaureate, 1970–2010*. Berlin: VDM Publishing House Ltd.

Berting, R. (2010). From local or international to colloquial or cosmopolitan – Refining how we look at the populations of international schools. *International Schools Journal, 29*(2), 30–40.

Bonk, C. J. (2009). *The world is open: How web technology is revolutionizing education*, San Francisco: Jossey-Bass.

Boyer, E. L. (1994, March). Creating the new American college. *Chronicle of Higher Education*, 8–48.

Brown, C., & Lauder, H. (2011). The political economy of international schools and social class formation. In R. Bates (Ed.), *Schooling internationally: Globalisation, internationalisation and the future for international schools* (pp. 39–58). Abingdon: Routledge.

Bunnell, T. (2006a). Managing the role stress of public relations practitioners in international schools. *Educational Management Administration and Leadership, 34*(3), 385–409.

Bunnell, T. (2006b). The growing momentum and legitimacy behind an alliance for international education. *Journal of Research in International Education, 5*(2), 155–176.

Bunnell, T. (2007). The international education industry: An introductory framework for conceptualizing the potential scale of an 'alliance'. *Journal of Research in International Education, 6*(3), 349–367.

Bunnell, T. (2011). The International Baccalaureate and 'growth scepticism': A 'social limits' framework. *International Studies in Sociology of Education, 21*(2), 161–176.

Caffyn, R. (2011). International schools and micropolitics: Fear, vulnerability and identity in fragmented space. In R. Bates (Ed.), *Schooling internationally: Globalisation, internationalisation and the future for international schools* (pp. 59–82). Abingdon: Routledge.

Cambridge, J., & Thompson, J. (2004). Internationalism and globalization as contexts for international education. *Compare: A Journal of Comparative Education, 34*(2), 161–175.

Cloke, P., & Little, J. (Eds.). (1997). *Contested countryside cultures: Rurality and socio-cultural marginalisation*. London: Routledge.

Deleuze, G., & Guattari, F. (1987). *A thousand plateaus: Capitalism and schizophrenia*. Bath: Bookcraft.

Dolby, N., & Rahman, A. (2008). Research in international education. *Review of Educational Research, 78*(3), 676–726.

EdStats. (2006). *World Bank education statistics*. wwwr.worldbank.org/education/edstats. Accessed 13 Jan 2008.

Ellwood, C. A. (2004). *Sociology and modern social problems*. Whitefish: Kessinger Publishing.

Glass, G. V. (2010). Potholes in the road to virtual schooling. *School Administrator, 67*(4), 32–35.

Green, B. (2008). *Spaces and places: The NSW rural (teacher) education project*. Wagga Wagga: Charles Sturt University, Centre for Information Studies.

Green, B. (Ed.). (2009). *Understanding and researching professional practice*. Rotterdam: Sense Publishers.

Halsey, J. R. (2006). Towards a spatial 'self-help' map for teaching and living in a rural context. *International Education Journal, 7*(4), 490–498.

Halsey, R. J. (2012, March). Rural reflections on Gonski. *Education Review*, np.

Hayden, M. (2006). *Introduction to international education*. London: Sage Publications Ltd.

Hayden, M. C., & Thompson, J. (2011). Teachers for the international school of the future. In R. Bates (Ed.), *Schooling internationally: Globalisation, internationalisation and the future for international schools* (pp. 83–100). Abingdon: Routledge.

Hill, I. (2007). International education as developed by the International Baccalaureate Organization. In J. Thompson, M. Hayden, & J. Levy (Eds.), *The SAGE handbook of research in international education* (pp. 25–38). London: Sage.

International Middle Years Curriculum. (2010). *International Middle Years Curriculum*. Retrieved April 18, 2010, from http://www.internationalmiddleyearscurriculum.com/

International Primary Curriculum. (2010). *International Primary Curriculum*. Retrieved April 18, 2010, from http://www.internationalprimarycurriculum.com/

IBO. (2003a). *Programme standards and practices*. Cardiff: IBO. www.ibo.org/documentlibrary/programmestandards. Accessed 30 Mar 2006.

IBO. (2003b). *IB learner profile booklet*. Cardiff: IBO. www.ibo.org/ibla/conference/.../TheLearnerProfileinActionFabian.ppt. Accessed 30 Mar 2006.

IBO. (2009). *A continuum of international education*. IBO. www.ibo.org/communications/powerpoint/.../Continuumppt22.12.08Eng.pp. Accessed 20 Oct 2010.

IBO. (2011a). *IB fast facts. One page of key information about the IB*. Retrieved from www.ibo.org/facts/fastfacts/

IBO. (2011b). *International Baccalaureat Organisation*. Retrieved from www.ibo.org

IBO. (2011c). *Programme standards and practices*. Cardiff: IBO. Retrieved from www.ibo.org/documentlibrary/programmestandards/

IBO. (2012). *Mission and strategy*. www.ibo.org/mission. Accessed 1 Jan 2013.

Kristiansen, S., & Pratikno. (2006). Decentralising education in Indonesia. *International Journal of Educational Development, 26*(5), 513–531.

McConaghy, C, & Bloomfield, D. (2004). Beyond the line, beyond the self. *Journal of Curriculum Theorising*, (Fall), 93–112.

McKenzie, M. (1998). Going, going, gone… global! In M. Hayden & J. Thompson (Eds.), *International education: Principles and practice* (pp. 242–252). London: Kogan Page.

Miles, R., Marshall, C., Rolf, J., & Noonan, S. (2004, May 13). *The attraction and retention of professionals in regional areas*. National Rural Health Alliance Inc., Fact Sheet. http://www.bowenbasin.cqu.edu.au/pdfs/dotars_colloq. Accessed 11 Feb 2006.

Moegiadi, A., & Jiyono, C. (1991). *Research report on community participation in education at the primary level in Indonesia*. Office of Educational and Cultural Research and Development.

Ornstein, A. C., & Hunkins, F. P. (2004). *Curriculum foundations, principles, and issues* (4th ed.). Boston: Allyn & Bacon.

Pearce, R. (1994, November 27–29). Globalization: Learning from international schools. *Mobility*.

Porter, P., & Vidovich, L. (2000). Globalization and higher education policy. *Educational Theory, 50*(4), 449–465.

Quist, I. (2005). The language of international education: A critique. *IB Research Notes, 5*(1), 2–6.

Reid, J., Green, B., White, S., Cooper, M., Lock, G., & Hastings, W. (2009, May). *Understanding complex ecologies in a changing world*. Paper presented at the AERA annual conference. Denver: American Educational Research Association.

Sharplin, E. (2009, February). *Getting them out there: A rural education field trip*. Presented at the International Symposium for Innovation in Rural Education, Armidale, Australia.

Tonts, M. (2011, September). *Sustainability and globalization – Partners or protagonists?* Paper presented at the Rural National Summit, Flinders University, Adelaide.

Trinidad, S., Sharplin, E., Lock, G., Ledger, S., Boyd, D., & Terry, E. (2010, August). *Developing strategies at the pre-service level to address critical teacher attraction and retention issues in Australian rural, regional and remote schools*. Paper presented at the National Rural Education Conference, Mooloolaba, QLD, Australia.

Van Schaik, B. (2009). *Indonesia's education policy: Enabling innovation and growth*. Unpublished M.Sc. thesis, Delft University of Technology, Delft, The Netherlands.

Wahyudi, I. (2004). *Symbolism, rationality and myth in organizational control systems: An ethnographic case study of PBS Jakarta Indonesia*. Unpublished Ph.D. thesis, The University of Wollongong, Australia.

Wakerman, J. (2004). Defining remote health. *Australian Journal of Rural Health, 12*(5), 210–214.

White, S., Green, B., Reid, J. A., Lock, G., Hastings, W., & Cooper, M. (2008, July). *Teacher education for rural communities: A focus on incentives*. Paper presented at the Australian Teacher Education conference, Sunshine Coast, QLD, Australia.

Zhao, Y. (2010). Preparing globally competent teachers: A new imperative for teacher education. *Journal of Teacher Education, 61*(5), 422–431.

Chapter 3
Literature Review

3.1 Introduction

The previous chapter contextualized the three background fields in which the study at the core of the book is located. It introduced the IB's Primary Years Programme (IBPYP), it gave an outline of the Indonesian educational context, and it described issues related to remote schooling. This chapter now presents a review of key concepts underpinning the study. It is organized into two main sections. It begins by fore-grounding the ever-changing macro level phenomenon of globalization. The second section then details the changing face of international education, and international schools and teachers, as well as the ideological constructs they espouse such as 'international mindedness'.

3.2 Globalization

The term 'globalization' is not new in educational discourse (Dabbagh and Bannan-Ritland 2005). However, it is difficult to "pinpoint when the term globalization was actually coined and incorporated into academic language" (Al-Rodhan 2006, p. 1). Over the last decade there has been unprecedented debate about its complexity and ambiguity, particularly in regard to education (Bates 2011a, b; Brown and Lauder 2011; Held et al. 1999; Henry 2001; Rizvi and Lingard 2010; Walker 2007). The link that Dabbagh and Bannan-Ritland (2005) have established as existing between globalization and socio-cultural dimensions of society is useful in framing considerations. On this, Rizvi and Lingard (2010, p. 23) remind us that "the contemporary processes of globalization are reshaping most aspects of our sociality" by affecting the ways "in which we both interpret and imagine the possibilities of our lives". They point to the need to imagine different forms of the phenomenon beyond its historical, technological, ideological and present social imaginary.

© Springer International Publishing Switzerland 2014
S. Ledger et al., *Global to Local Curriculum Policy Processes*,
Policy Implications of Research in Education 4, DOI 10.1007/978-3-319-08762-7_3

Many images of globalization have been presented within the literature in economic, political, social and cultural terms (Al-Rodhan 2006; Appadurai 1996; Currie et al. 2003; Nye 2002; Peters 2003; Porter and Vidovich 2000). Less attention, however, has been given to globalization and educational policy, curriculum and paedagogy (Hayden and Thompson 2008; Rizvi and Lingard 2010; Winter 2012; Yates and Grumet 2011). This is the focus of the present section of this chapter. It elaborates on the complex and dynamic nature of globalization and its interconnectivity with education.

Globalization is considered to be a most significant phenomenon of the twenty-first century, yet it is not well understood (Milton-Smith 2008). Thus, it is likely that definitions of the notion will be refined to reflect the processes involved in change and innovation. There is also a general acceptance that globalization is "an evolving phenomenon that is so named because of the context in which it is developed" (Al-Rodhan 2006, p. 6). It will continue to be a fluid concept influenced by the context in which it exists and the impact it has in different spheres (O'Rourke and Williamson 2004).

The current wave of globalization is often presented as a multi-faceted phenomenon influenced by profound technological advances and policy decisions similar to that of an earlier 1950s post-war wave, but proceeding much faster and reaching much deeper. It has had an impact on educational policy at all levels, from global to local, with, for example, "hybridized curriculum policies being produced in different national contexts as a result of the intersection of international, national and local forces" (Winter 2012, p. 295). International schools are good examples of this trend of hybridizing global, national and local education policies and practices. At the same time, as Walker (2011) points out, there is a lack of literature about the impact of globalization on education. He suggests that it is still too early to see its effects in this domain with any clarity and he calls for more research in the area.

Globalization, of course, has an impact on the education sphere in specific contexts (Taylor and Henry 2000). These contexts are intertwined and porous. On this, Marginson and Rhoades (2002) coined the concept of a 'glo-na-cal agency heuristic' to help capture the dynamic interactions between different contexts at global, national and local levels. It is argued that globalization at a macro level is influenced by technological, economic, political, and social change (Appadurai 1996; Knight 2001). At a meso level, globalization is often affected by a nation's individual history, traditions, culture and priorities (Ruddy 2008). At the local level, "place and space matters" and forces of globalization are "felt" (Green 2009, p. 390).

Rather than define globalization, some commentators describe different types. For Bottery (2000), it has six forms: economic, political, cultural, demographic, managerial and environmental. Stearns (2003, p. 154) describes globalization as "the acceleration of interregional contacts in speed, in increased volume, and in widening range." Knight (2001, 2003) takes a different approach yet again. Instead of describing types of globalization, she speaks of a process of globalization, consisting of a flow of technology, economy, knowledge, people and ideas across borders. Others have offered similar views, suggesting that the phenomenon incorporates the movement of socially constructed global ideologies (Appadurai 1996; Held and McGrew 2002; Marginson and Rhoades 2002; Rizvi and Lingard 2010). Furthermore, there are those who discuss globalization as a global culture, or as Westernization or Americanization, suggesting homogenization of values (Currie et al. 2003).

Wylie (2011) argues that the process of globalization promotes the hegemonic interest of the West. On this, Rizvi and Lingard (2005) discuss how Western interests are transmitted through global forces and can result in uneven benefits that have the ability to create greater social stratification. In a similar vein, Dabbagh and Bannan-Ritland's (2005) description captures the concern that globalization is both politically and economically motivated. Others yet again, instead of describing types of globalization, or the process of globalization, have attempted to measure the rate and dynamics of the phenomenon in terms of economic, political, technological, cultural and social changes (Andersen and Herbertsson 2005). Examples of such attempts include the Organisation for Economic Co-operation and Development's (OECD) (2005) *Economic Globalization Indicators* and the Geneva Centre for Security Policy's (2008) *Globalization Matrix*. More recently, the matrix of Al-Rodhan (2006) has provided an analytic tool that highlights the impact that globalization has on policy makers.

Overall, then, globalization is an ever-changing process. It has become a backdrop to many discussions due to its influence. Yet, making meaning of globalization is problematic due to its dynamic nature, unpredictability and pervasiveness. It can represent a double-edged sword that has the capacity to both connect and disconnect individuals, systems and nations. In the words of Porter and Vidovich (2000, p. 449), globalization is a concept "considered as both a sought-after dream and a dreaded devil, an empirical reality and rhetorical myth". Also, issues of equity and access, power differentials, and Western-dominated discourses, have emerged surrounding it effects. The following discussion now considers various aspects of globalization in terms of the impact it has on education.

3.2.1 *Globalization, Internationalization and Education*

The focus here is on the contested differences and interconnected relationship between globalization and internationalization, and the role they both play in the field of education. In terms of defining 'global' and 'international', the educational literature defines global relations as super-territorial (Scholte 2005), or supra-national (Vidovich 2007), whereas international relations occur across borders, involving bilateral or multilateral exchanges between several nations. 'Internationality' relates to one or more nations, whereas 'globality' transcends geography (Currie et al. 2003; Scholte 2005). Both constructs are interconnected and interdependent (Yang 2002). The definition of globalization of education put forward by Spring (2009, p. 1) as "the worldwide discussions, processes, and institutions affecting local educational practices and policies" helps capture the dynamic and complex nature of the phenomenon. Accompanying the forces of globalization is the process of internationalization of education (Yang 2002).

The sub-sections below detail core themes that are evident in the literature in relation to both globalization and internationalization. These are 'contexts', 'power', 'technology', 'organization as vehicles to transmit global ideologies', and 'the marketization of education'.

3.2.1.1   Contexts

Globalization was initially conceived of as a top down force; that is, as a macro level phenomenon. Over time, however, the meaning has shifted to include localized contexts (Green 2009). The construct of a 'glo-na-cal agency heuristic' (Marginson and Rhoades 2002), where global, national and local perspectives are identified, captures this shift and has been quite extensively used in policy analysis related to higher education. Zadja (2005), in the *International Handbook on Globalization – Education and Policy Research*, examined global pedagogies and policies in over 25 different countries and found great variety, leading him to conclude that globalization does not necessarily create convergence across the globe. Overall, the literature exposes the complex interplay of global and local dimensions to the policy process, and also underscores the importance of studying local contexts, when analysing global policy trends.

3.2.1.2   Power

Power differentials between the macro (global), meso (national) and micro (local) levels of policy processes increasingly dominate educational discourse. On this, Taylor and Henry (2000, p. 502) recognize uneven power relationships that accompany globalization, when they state that it "exerts simultaneous impulses for convergence and fragmentation, for universalism and localism". Globalization is also a powerful influence on the structural arrangements and ideologies that dominate life in schools. In doing so, it has the capacity to cause tensions, both unprecedented and unpredictable (Apple 1979, 2004). The cultural life of schools is influenced and often dominated by a combination of local, national and global demands (Caffyn 2011; Yates and Grumet 2011). The globalization process allows the cultural life experienced by students and teachers in schools to be infiltrated by a wide range of external influences.

At times, global ideologies, products and forces can be in conflict with local cultural demands and desires. As a result, power inequities and relationships are affected. When a clash of cultures occurs between international and local forces, interpersonal and intercultural relationships can be fractured in a manner that can result in conflicts or compromises (Caffyn 2011). Relationships between networks of people, ideologies and technology can also fracture when there are conflicts between ideologies at the macro and micro levels.

English has emerged as the language of globalization as a result of technological advances. International schools recruit most of their teachers from English-speaking countries (Hayden and Thompson 2011). This perceived Western-dominated practice could trigger tension between global forces and local cultures, especially if teachers are not prepared to teach in multinational, multilingual and multicultural settings (Bernstein 2000; Fail 2011; Wylie 2011). On this, Hayden and Thompson (2008, p. 3) highlight the need for teachers in international schools to be 'culturally sensitive'. Taking a different perspective, Wylie (2011, p. 29) shows concern that international schools may be "devaluing indigenous culture, beliefs and identity, where the loss of language results in the disruption of cultural reproduction". On the other hand, international school systems that provide students with an English language experience could be seen as empowering their students by offering an internationally recognized transferable skill.

3.2.1.3 Technology

In a globalized world, technological advances have the ability to both marginalize and be inclusive. They also have the ability to connect and disconnect policy players and educational consumers. In other words, while technology allows international students to remain connected with their family and friends in their home country, it can, at the same time, disconnect them from the local culture and population (Allen 2002).

The range of technologies being employed in schools is diverse. It includes knowledge portals, tele-learning and virtual classrooms (Levin and Schrum 2002). Schools are using technology to provide one-on-one web-based personalized instruction for their students, seeking to connect them to educational products and programmes around the world. In this regard, flexible learning technologies have the capacity to facilitate further removal of cultural specificity.

Technology has also blurred the concept of 'place and space' (Green 2009). Rizvi and Lingard (2010) alerted us to this when they use the term 'transnational public space'. They argue that technology renders any strictly bounded sense of community, or relationality, borderless. They conclude from this that the once-identified notion of 'here and there' is now the 'here is there' borderless context. This situation has, in the view of some, opened up educational opportunities and made it possible for anyone to learn anything from anyone at any time (Bonk 2009). Technology, it is held, will transform how access to international education will be gained and, ultimately, will provide a re-conceptualization of the terms 'school' and 'schooling' in the future.

3.2.1.4 Global Organizations as Vehicles to Transmit Ideologies

Globalization and internationalization can facilitate the transmission of ideologies by means of a range of global organizations and their networks of technologies, organizational structures and associated groups; they have the capacity to promote and create a ruling consciousness (Lauder 2007). This consciousness can be interpreted as another opportunity to promote the transmission of Western ideologies, language and cultural desires (Hill 2007). Global organizations are vehicles that transmit these social constructs. One such construct has developed into what is commonly referred to as 'international mindedness', 'global citizenship' and 'cosmopolitanism', or more recently, into what Zhao (2010) terms 'global competencies'. These social constructs are embedded in education policies and discourses related to international organizations and schools.

Hayden and Thompson (2008) offer a detailed outline of the role of particular international organizations that have had an impact on international education. Their UNESCO-funded report provides a comprehensive coverage of the growth of international education. It also highlights the role of such global organizations involved in international education as the United Nations, the World Bank, the International Monetary Fund, and the OECD. A variety of international educational 'brands' has also emerged over the years that seek support and favour from these large global organizations. Many of these 'brands' have originated from the migration of national curricula around the globe. They include the Cambridge Local Examinations Syndicate (UK), International School Services (USA), Yew Chung Education Foundation (China), International Schools Association (USA) and the European Council of International Schools (EU).

Educational brands that are associated with particular nation states also exist. These include the long-standing Global Education Management System of schooling founded by Sunny Varkey in the mid-1960s, the United World Colleges established in 1962, the IBO established in 1968, the International Primary Curriculum established in 2000, and the International Middle Curriculum established in 2010. On this, Hayden and Thompson (2008) characterized international schools as organizations that offer curricula not of the host country. Also, there are schools that have an internationally recognized marketable brand, some not-for-profit and others commercial.

Affiliated international curricular and assessment organizations have also emerged, aligning themselves to each of the above-mentioned large organizations. As a result, they are transforming themselves into manufacturers of globally-branded educational goods and services. They have, in part, become global participants in the social, cultural and economic dimensions of marketization and globalization. Specific examples of the growth in this field of affiliated groups include the extensive range of professional development opportunities and conferences offered that target these organizations, the Australian Council of Educational Research that developed the International Schools Assessment tool in 2005, and a wide range of publishing houses producing books and resources written specifically to cater for, and capture the essence of, each educational institute they represent. Further examples include such external accreditation organizations as the Council for International Schools, the Northern European International Schools Association, and the Western Association of Schools and Colleges. The growth of such groups, companies and publishers affiliated with international educational organizations is indicative of the impact globalization has had on the educational landscape and the involvement of these organizations in the transmission of international curriculum policy. Furthermore, their exponential growth adds to the debate about the marketization and commodification of education.

3.2.1.5 Marketization of Education

Globalization has been associated with the ascendancy of a market ideology in education over the last three decades, particularly in regard to international education and schooling. The impact of globalization has seen the international schools' network develop into both the product and the process for internationalizing education (MacDonald 2006). This network of international schools has been referred to as 'a franchised outlet' (Cambridge 2002; Hayden and Thompson 2008; Wylie 2011) that readily distributes international education to a wide range of locations. The franchise guarantees a high profile, a positive reputation and a 'brand proposition' that help schools attract customers (Bates 2011b; Cambridge 2002).

The relationship is also regulated by quality assurance mechanisms, accreditation processes and support organizations comparable with how most franchised businesses are regulated. It is argued here that the IBPYP falls within this quasi-franchised educational branding paradigm and, in doing so, places itself firmly within the social, cultural and economic dimensions of globalization. The potential tension between the inclusive principles that the IBPYP espouses on the one hand, and the IBPYP being labelled as a global policy product on the other, is further evidence of the push/pull dynamics and the double edged sword associated with globalization (Porter and Vidovich 2000).

The franchise metaphor for the multi-million dollar industry of international education (Bates 2011b; Bunnell 2011; MacDonald 2006) supports a 'transnational capitalist class', a term coined by Sklair (2001) to characterize a group which supports global free market capitalism. Sklair claims that international education is a service, or product, consumed predominantly by two client groups. The first client group is made up of the globally mobile workforce employed by multinational companies, governmental and non-governmental organizations, and parastatal organizations that are indirectly controlled by government. The second group includes members of local economic and social elites who have a disinclination to use the local educational system of a given country. The rise in the transnational middle class is a catalyst for the expansion of the international education industry. Such expansion could move it from granting elite access to a more general status that could have an impact on state and national schooling (Bates 2011b).

3.2.1.6 Interconnections Between Globalization and Internationalization

For the purpose of this work, globalization is taken as being "intimately connected with the way we view the world" (Bottery 2006, p. 96) and a "dynamic phenomenon expressed in particular histories and political configurations" (Rizvi and Lingard 2010, p. 20). Such approaches embrace the interdependence that Dabbagh and Bannan-Ritland (2005) state exists between technological, economic, political and socio-cultural outcomes of globalization. Yet, it is important to emphasise that while the impact of globalization on education is considered to be one of the most significant phenomena of the 21st century, it is not well understood (Milton-Smith 2008). In highlighting this, Milton-Smith (2008) maintains that there is a tendency to focus too much on macro accounts at the expense of the micro experiences. What is needed is an approach that considers both macro constraint and micro agency.

Internationalization of education has been defined as "the process of integrating an international perspective in the teaching/learning, research and service functions" (Knight 2001, p. 229). Such a definition, like others (Currie et al. 2003; Scholte 2005), although contentious, implies that internationalization of education is a partly-planned process and an integrated phenomenon that is usually agreed upon by one, or more, partners. The planned process of internationalization relies on policy, organization and resources for enactment.

The planned internationalization processes that are currently evident in higher education and national school policy settings (Ruddy 2008) have both economic and social rationales. On this, Hayden and Thompson (2008, p. 26) describe how "prestigious independent schools establish their marketable brands as 'franchises' in, inter alia, China, Thailand and Dubai". Enhanced intercultural understandings often sit alongside the economic benefits of internationalization of education.

Notwithstanding the foregoing positions, there is still a lack of consensus on the meaning of globalization and internationalization of education other than that they are inextricably linked and affected by technology and change. Hill (2007) highlights the inequities that accompany globalization and internationalization of education, as do Knight and deWit (1997), and Yang (2002, 2005). The need to develop mutual understanding, respect and relationships, as well as interactions between different national states and cultures has been highlighted by all of these authors as an important component of the internationalization of education.

Forces of globalization and internationalization are occurring in a world where social, economic, environmental and political issues rapidly transcend borders. They are causing substantial time-space compression in a shrinking world. Also, globalization itself is an unpredictable phenomenon forged by, and forging technologies and change that permeate all facets of society, including education. As a result of its unpredictability it continues to be a source of political, economic and social conflict affecting global, national and local contexts of educational policy processes.

3.3 International Education

The conceptual maps that we are currently using to construct our modern sense of an emergent field of international education are largely untested and incomplete. (Sylvester 2002, p. 91).

Notions of international education are value laden, full of anomalies, and contestable. They have given rise to a field of study with research trajectories that focus primarily on comparative and international education, the internationalization of higher education and K-12 schooling, international schools, international teachers and teacher education, and the link between globalization and education (Dolby and Rahman 2008). The study reported in the following chapters focused on the link between globalization and education, the internationalization of K-6 schooling in international schools, and the role of the teacher within this context.

This section of the present chapter, which locates the study reported here within the relevant corpus of research literature, is divided into three subsections. The first sub-section presents international education as a field of study and considers the ideological constructs it espouses, including 'international mindedness' and 'intercultural learning'. The second sub-section provides an outline of the changing face and types of remote international schools and teachers. The final sub-section explores the settings in which international schools are located and the teaching cohorts within them.

3.3.1 International Education as a Field of Study

The terms 'international education' and 'internationalization' have been located predominantly in discourses surrounding higher education, particularly in relation to the global market of cross-border degrees (Ruddy 2008). Related discussions focus on issues of globalization, attraction and retention of students, financial imperatives, intercultural understandings, power inequities, and education as currency (Marginson 2007a, b). Lately such discussion has also been emerging within discourses surrounding schooling. In the remainder of this sub-section, the consideration of international education largely focuses on international education in schools. In doing so, however, it also acknowledges the similarities and possible cross-fertilization of ideas across the two fields.

International education is a socially constructed field of study that encompasses international policies, international curriculum, international schools, teachers, students, communities, cultures, professional development and international resources. While these can be separated for heuristic purposes, they are inherently interconnected and intertwined. This is because the function of international education is dynamic. Consequently, the meaning of the term has expanded and multiple dialogues proliferate (Bagnall 2008a, b, 2010; Hayden 2006; Roberts 2003). Also, as Garavalia (1997) and Wylie (2008) suggest, definitions of international education are dependent upon context and audience. At the same time, Wylie (2008, p. 5) argues that definitions of international education are "contested and context dependent, international education and the associated models are expanding into mainstream discourses".

Although defining international education can be problematic, many typologies, categories and descriptions have been presented. Roberts (2003, p. 2) outlines eight key features of international education, namely, "content, context, delivery, intention, derivation, assessment, governance and currency". The inclusion of 'derivation' in this list reflects Ball's (1994) and Vidovich's (2007) acknowledgement of the important role that the 'context of influence' and 'power' play in the policy process. Furthermore, Roman (2003) suggests we consider 'in whose interest?' or to 'what normative end?' international education exists. Likewise, Matthews and Sidhu (2005) encourage the development of an awareness of the normalizing discourses of nationality, race and ethnicity in international education policy construction and enactment. Such attention means that international education as an emerging field of study is generating a wide range of research areas related to context, power, purpose and influence, linked to the forces of globalization and internationalization of education.

The contested nature of international education is also contributing to the debate surrounding the idea of international schools and teachers being a common global currency (Bates 2011b; Bunnell 2007; Cambridge 2011; Hayden 2006; Sylvester 2002). This refers to the transfer of knowledge and expertise between national systems of education (Lauder 2007; Lowe 1998). In a globalized world, global branding of educational products, curricula, and key concepts such as 'international mindedness' are specific examples of educational currency.

One of the claims for the development of international education is that it "has the capacity and the commitment to develop ideas and predispositions towards global citizenship among pupils" (Marshall 2011, p. 182). This is also often identified as the promotion of international mindedness. This concept of international mindedness has emerged alongside such notions as 'global citizenship', 'cosmopolitism', 'intercultural studies', 'global knowledge' and '21st century competencies' (Marshall 2011; Urry 2000; Weenink 2008; Yates and Grumit 2011). Hayden and Thompson (2011, p. 22) see its origin as being in the deliberations of the Conference of Internationally Minded Schools in 1951, an organization "which was later subsumed by the International Schools Association".

The move toward developing international mindedness has paralleled the development of international schooling. Also, over the last 20 years the *IB Learner Profile Booklet* (IBLP), which has emerged as the ideological core for each IB programme, has become a tool for internationalization in IBPYP schools. The IBLP provides a list of ten attributes that embody the IBO's mission statement. It promotes the notion of students as inquirers, knowledgeable, thinkers, communicators, principled, open-minded, caring, risk-takers, balanced and reflective.

The IBLP is embedded in all IBPYP documents. For example, the *Programme of Inquiry and Scope and Sequence Document* (IBO 2003a) utilises the subject area of Personal and Social Education as a means of promoting 'the learner profile' in its text. It states:

> The expectations of PSE emphasize attitudes, behaviours and skills that are closely aligned with the PYP student profile. ... Students must be prepared to address moral issues in their lives and should act upon a set of positive values such as justice, respect for human rights and dignity. It is through exposure to new and difficult issues in a non-threatening environment that students are able to develop their own positive values and prepare for their role as international citizen. (IBO 2003b, p. 6.1)

The IB literature also acknowledges that the development of internationally-minded students can come about through the enactment of the *IB Learner Profile Booklet* (IBO 2003b) and it highlights the importance of such environmental factors as setting, teachers and community members in this development.

Notions about international education and international mindedness are not without critics. Roman (2003), for example, argues that there are competing definitions of global citizenship and international mindedness. Also, there is concern that if educators are not careful they can reinforce binaries between 'us and other' and 'West versus other' (Davies 2006). On this, the developing concept of 'othering' is emerging in discourses on international education. Similarly, Roman (2003) cautions educators to be mindful with regard to how power relationships can be reinforced in this construction, as do others (Davies 2006; Matthews and Sidhu 2005; Merryfield and Masataka 2004). Likewise, Schweisfurth (2006, p. 42) suggests that "even education which aims at creating global perspective in learners is a distinctly culture-bound exercise".

Further, there are inherent difficulties in enacting international mindedness. Roman (2003, p. 272) refers to the danger of "intellectual tourism". He specifies that such tourism can occur via travel, or cyberspace, and can lead to a sense of superiority on the part of those from Western cultures who may see problems and issues as only belonging to cultures other than their own. This point serves to highlight that while there is a need for global citizenship education and the creation of critical thinkers in international schooling, it should not simply refer to a critical examination of 'other', but an examination that looks both ways (Curry 2006). In other words, internationally-minded students should engage with their own localized contexts and with 'others' to see merit in both.

When critiquing international education it is also valuable to consider that identifying 'differences' can direct discussion and debate in new fields of study, such as that on international mindedness. In a world where there is migration, leading to complex cultural identities (Davies 2006), there is a need to critically consider power relationships and identity within international school settings. Simplistic understandings and misunderstandings occur when complexities are ignored (Zhao 2010).

3.3.2 The Changing Face of International Schools and Teachers

International schools are scattered throughout the world within a range of urban, rural and remote settings. They are connected through curriculum, paedagogy and assessment and are networked through organizations, technology and communication systems (Wylie 2011). Within these contexts, dynamic ideological tensions occur and organizational differences exist.

International schools expanded at a rapid rate between 2000 and 2010, with the number doubling to 5000. The most rapid growth occurred in Asia, Europe, Africa and the Americas (Bates 2011b). However, determining whether a school is 'international', or not, is problematic. Gellar (2002) suggests that the term international has little or no meaning and is often attached to schools with little understanding of its implications. On this, the International Schools Association argues that the true measure of a school is not to be found in its name, but in the manner in which it lives its philosophy on a daily basis.

Given the changing economic climate, technological advances and ease of travel, the number of international schools continues to increase to meet demand. Tied to this increase is a growth in diversity among schools. The recent work of Bagnall (2008a), Caffyn (2011), Hayden and Thompson (2011), Roberts (2006), Sylvester (2002) and Wylie (2006), has contributed to the development of related typologies, categories and classifications of international schools. Nevertheless, as Hayden and Thompson (2011) suggest, the growing number of international schools and school types continues to make the task of clarifying a difficult one. They argue that there is still value in going back to a classification of nearly a quarter of a century ago and a position that we should think in terms of a spectrum with ideological and market forces at opposite ends.

Hayden (2006, p. 6) reported that the "one-to-one correspondence between international schools and international education should be rejected", even though the term 'international school' often refers to students and teachers who attend an international school, or experience an international education. She then went on to focus her discussion on the reasons why schools wish to describe themselves as international. These reasons primarily relate to policy, curriculum type, location and student demographics. The conclusion she draws is that schools choosing to be international schools do so for a range of contextually-based reasons.

International schools can be classified both structurally and ideologically. Sylvester (2007) and Wylie (2008) have presented matrices to help locate international schools on a continuum, yet also highlight the diversity and difficulty of the task. International schools have also been categorized by the contexts in which they are located (Hayden and Thompson 2011). However, with online technological advances and flexible learning opportunities, curricula can readily be transported across borders. Many students can now stay at home, be overseas, or be in an isolated location, whilst at the same time be receiving an international education (Van Der Wende 2001). This situation leads to complexity when trying to classify international schools.

At the same time, many international schools have common characteristics related to structure, ideology and context. According to Hayden (2006), they are often private, or fee paying, they have homogeneous groupings linked to international organizations and multinational companies, they offer English as a world language, and they provide more flexibility than is provided by a national system of education. Recognizing these characteristics brings one to realise the nuances within the term 'international school'. Thus, regardless of how international schools are classified, it can be concluded that diversity is evident in them and that they are full of complexities and affected by micro-politics (Caffyn 2011).

Many of the attempts to describe international schools have also been recorded in the current evidence-based education literature and there have been demands for greater clarification of terms (Bagnall 2008a; Garton 2000; Hardman 2001; Hayden 2006; Hill 2007; Sylvester 2007). The following typology by Hill (2007), identifying four distinct international school types, is widely used:

- National school abroad with national programme of home country.
- National school in home country with international programme.
- International school with international programme.
- International school and national programme of one or more countries.

Taking a different approach, Hayden's (2006) groupings are based on the philosophy and curriculum taught in the school. These include the European Schools founded in 1953 which have a heavy focus on acquiring at least two languages and are Eurocentric, the United World Colleges founded in 1962 which follow Kurt Hahn's ideology of peace, and the English Schools Foundation founded in 1967 to deliver a British-style curriculum internationally. In addition to these categories, Hayden presented 'other groupings' to include national schools that embrace an international curriculum, Christian missionary schools or benefactors in developing countries, multi-national company schools, and the rising number of schools with links to independent schools in England whose recruitment of students is related to the economic climate in China, Thailand and Hong Kong. Then there are the Yew Chung International schools founded in 1932 that encourage a bicultural and dual language philosophy, and also the Aga Khan Academies, founded in 2000 by the Aga Khan Development Network, that are expanding an integrated network of schools in Africa and Asia to provide access to education of an international standard.

Hayden and Thompson's (2011) recent United Nations Educational, Scientific and Cultural Organization (UNESCO) publication, with its global representative list of international school types, is indicative of how, as the number of international schools grow, so too will their range of contexts and categories. Also, as a result of globalization and marketization, international schools are changing in form, function and population. The traditional international school that catered for the 'elite' foreign diplomat, or entrepreneur, is now catering for a much wider student population, including that associated with multi-national corporations, non-governmental organizations and mobile blue-collar workers. Hayden and Thompson (2011, p. 86) make reference to this phenomenon as the 'modern' international school type that has emerged in response to market demand to cater for the children of expatriates and affluent locals, "established on a for-profit, proprietary basis by an individual owner, or commercial organization".

One should also not forget that linked to the rise in international schools that cater for the large mining sector in areas such as Indonesia, South America and Africa, is the global phenomenon of 'fly in and fly out' workers. The number of

English-as-second language students entering international schools is increasing due to this development. Zhao (2010) sees such a changing environment for schools as an opportunity to promote the 'global enterprise essence'. In his speech (Zhao 2010) at the 'Alliance for International Education' biennial conference held in Melbourne, 2010, he challenged international schools to lead the way in the age of globalization by re-inventing themselves and developing 'niche' markets.

The changing landscape of international education, schools and teachers is also influenced by what Rischard (2003, pp. 3–4) labels a 'demographic explosion' that "will change the world and force us to re-evaluate our understanding of the world". This has led to changes in how teachers in international schools are conceptualized (Rischard 2003). On this, Cambridge (2002) describes a teacher hierarchy evident in many international school settings:

> A tripartite organizational structure occurs consisting of a long term administrative core . . . , a fringe of relatively highly paid professional expatriates . . . on shorter term contracts, and local staff hired at lower rates of remuneration, who are likely to be longer term. (Cambridge 2002, p. 159)

This classification provides a starting point for identifying and acknowledging the diversity of the teaching force within international schools (Hayden and Thompson 2011).

Teachers, of course, are at the heart of any educational reform (Ornstein and Hunkins 2004; Sungaila 1992). Thus, it is reasonable to suggest that principals of international schools may best influence learning through the teachers they hire. Teachers account for the vast majority of expenditure in such schools and their impact on learning can outweigh the impact of any education programme, or policy (Hattie 2009). On this, there has been agreement for some time (Brophy 1989; Egan 2001; Hayden 2006; Stigler and Hiebert 1999), that teachers' beliefs are of central importance in influencing teaching practice and the micro-political world in which they are situated

Several studies have examined teachers' perspectives on the development of international education. Some of the research has focused on the IB curriculum (Bagnall 2008b; Brok and Koopman 2007; Hayden 2006; Hayden and Thompson 2011; Snowball 2007; Walker 2004). Others have looked at teachers' tacit knowledge (Hall 2010). While these studies examined the ideology of international education, including that of the IBPYP, they did not explore the personal dimension of the practitioner's enactment of policy, or the role and influence that other key stakeholders can play. Also, the diverse nature of stakeholders in the international school system is not addressed to any great extent in the research literature. This means that there is only a small corpus of empirical knowledge available on the role of the IBPYP coordinators, principals, regional accreditation personnel, school boards and parents.

Studies have been conducted, however, that focus on teachers' nationality and the reasons why they move into the world of international schooling (Bagnall 2008a, b; Cottrell 2002; Hayden and Thompson 2011; Richards 1998). Hayden (2006, 2010)

suggests that a number of teachers who experienced global mobility in their childhoods make up a significant proportion of the international teaching workforce because they want to recreate the lifestyle they had as a result. Hardman (2001) categorized teachers applying for positions in international schools as either child-less career professionals, mavericks, or career professionals with families. Similar categories were found to apply in relation to administrators.

On the international teaching circuit, colloquial terms are often used to depict teachers' motivations for becoming involved in international education. The terms 'mercenaries', 'missionaries' and 'misfits' are stereotypes that have emerged in discourses related to volunteers and aid workers in developing countries. Cogitating these stereotypes can be useful in providing "entry points for exploring the tensions and contradictions in ways in which people working in the industry view themselves and others" (Stirrat 2008, p. 1).

3.3.3   International School Settings

Just as international schools are diverse and dynamic, so too are international school settings. A school's location can be a contributing factor to teacher attraction and retention, with various types being "conducive to encouraging short, medium or long term stays" (Hayden 2006, p. 76). Schools that tend to be encourage short, or medium, stays are those in rural and remote areas, and those in low socio-economic urban centres. The category also includes large international schools in cities, particularly in Asia, South America and Africa, where environmental, political, and economic factors can have a negative impact on one's lifestyle.

The environment and culture of most traditional international schools in privileged settings tend to have the capacity to act to ensure that staff will remain on for somewhat long periods. These schools tend to be those that offer long-term opportunities for teachers and their families. If they are in large urban centres they can provide access to higher education and an attractive lifestyle. Such schools also usually offer attractive salaries (Hayden and Thompson 2011). Also, urban international schools can act as training centres catering for up-and-coming international school teachers, or new graduates trying to make their mark in the field. Here, they may find themselves surrounded by experienced mentors of mature age.

It is difficult to find exact numbers of teachers working in the large international schools, especially given what has already been said about the ambiguity of the term 'international school' and the borderless world that exists. Bunnell (2007) has presented the most comprehensive statistics to date, albeit somewhat dated, incomplete and containing discrepancies. His data were collected from the Council of International Schools, showing that international schools have an annual growth of eight per cent. He concluded that the international school sector is equivalent in size to education systems in Sweden, or Florida (USA).

3.4   Conclusion

The previous chapter contextualized the three background fields in which the study at the core of this book is located. It introduced the IBPYP, gave an outline of the Indonesian educational context, and described issues related to living, working and schooling in remote settings. This chapter has presented a complementary body of research literature.

The chapter was organized in two main sections. It began by fore-grounding the ever-changing macro level phenomenon of globalization. The second section detailed the changing face of international education and international schools and teachers, as well as the ideological constructs they espouse such as 'international mindedness'. Several converging and diverging themes were highlighted. It was also emphasised that the impact of globalization on localized contexts is the focus of a developing field of study and that limited empirical research has been conducted on the relationship between international curriculum policy and how it is adapted to suit local contexts, including remote settings. The study reported in the following chapters is a response to this observation.

References

Allen, K. (2002). Atolls, seas of culture and global nets. In M. C. Hayden, J. J. Thompson, & G. Walker (Eds.), *International education in practice: Dimensions for national and international schools* (pp. 112–135). London: Kogan Page.

Al-Rodhan, N. (2006). *Historical milestones for globalization. Programme on the geopolitical implications of globalization and transnational security.* Geneva: Geneva Centre for Security Policy.

Andersen, T., & Herbertsson, T. T. (2005). Quantifying globalization. *Applied Economics, 37*(10), 1089–1098.

Appadurai, A. (1996). *Modernity at large: Cultural dimensions of globalization.* Minnesota: University of Minnesota Press.

Apple, M. W. (1979). What correspondence theories of the hidden curriculum miss. *The Review of Education, 5*(2), 101–112.

Apple, M. W. (2004). *Ideology and curriculum.* New York: Routledge Falmer.

Bagnall, N. F. (2008a). *International schools as agents for change.* New York: Nova Science.

Bagnall, N. F. (2008b). Case studies of four international schools. In N. F. Bagnall (Ed.), *International schools as agents for change* (pp. 109–125). New York: Nova Science.

Bagnall, N. F. (2010). *Education without borders: Forty years of the International Baccalaureate, 1970–2010.* Berlin: VDM Publishing House.

Ball, S. J. (1994). *Education reform: A critical and post-structural approach.* Buckingham: Open University Press.

Bates, R. (Ed.). (2011a). *Schooling internationally: Globalisation, internationalisation and the future for international schools.* Oxford: Routledge.

Bates, R. (2011b). *Learning to teach internationally: What international teachers need to know.* Paper presented at the Australian Teacher Education Association annual conference, Melbourne, July 2011.

Bernstein, B. B. (2000). *Paedagogy, symbolic control, and identity: Theory, research, critique.* Lanham: Rowman & Littlefield.

Bonk, C. J. (2009). *The world is open: How web technology is revolutionizing education.* San Francisco: Jossey-Bass.

Bottery, M. (2000). *Education, policy and ethics.* London: Continuum International Publishing Group.

Bottery, M. (2006). Education and globalization: redefining the role of the educational professional. *Educational Review, 58*(1), 95–113.

Brok, P., & Koopman, G. J. (2007). International education. In M. Hayden, J. Thompson, & J. Levy (Eds.), *The Sage handbook of research in international education* (pp. 233–246). London: Sage.

Brophy, J. E. (1989). *Advances in research on teaching: A research annual.* Greenwich, CT: JAI Press.

Brown, C., & Lauder, H. (2011). The political economy of international schools and social class formation. In R. Bates (Ed.), *Schooling internationally: Globalisation, internationalisation and the future for international schools* (pp. 39–58). Oxford: Routledge.

Bunnell, T. (2007). The international education industry: An introductory framework for conceptualizing the potential scale of an 'alliance'. *Journal of Research in International Education, 6*(3), 349–367.

Bunnell, T. (2011). The International Baccalaureate and 'growth scepticism': a 'social limits' framework. *International Studies in Sociology of Education, 21*(2), 161–176.

Caffyn, R. (2011). International schools and micropolitics: Fear, vulnerability and identity in fragmented space. In R. Bates (Ed.), *Schooling internationally: Globalisation, internationalisation and the future for international schools* (pp. 59–82). Oxford: Routledge.

Cambridge, J. (2002). Recruitment and deployment of staff: A dimension of international school organization. In M. Hayden, J. Thompson, & G. Walker (Eds.), *International education in practice: Dimensions for national and international schools* (pp. 158–169). London: Kogan Page.

Cambridge, J. (2011). International curriculum. In R. Bates (Ed.), *Schooling internationally: Globalisation, internationalisation and the future for the international schools* (pp. 121–147). Oxford: Routledge.

Cottrell, A. B. (2002). Education and occupational choices of American adult third culture kids. In M. G. Ender (Ed.), *Military brats and other global nomads: Growing up in organization families* (pp. 229–253). Westport: Praeger.

Currie, J., DeAngelis, R., deBoer, H., Huisman, J., & Lacotte, C. (2003). *Globalizing practices and university responses: European and Anglo-American differences.* Westport, CT: Greenwood Publishing Group.

Curry, C. E. (2006). Going international: Teaching and learning culture from the outside in. *The English Journal, 95*(6), 23–27.

Dabbagh, N., & Bannan-Ritland, B. (2005). *Online learning: Concepts, strategies, and application.* Upper Saddle River: Pearson/Merrill/Prentice Hall.

Davies, J. (2006). Affinities and beyond!! Developing ways of seeing in online spaces. *E-Learning., 3*(2), 217–234.

Dolby, N., & Rahman, A. (2008). Research in international education. *Review of Educational Research, 78*(3), 676–726.

Egan, K. (2001). Why education is so difficult and contentious. *Teachers College Record, 103*(6), 923–941.

Fail, H. (2011). Teaching and learning in international schools: A consideration of the stakeholders and their expectations. In R. Bates (Ed.), *Schooling internationally: Globalisation, internationalisation and the future for international schools* (pp. 101–120). Oxford: Routledge.

Garavalia, B. J. (1997). International education: How it is defined by U.S. students and foreign students. *The Clearing House, 70*(4), 21–221.

Garton, B. (2000). Recruitment of teachers for international education. In M. Hayden & J. Thompson (Eds.), *International schools and international education: Improving teaching, management and quality* (pp. 85–95). London: Kogan Page.

Gellar, C. (2002). International education's internationalism: Inspirations from cosmopolitanism. In M. Hayden, J. Thompson, & G. Walker (Eds.), *International education in practice* (pp. 90–99). London: Kogan Page.

Geneva Centre for Security. (2008). *Globalization matrix*. Geneva: Centre for Security.

Green, B. (Ed.). (2009). *Understanding and researching professional practice*. Rotterdam: Sense.

Hall, R. (2010). *Learning beyond borders. B sides*. Retrieved from http://ir.uiowa.edu/bsides/16

Hardman, J. (2001). Improving recruitment and retention of quality overseas teachers. In S. Blandford & M. Shaw (Eds.), *Managing international schools* (pp. 123–135). London: RoutledgeFalmer.

Hattie, J. (2009). *Visible learning: A synthesis of over 800 meta-analyses relating to achievement*. London: Routledge.

Hayden, M. (2006). *Introduction to international education*. London: Sage.

Hayden, M. C., & Thompson, J. J. (2008). *International schools: Growth and influence*. Paris: UNESCO.

Hayden, M. C., & Thompson, J. (2011). Teachers for the international school of the future. In R. Bates (Ed.), *Schooling internationally: Globalisation, internationalisation and the future for international schools* (pp. 83–100). Oxford: Routledge.

Held, D., & McGrew, A. G. (2002). *Governing globalization: Power, authority and global governance*. Cambridge: Polity.

Held, D., McGrew, A., Goldblatt, D., & Perraton, J. (1999). *Global transformations: Politics, economics and culture*. Cambridge: Polity Press.

Henry, M. (2001). *Policy approaches to educational disadvantage and equity in Australian schooling*. Paris: International Institute for Educational Planning.

Hill, I. (2007). International education as developed by the International Baccalaureate Organization. In J. Thompson, M. Hayden, & J. Levy (Eds.), *The SAGE handbook of research in international education* (pp. 25–38). London: Sage.

IBO. (2003a). *Programme of inquiry and scope and sequence document*. www.ibo.org/documentlibrary/programmestandards. Accessed 1 Mar 2004

IBO. (2003b). *IB learner profile booklet*. Cardiff: IBO. www.ibo.org/ibla/conference/.../TheLearnerProfileinActionFabian.ppt. Accessed 30 Mar 2006.

Knight, J. (2001). Monitoring the quality and progress of internationalization. *Journal of Studies in International Education, 5*(3), 228–243.

Knight, J., & DeWit, H. (Eds.). (1997). *Internationalisation of higher education in Asia Pacific countries*. Amsterdam: European Association for International Education.

Lauder, H. (2007). International schools, education and globalization: Towards a research agenda. In M. Hayden, J. Thompson, & J. Levy (Eds.), *The Sage handbook of research in international education* (pp. 444–461). Thousand Oaks: Sage.

Levin, B., & Schrum, L. (2002). *Leading technology-rich schools: Award-winning models for success*. New York: Teachers College Press.

Lowe, L. (1998). The international within the national: American studies and Asian American critique. *The Futures of American Studies, 40*, 29–47.

MacDonald, J. (2006). The international school industry: Examining international schools through an economic lens. *Journal of Research in International Education, 5*(2), 191–213.

Marginson, S. (2007a). The public/private divide in higher education: A global revision. *Higher Education, 53*(3), 307–333.

Marginson, S. (2007b). The new higher education landscape: Public and private goods, in global/national/local settings. In S. Marginson (Ed.), *Prospects of higher education: Globalization, market competition, public goods and the future of the university* (pp. 29–78). Rotterdam: Sense.

Marginson, S., & Rhoades, G. (2002). Beyond national states, markets, and systems of higher education: A glonacal agency heuristic. *Higher Education, 43*(3), 281–309.

Marshall, H. (2011). Instrumentalism, ideals and imaginaries: Theorising the contested space of global citizenship education in schools. *Globalisation, Societies and Education, 9*(3–4), 411–426.

Matthews, J., & Sidhu, R. (2005). Desperately seeking the global subject: International education, citizenship and cosmopolitanism. *Globalisation, Societies and Education, 3*(1), 49–66.

Merryfield, M. M., & Masataka, K. (2004). How are teachers responding to globalization. *Social Education, 68*(5), 354–359.

Milton-Smith, M. (2008). *A conversation on globalisation and digital art.* Unpublished PhD thesis. University of Western Australia, Perth.

Nye, J. (2002). Transnational relations, interdependence and globalization. In M. Brecher & F. P. Harvey (Eds.), *Millennial reflections on international studies* (pp. 165–175). Ann Arbor: University of Michigan Press.

O'Rourke, K., & Williamson, J. (2004). Once more: When did globalisation begin? *European Review of Economic History, 8,* 109–117.

OECD. (2005). *Economic globalization indicators.* Retrieved from www.oecd.org. Accessed 2 May 2006.

Ornstein, A. C., & Hunkins, F. P. (2004). *Curriculum foundations, principles, and issues.* Boston: Allyn & Bacon.

Peters, M. A. (2003). Education policy in the age of knowledge capitalism. *Policy Futures in Education, 1*(2), 361–380.

Porter, P., & Vidovich, L. (2000). Globalization and higher education policy. *Educational Theory, 50*(4), 449–465.

Richards, N. (1998). The emperor's new clothes? The issue of staffing in international schools. In M. Hayden & J. Thompson (Eds.), *International education: Principles and practice* (pp. 173–183). London: Kogan Page.

Rischard, J. (2003). *High noon: 20 global problems, 20 years to solve them.* New York: Basic Books.

Rizvi, F., & Lingard, B. (2005). Globalization and education: Complexities and contingencies. *Educational Theory.* doi:10.1111/j.1741-5446.2000.00419.x/full.

Rizvi, F., & Lingard, B. (2010). *Globalizing education policy.* London: Taylor & Francis.

Roberts, B. (2003). What should international education be? From emergent theory to practice. *International Schools Journal, 22*(2), 69–79.

Roberts, R. L. (2006). *The effects of resources and experience on the self-concept of a group of global nomads: Missionary kids.* Unpublished Psy.D. thesis, Alliant International University, San Francisco, CA.

Roman, L. G. (2003). Education and the contested meanings of 'global citizenship'. *Journal of Educational Change, 4*(3), 269–293.

Ruddy, A. (2008). *Internationalisation: Case studies of two Australian and United States universities.* PhD thesis, Murdoch University, Perth.

Scholte, J. A. (2005). *Globalization: A critical introduction.* London: Palgrave Macmillan.

Schweisfurth, M. (2006). Education for global citizenship: Teacher agency and curricular structure in Ontario schools. *Educational Review, 58*(1), 41–50.

Sklair, L. (2001). *The transnational capitalist class.* Malden: Blackwell.

Snowball, L. (2007). Becoming more internationally minded: International teacher certification and professional development. In M. Hayden, J. Thompson, & J. Levy (Eds.), *The Sage handbook of research in international education* (pp. 247–255). London: Sage.

Spring, J. (2009). *Globalization of education: An introduction.* New York: Taylor & Francis.

Stearns, P. (2003). Treating globalization in history surveys. *The History Teacher, 36,* 154–172.

Stigler, J. W., & Hiebert, J. (1999). *The teaching gap: Best ideas from the world's teachers for improving education in the classroom.* New York: Free Press.

Stirrat, R. (2008). Mercenaries, missionaries and misfits: Representations of development personnel. *Critique of Anthropology, 28*(4), 406–425.

Sungaila, H. (1992). Educational reform and the new 'theory of chaos'. In F. Crowther & D. Ogilvia (Eds.), *The new political world of educational administration* (pp. 69–87). Hawthorn: Australian Council for Educational Administration.

Sylvester, R. (2002). Mapping international education: A historical survey 1893–1944. *Journal of Research in International Education, 1,* 90–125.

Sylvester, R. (2007). Historical resources for research in international education. In M. Hayden, J. Thompson, & J. Levy (Eds.), *The Sage handbook of research in international education* (pp. 185–195). London: Sage.

Taylor, S., & Henry, M. (2000). Globalization and educational policy-making: A case study. *Educational Theory, 50*(4), 487–503.

Urry, J. (2000). *Sociology beyond societies: Mobilities for the twenty-first century.* London: Routledge.

Van der Wende, M. (2001). Internationalisation policies: about new trends and contrasting paradigms. *Higher Education Policy, 14*(3), 249–259.

Vidovich, L. (2007). Removing policy from its pedestal: Some theoretical framings and practical possibilities. *Educational Review, 59*(3), 285–298.

Walker, G. (2004). *To educate the nations: Reflections on an international education.* Great Glemham: Peridot Press.

Walker, G. (2007). Challenges from a new world. In M. Hayden, J. Thompson, & J. Levy (Eds.), *The Sage handbook of research in international education* (pp. 404–411). London: Sage.

Walker, G. (2011). *East is East and West is West.* Geneva: International Baccalaureate Organisation.

Weenink, D. (2008). Cosmopolitanism as a form of capital: Parents preparing their children for a globalizing world. *Journal of Sociology, 42*(6), 1089–1106.

Winter, C. (2012). School curriculum, globalisation and the constitution of policy problems and solutions. *Journal of Education Policy, 27*(3), 295–314.

Wylie, J. (2006). Cultural geographies in practice: Smoothlands: fragments/landscapes/fragments. *Cultural Geographies, 13*(3), 458–465.

Wylie, M. (2008). Internationalizing curriculum: Framing theory and practice in international schools. *Journal of Research in International Education, 7*(1), 5–19.

Wylie, M. (2011). Global networking and the world of international education. In R. Bates (Ed.), *Schooling internationally: Globalisation, internationalisation and the future for international schools* (pp. 21–38). Oxford: Routledge.

Yang, R. (2002). *The third delight: Internationalization of higher education in China.* London: Routledge.

Yang, R. (2005). Internationalisation, indigenisation and educational research in China. *Australian Journal of Education, 49*(1), 66–88.

Yates, L., & Grumet, M. (Eds.). (2011). *Curriculum in today's world: Configuring knowledge, identities, work and politics World yearbook of education 2011.* Oxford: Routledge.

Zajda, J. I. (2005). *International handbook on globalisation education and policy research: Global pedagogies and policies.* Dordrecht: Springer.

Zhao, Y. (2010). Preparing globally competent teachers: A new imperative for teacher education. *Journal of Teacher Education, 61*(5), 422–431.

Chapter 4
The Research Approach

4.1 Introduction

The study of the IBPYP curriculum policy process in remote international schools in Indonesia outlined in later chapters is, as already pointed out, located within the broad context of globalization and internationalization. Recognition of the gap between policy and practice and the potential interconnectivity of curriculum policy processes, internationalization and remote contexts presented in Chaps. 2 and 3 gave rise to the study. It also led to a decision that it should be undertaken using a qualitative research design. This chapter now details the conceptualization of the study and how the research aim and research questions were addressed. It explains the theoretical base that guided the study and outlines the processes involved in data collection and analysis.

The chapter focuses in particular on how the interpretivist paradigm and the critical theory paradigm were drawn upon to complement each other at different stages of the policy analysis. This theoretical eclecticism was used to capture how policy actors made meaning of the IBPYP, and to uncover the power relationships that existed within the policy process. Equally, while an investigation of the perspectives of individual administrators and teachers was central to the study, the analysis was also informed by a broader framework based on the notion of a policy trajectory (Ball 1994; Rizvi and Lingard 2010; Vidovich 2007). Adopting such a perspective, the framework highlights the interrelatedness between contexts and levels (macro to micro) along the policy trajectory. As already indicated, the macro level refers to the International Baccalaureate Organisation (IBO) and the forces of globalization and internationalization, the meso level relates to the Indonesian national context as well as the IB Asia Pacific regional office, and the micro level refers to select remote international schools in Indonesia.

The remainder of this chapter is divided into six sections. First, the research aim and research questions are presented. Section 4.3 outlines the theoretical framework that guided the study. Section 4.4 describes the conceptualization of a policy

© Springer International Publishing Switzerland 2014   57
S. Ledger et al., *Global to Local Curriculum Policy Processes*,
Policy Implications of Research in Education 4, DOI 10.1007/978-3-319-08762-7_4

trajectory framework. Section 4.5 outlines the data collection and analysis processes employed. Section 4.6 elaborates the way in which 'trustworthiness' was enhanced. Finally, ethical considerations are dealt with in Sect. 4.7.

4.2 The Research Aim and Research Questions

The aim of the study, it will be recalled, was to explore the dynamics of curriculum policy processes involved in the adoption, production and enactment of the International Baccalaureate Primary Years Program (IBPYP) in three remote international schools in Indonesia. This involved analysing the conceptual terrain of these international schools as they worked toward authorization, or re-authorization, of the IBPYP. The aim was pursued through a set of research questions based on the conceptualization of the approach to policy analysis adopted as a 'policy trajectory study'. The policy trajectory is conceived in terms of the series of 'contexts' outlined by Ball, (1994), namely, the context of influence, the context of policy text production, the context of practices, and the context of outcomes. The policy trajectory approach of Vidovich (2007) and Rizvi and Lingard (2010), derived from Ball's (1994, 2006) conceptualization of the policy process, incorporates both the macro constraints (wider policy agendas) and the micro agency of policy actors within individual educational institutions. Policy analysis conceived of in this way stresses the importance of considering ongoing interrelatedness across the differing levels and contexts of curriculum policy processes.

The policy contexts noted above were used to frame the research questions and structure of the whole study. The questions are as follows:

Research Question 1
What were the key influences that impacted on the initiation of curriculum policy reform at the case-study schools? (identifies global, regional, national and local level influences).

Research Question 2
What were the key features of the curriculum policy texts in the case-study schools, and how were they produced? (details the curriculum policy intent)

Research Question 3
What were the subsequent policy practices evident in the case-study schools? (examines enactment of policy reform)

Research Question 4
What were the anticipated outcomes and implications of curriculum policy reforms for the case-study schools, international education and remote education? (meta-analysis of findings and longer term consequences)

The research questions were designed to generate understandings on how teachers and educators located along the trajectory made meaning of the IBPYP policy and its associated concepts. They capture the dynamic nature of international education in practice and respond to Caffyn's (2010) call to identify the micro-politics of schools when trying to understand their complexities within a global framework (Milton-Smith 2008). The theoretical framings that guided the study and suggested the research design and methods of data collection and analysis are now considered. These are followed by a further explication of the concept of a 'policy trajectory'.

4.3 Theoretical Framings

Unless we have a theoretical understanding of the social terrain we are traversing our research is likely to fail. (Walter 2010, p. 19)

This section of the chapter outlines the theoretical framework adopted for the study. It is premised on the view that paradigms are 'the overarching set of thoughts and beliefs that colours and filters, existing and emergent research theories and research programs' (Bales 2002, p. 7). It also embraces the 'theoretical eclecticism' espoused by Ozga (2001) and Cibulka (1994). In particular, it was inspired by Peters and Humes (2003, p. 109) who argue that "greater theoretical sophistication and creativity involves more than one theory alone".

Specifically, the framework involved recognizing the value of using the interpretivist paradigm and the critical theory paradigm to complement one another in order to add depth at different stages of the policy analysis. Interpretivism was employed to guide data collection and early analysis, while critical theory was adopted to facilitate meta-analysis. Drawing on two paradigms in this way presents an approach to policy analysis aimed at capturing its multifaceted and ambiguous nature. This is now taken up in more detail.

4.3.1 Interpretivist Theory

Locating a study within the interpretivist paradigm is very helpful in trying to understand and explain the human and social reality of educators in the field of international education. Its micro-level emphasis and the focus on individual motives and interpretations of the world are primarily associated with qualitative social research methods (Walter 2010). On this, O'Donoghue (2007) stresses Habermas' (1972) point that interpretivism is the paradigm adopted by those pursuing an interest in understanding the meaning behind something. In the case of the study reported in this book, the research at the micro level was aimed at generating an understanding of the policy processes investigated through seeking out the meanings individual actors made of the IBPYP policy and examining how they translated it into practice in their particular schools.

One of the strengths of interpretivism is its uniqueness in exploring in detail what occurs 'in situ'. It addresses Caffyn's (2010, p. 2) concern that the "social, political structure of a school . . . and the psychodynamics and emotions that are experienced at a local level are often ignored". He sees it as important to raise this matter because of the stress he places on issues of identity and of finding meaning at the micro level. This, in turn, requires recognizing that meaning is socially constructed. It is for this reason that O'Donoghue (2007, p. 9) states that micro-sociology researchers must "emphasize social interaction as the basis for knowledge".

It was valuable to underpin the study being reported here with the interpretivist paradigm because of its suitability to explore details, context and holistic aspects of participants' life experiences by concentrating on interpretations and process (Punch 2000). It embraces a view that people actively construct knowledge and formulate interpretations from the interactions they have with the environment in which they find themselves (Coutas 2008). This is to say that the interpretations are socially constructed. This was important to realise in seeking to explore the complex nature of the world of international schools and the multiple worlds that exist within their local social contexts.

Accordingly, teachers' perspectives of IBPYP policy, international education and international mindedness were explored to better understand how they made meaning of each of these constructs. It was recognized that the perspectives held by teachers can direct interpretation and enactment of policy, but can also be unpredictable and dynamic (Audi 1999; O'Donoghue 2007). It was also recognized that teachers at the micro level may transfer their own values, beliefs and ideologies onto their pupils and others in a school. In doing so they can become transmitters of international policy and, more generally, transmitters of social reform.

Focusing on educators' perspectives led to the adoption of research and theoretical insights from within the discipline of sociology (Walter 2010). In particular, 'perspectives' is a central concept within the micro-sociology school of symbolic interactionism. Drawing on this school, O'Donoghue (2007, p. 31) describes perspectives as:

> . . . .capturing the notion of a human being who interacts, defines situations and acts according to what is going on in the present situation . . . perspectives are conceptualized as dynamic and changing guides to interpretation and then to action, such action can never be totally predictable.

Thus, the study reported here sought to captures the interactions and perspectives involved at the micro-political level of IBPYP policy enactment at the three school sites and beyond.

Perspectives, however, have multiple descriptions and are difficult to identify. They have been defined as the "extraction and use of information about one's environment and one's own body" (Audi 1999). Woods' (1993, p. 7) definition, as "frameworks through which people make sense of the world" is particularly helpful for educational research. Equally useful is Charon's (2009) view that perspectives are how we filter information and create meaning. This is in accord with Crotty's (1998) belief that we create meaning through the interactions with the world and objects within it. To summarize on this, the construction of meaning is dynamic, situational and contextual. Therefore, the perspectives sought within the research project reported here focused on the construction of knowledge 'in situ' about IBPYP by the teaching cohorts within the remote international case study schools.

Considering the matter in relation to the broader policy dimension of the study, the view adopted is that the actors or agents in the process are those who action policy. Also, teachers' and administrators' experiences can affect the understandings that they hold. These understandings can, in turn, be either confirmed, or re-moulded, with new experiential inputs and reworked understandings can inform the next set of actions taken. Rizvi and Lingard (2010, p. 8) relate this to the notion of 'social imaginary' and suggest that "policies are not only located within discourse, but also in imaginaries that shape thinking about how things might be".

In summary, the theoretical framework employed in the study reported here drew upon the interpretivist paradigm as a guide for analysing policy 'in situ' by directing the investigation of the perspectives of local policy actors. These were sought about IBPYP policy, policy processes, pedagogy and the social constructs of 'international education' and 'international mindedness'. The paradigm guided the data collection stage of the study and early analysis of data generated at the case study schools. The role of the critical theory paradigm in complementing this work, especially when it came to the meta-analysis of findings, is now detailed.

4.3.2 Critical Theory

This section examines the use of 'critical theory' within policy analysis studies and the role it played in the study reported in this book. Emerging from work of philosophers, sociologists and the social sciences in the 1930s, critical theory has been used to critique society rather than explain how societies function (Horkheimer 1972). Habermas, one of its most influential proponents, has played an important role in promoting its strong position in empirical research projects. An associated rigorous approach to research that minimizes subjectivity and bias was developed. Nevertheless, it has been criticized for being overly philosophical, overtly political, densely written and full of scepticism (Agger 1991; Leonardo 2004; Moore 2007). As Moore (2007, p. 27) has concluded, its social and historical contextualization of knowledge has become "a kind of systematically deconstructing relativism with a built-in scepticism"

For the purposes of the research reported here, the critical theory paradigm was chosen to complement the interpretivist paradigm as it looks beyond rhetoric and examines patterns of inequality and results of real-life struggles (Pitman and Vidovich 2012). In doing so, it provides a tool that can "show us our world and ourselves through new and valuable lenses ... and can strengthen our ability to think logically, creatively and a good deal of insight" (Tyson 2006, p. 3). This is a view that in an ever-changing world new and multiple lenses are required to effectively analyse data and keep up with technological, economic and social changes.

For the study, Crotty's (1998) explanation of critical theory, that meaning is socially constructed to support a particular hegemonic interest or power structure, was adopted. It led to recognition that the power structures at different stages of the policy process and within different contexts would need to be explored through critical theory's 'power lens'. In other words, it was seen that critical theory would provide the researchers with an opportunity to gain insights into the dynamic nature of power relations at the case study schools and beyond as policy in relation to the IBPYP was constructed, interpreted and enacted. In other words, being 'critical' in analysis would help us "deconstruct the many 'taken-for-granteds' in the policy processes and policy texts" (Bottery 2006, p. 69).

The result was that critical theory and the associated 'power lens' were employed to examine the assumptions and values in the relevant texts and contexts. IBPYP documents were reviewed to analyse the power differentials between macro, meso and micro level policy actors, and comparisons were made horizontally (cross case analysis at the micro level) and vertically (between macro, meso and micro levels) for the meta-analysis. Overall, critical theory positioned the study by explicitly critiquing the social and historical context in which policy text and policy practices were situated.

Returning to the issue more generally, many academics have been influential in shaping the conceptualization of power issues within the policy process (Ball 1994, 2007; Blase 1991; Caffyn 2011; Vidovich 2002, 2007). Caffyn (2010) builds on Blase's (1991) idea that micro-political and macro-political factors frequently interact and suggests that cooperative and conflicting actions and processes are part of the realm of micro-politics and power differentials. Thus, uncovering micro-politics evident in specific global, regional, national and local contexts can enable one to achieve a deep understanding of the complexities of the policy process.

Critical theory can provide the lens to guide the latter task. It highlights the importance of identifying the dynamics of power relationships. On this, Jacobs (2010) suggests that power is contingent on the relationships between individuals within the policy process. Being cognizant of this view, not only did the study reported here investigate the micro level perspectives of participants, it also investigated the interrelatedness of stakeholders and documents along the policy trajectory. In particular, it emphasized the role of ideology and language employed by teachers and administrators in shaping outcomes (Fairclough 2003, 2007). Power paradigms implicit in the constructs of globalization and internationalization were also highlighted, thus responding to Rizvi and Lingard's (2010) call for their inclusion in policy analysis studies.

It was also important not to overlook the role that globalization can play in educational policy. This is of interest since critical theorists seek to explicate the links between how power is situated and how it flows between groups in society (Moore 2007). Yet, the link between globalization and education is still under-researched and understudied. Nevertheless, three schools of thought concerning globalization and education have emerged (Held et al. 1999). The first two are driven by economics, represented by the 'hyperglobalists' who view globalization as an important phenomenon and the 'sceptics' who use statistics to support their opposition to a single global economy. The third school of thought, on the other hand, is represented by the 'tranformationalists', who see globalization as a driving force between social, political and economic changes. Informed by these positions, the study also endeavoured to capture the interconnectivity of globalization and education in its analysis of the IBPYP policy process.

4.4   A Policy Trajectory Framework

A comprehensive review of the construct of 'policy' was presented in Chap. 3. It revealed that policy is difficult to define and is conceptually diverse (Rizvi and Lingard 2010). Ball (1990, p. 9) discussed the "messy realities" of policy and Boyd (1999, p. 227) talked about the "complexities, contradictions and paradoxes that perplex the field". Making sense of policy research in education therefore can be a complex, problematic, messy and unpredictable process. One way to address this, we hold, is to employ the 'policy trajectory' framework (Vidovich 2007) employed in the study reported here. As authors, we recognized the shifts that have taken place in policy research from the traditional linear frame factor approach of the past to a more cyclic process approach of the 1980–1990s (Ball 1994), to the current complex multi-dimensional approach presented by Bottery (2000), Rizvi and Lingard (2010) and Vidovich (2007). The study, as a result, aligned itself to a description of policy as a process and product involving negotiation, contestation and struggle along the trajectory.

The principal feature of Ball's (1994) conceptual framework for policy analysis relevant to the study is his conceptualization of the policy trajectory that was later further developed by Vidovich (2002, 2007, 2013) and Rizvi and Lingard (2010). Bowe et al. (1992) originally identified three contexts of the 'policy trajectory' namely, policy influence, policy text production and policy practices. The 'context of influence' involves the policy actors, environment and agencies that have an impact on policy at the global, national and local levels. The 'context of policy text production' is where policy is articulated and includes the struggles, the discourses and the format of texts as policy is produced. The 'context of practices' refers to how policy actors interpret and enact policy, predominately on a micro level. Ball (1994) later added two more contexts: 'outcomes' and 'political strategies'. The 'context of outcomes' relates to issues of "social justice, equity and individual freedom" (Ball 1994, p. 26) and the 'context of political strategies' refers to the political and social inequalities arising from policy consequences. This conceptualization of the policy trajectory recognizes the plurality of contexts and multiple trajectories inherent in the policy process. The additional contexts added by Ball, and noted above, helped frame the meta-analysis in the study reported here as they deal with issues of power and social justice.

Ball's two additional contexts of 'outcomes' and 'policy strategies' were encapsulated as one and referred to as policy 'outcomes'. This supported Rizvi and Lingard's (2010) preference to use the term 'outcomes' to encompass Ball's final two contexts as they both deal with power and inequity. Vidovich's (2007, 2013) approach derived from Ball's (1994) model incorporates both the macro constraints and the micro agency of participants (global, national and local policy agendas). She developed the 'policy trajectory' approach for application in empirical research. This helped to provide specific questions for the collection and analysis of data at macro, meso and micro levels. It also helped to address one of the criticisms of Ball's (1994) early policy trajectory, namely, the omission of the broader context of globalization and its impact on the policy process.

For the study being reported here, Vidovich's (2007) model informed the structure of the research questions. These questions guided data collection and analysis along the policy trajectory from the world of globalization and IB (macro-level), to the regional and national worlds of IB Asia Pacific regional office and the Indonesian Ministry of Education (meso level), and the local world of remote international schools in Indonesia (micro level). The interrelatedness and interconnectivity of each element in the policy process is captured in the design of the research questions and the methods employed for data collection and analysis.

4.5 Data Collection and Analysis

The previous section outlined the theoretical framework that underpins this study. This section outlines the research techniques and methods used to collect, analyse and interpret the data obtained within the theoretical frame. The methods directed the study and enabled the research to address the research aim and questions. In this regard, Walter (2010, p. 8) provides a set of standards used as a backdrop for "planned and methodical research based around observing, analysing and interpreting our research data, conducted with professionalism and ethical integrity and transparent and rigorous in its approach." This part of the chapter section outlines the four subsections under which the activities undertaken to meet these standards can be considered. The first explains why a qualitative approach was employed in the construction, conduct and interpretation of the research. The second sub-section details the case-study methods undertaken. The third describes the data collection sources, namely, documents and interviews. The fourth sub-section explains the data analysis procedures employed in the study, highlighting how themes were generated from the data and discussing the approach to meta-analysis used.

4.5.1 Qualitative Research

Research design is the plan for systematic inquiry (Merriam 2009). An empirical research plan constitutes a choice primarily between quantitative or qualitative studies or a combination of the two. The strength of qualitative research is the flexibility in how and with whom it can be used. A qualitative approach to policy analysis was chosen in this instance as the most appropriate method for collecting and analysing data. A qualitative approach can provide an interpretation that is compelling for theoretical and significant reasons (Punch 2009). It was chosen because of its potential to best generate understanding of the adoption of the IBPYP curriculum policy reform in remote schools in Indonesia.

Qualitative research refers to a range of research methods, diverse in nature. It is a "complex, changing and contested field" (Punch 2009, p. 115). However within the diversity are key characteristics inherent in this study. First, it is naturalistic in design as the educators and policy makers are studied in their natural settings (Creswell 2005). Secondly, it relies on a qualitative research frame to understand the 'making of meaning' by asking open questions about phenomena as they occur in context (Pound et al. 2005; Schwandt 2001). Thirdly, the use of qualitative research can help the researcher seek insight into the subtle nuances of educational contexts and allow for exploration of unexplained phenomena (Kervin 2006).

The rationale for using a qualitative approach for the study reported here was to enable the researchers to collect rich, descriptive, contextually based data for analysis and for the generation of theory. A continuing interplay between data collection, analysis and theory describes the practice undertaken. It focused on contextual characteristics through description, understanding and interpretation (Gunzenhauser 2006). A detailed description of each setting in which the study was located was provided, including the geographical, economic, environmental and demographic environment.

More than one approach to collecting and analysing data was also adopted, so as to add breadth and depth to the policy analysis. Interviews were conducted and documents analysed within a case study approach. This combination is a recognized strength of qualitative research (Travers 2009). It can facilitate analysis of individual perspectives, help capture the 'voices' of participants, and accommodate the study of group interactions. Strategies were adopted aimed at interrogating and highlighting individuals' perspectives on the multiple worlds and multiple identities with which they engage. The 'worlds' under investigation included the world of the IB, the world of international schools, the national world, and the micro-political local world of school communities. These world-views were seen as acting as an axiological filtering system for any new information (Mansfield and Volet 2010). The view was that traversing through each of these worlds helped participants to socially construct and formulate meaning of such constructs and concepts as international curriculum policy and the process of 'becoming' an international teacher.

The use of a qualitative research approach allowed the researchers to move between the human element of interviews to the world of written communication, including that of relevant policy documents located along the policy trajectory. An analysis of written texts helped to uncover the explicit and implicit meaning of language and its role in achieving specific ideological objectives. It also uncovered what Crotty (1998) and Travers (2009) have termed the hidden use of power. This was to take note of Vidovich's (2007) claim that power differentials are important factors that need examination in any policy trajectory analysis. While policy texts are the tangible face of policy, their contexts of production can differ from their contexts of reception and lead to policy 'slippages' (Bottery 2006) and 'misinterpretations'.

4.5.2 Case Studies

The multiple case-study design of the research being reported here allowed for discoveries, insight and understandings to take place (Merriam 2009) at the micro level of the policy trajectory. Case studies were considered the 'best fit' for the policy analysis as they allowed flexibility and facilitated opportunities to capture the complexity of each case (Anderson 1986; Punch 2008; Stake 1995). On this, Walford (2001, p. 162) suggests that "micro-level case studies must relate to particular research questions that are answerable through studying the sites". The paradigm most naturally suited to case-study research with its emphasis on the interpretive and subjective dimensions is one that seeks to understand and interpret the world in terms of actors. In this case the actors are 'policy actors'.

Case studies were chosen because they "are distinguished less by the methodologies that they employ than by the subjects or objects of their inquiry" (Hitchcock and Hughes 1995, p. 316). This is a view pertinent to studies to be conducted 'in situ'. Significance rather than frequency is a hallmark of the decision to engage in case studies. Morrison (2002, p. 185) suggests that they provide "an insight into the real dynamics of situations and people". This makes them ideal for studying teachers enacting IBPYP policy in small remote schools within Indonesia.

Case studies have many other advantages, some of which have been outlined by Gomm et al. (2000). They can explore unique phenomena – 'how' things happen – and facilitate an appreciation of the complexity rather than the generalizability of findings. Conversely, a case-study approach has to contend with some who argue that the case-study method is the logically weakest way of knowing. Yet, case studies push one to seek to gain access to places where most of us might not usually have an opportunity to go. They allow us to experience (vicariously) unique situations, individuals and cultures. Case studies also allow us to view the world through the lenses of the researchers who are influenced by their own theoretical biases, personal experiences and tacit knowledge (Polanyi 1967; Zhenhua 2004). These individual differences make each case study research project that is undertaken, 'unique'.

The multiple site case-study method used here involved three remote international schools in Indonesia adopting the IBPYP as curriculum policy reform. The notion was that the case studies would give voice to those experiencing change and those who were most directly affected by it (Hargreaves et al. 1998), namely, the teachers and administrators in the remote locations. The great strength of case studies is that they can provide vicarious experience in the form of full and thorough knowledge of the particular. The unique situations that become evident at each site and the findings of each case cannot be used to make gross generalizations. On this, Rosenmund (2000) indicates that case studies are closely connected with their specific contexts and that findings therefore should not be directly transferred. However, a cross-case analysis involving comparability of themes can deepen our understanding of, and indicate how we might explore further, the relationship between international education, remote contexts and policy enactment.

On designing the study being reported here, it was hoped that by giving full and detailed descriptions of each context (Gunzenhauser 2006) one could explore context-specific issues (micro level politics) that would provide 'food for thought' elsewhere in the growing number of contexts where the IBPYP operates. Some of the implications drawn from the research, it was held, would be relevant to other international schools, remote international schools and schools moving to internationalize their curriculum. This would facilitate what Stake (1994) calls 'naturalistic generalization' by building up the body of tacit knowledge on the basis of which people act. Yin (1984, p. 84), in his *Case-study Research: Design and Methods,* defines case-study research method as "an empirical inquiry that investigates a contemporary phenomenon within its real-life context; where the boundaries between phenomenon and context are not clearly evident; and in which multiple sources of evidence are used" (see also Yin 2011). The study being reported here employed Yin's definition to justify its choice of method. Specifically, it used case studies to investigate how international educational policy was translated into practice in three remote contexts in Indonesia with the phenomenon of globalization being ever-present.

4.5.3 Case-Study Sampling, Selection, and Data Collection

In qualitative research there is no need to work with a total research population group or with a statistical sample because the aim of the research is to uncover meanings and understandings, not generalizable findings. The rationale for selecting the three case studies was to provide rich detail and nuanced understandings of the context and of the stakeholder perspectives in each remote case-study international school setting implementing the IBPYP. Pseudonyms were used for each remote school to protect anonymity, particularly given the relatively low number of schools in the region. They were called Satu International School, Dua International School and Tiga International School.

In order to address the research questions in depth, non-probability sampling techniques and methods were used in the study, namely, purposive sampling and quota sampling. Purposive sampling enables researchers to select a sample population based on what they know about the target population and the purpose of the study. Quota sampling draws a sample of participants on the basis of total population at each case site (Babbie 2002). Thus, in the case of this study, while each case site was different in population size, all staff members at each case site were involved in the initial focus group interviews. Thirty-one participants were interviewed in total.

The rationale for choosing to select the particular three international schools was based on each school going through the IBPYP authorization or re-authorization process in remote locations. Other remote schools in different provinces of Indonesia were also implementing the IBPYP and could have been selected. However the chosen sites were selected based on concern for safety issues throughout Indonesia at the time of data collection.

Walford (2001) has highlighted the need when conducting comparative research for choice of research site to be directly linked to the research itself and not purely be based on ease of access, time, finance and convenience. Although the sample sites and participants for the research being reported here were selected purposively, safety issues were imperative. At the time of data collection in Indonesia, there was civil unrest, a natural disaster in Sumatra and the murder of three teachers in West Papua. These events restricted the research to three schools on two Indonesian islands rather than three schools on three islands, as was originally the plan.

The process of participant selection was systematic. All staff members at each school site were approached and asked to participate in a focus group interview. After the initial set of interviews, involving the total population of teachers at each case-study school, certain staff members were selected for follow up semi-structured, individual interviews. Staff selection at this stage of the process was purposive. Staff members at each site were chosen for individual interviews through identifying their interest and through their active participation in the focus group interviews.

Data were gathered from a variety of sources to strengthen the research (Yin 2011). While the case studies were undertaken at the micro level, the research also focused on the meso and macro levels of the policy trajectory. The major sources of data consisted of documents and interviews. Different sources were relied upon to different degrees at the three levels of the policy trajectory framework (Ball 1994; Vidovich 2007) that is, macro level (IB head office), meso level (IB Asia-Pacific regional office and Indonesian National Ministry of Education) and micro level (schools). The perspectives of educators and the enactment of policy were the focus of micro level interviews, whereas there was a heavy reliance on documents for analysing macro level and meso level policy processes. In addition to interviews and documents, profiles were developed of each case-study setting, thus following a process recommended by Gunzenhauser (2006). The profile of the environment in which the case-study site was located was documented to recognize the importance of 'place and space' in the policy process (Green 2008).

4.5.4   Document Study

Documentary data has certain advantages over other forms of data collection in that they are easy to collect, convenient to use and can supply information about activities that took place prior to the commencement of a research project

(Babbie 2002; Harber 1997). Documents for the study being reported were selected on the basis of knowledge gained from literature reviews and previous document analyses that determined those that were most appropriate. There were also cases in which the researcher was directed towards documents by interview participants, or in some cases were given them by participants. The use of documents enabled the researchers to view policy "holistically and comprehensively, to study it in its complexity and to study it in its context" (Punch 2000, p. 18).

During the course of the study understandings and triangulation of the interview data were sought through the analysis of documents. Attention was given to such matters as who composed the documents, the biases evident, the key categories and concepts used, and the theoretical issues and debates on which the documents cast light (Aminzade and Laslett 2002). Data from documents established the context for the data collected from interviews and equally data from the interviews served to fill gaps in the contexts and understandings not gained through the documented data. Both provided significant data that built up a comprehensive picture of the policy process along the trajectory.

Care was taken with regard to using documentary data in the analysis. Documents are social, economic and political constructions that reflect the interests and biases of the writer or those for whom they are written (Aminzade and Laslett 2002; Harber 1997). Curry (2006) believes that documents are not neutral, but instead are subjective in nature and imbued with values. The impact of globalization and internationalization is amongst the influences clearly affecting the discourses surrounding IB and IB-related documents and requires attention. The current push for 'global citizens' and 'international mindedness' of students is one such influence. The use of international policy in relation to IB programmes to internationalize curriculum and schools is another.

Macro and meso level policy documents have already been reviewed and analysed in Chap. 2 of this book. The case study findings outlined in later chapters detail how the texts were used in case study schools. The focus of the document analysis was primarily on the core IB policy documents. These documents included the IB's *Learner Profile* (IBO 2003) and the *Standards and Practices* (IBO 2005). These documents inform and span all IB programs. Documents specific to the IBPYP include *Making the PYP Happen* (IBO 2004), and sample programs of inquiry and units of inquiry used as planning documents. The IB website was also critiqued in terms of its messages. Particular meso level policy documents included those on regional IB policies such as the operating procedures and regional support materials required for authorization and re-authorization. The regional website was also reviewed for IBPYP content and recurring concepts. In addition, national documents from the Indonesian Ministry of Education were reviewed and policy texts related to international schools were scrutinized to position the research in its national Indonesian context.

At the micro level, pertinent school-based IB policy documents were critiqued because the case study schools were the focus of the study. These included the schools' mission statements, operating policies and procedures, standards and practices, IBPYP programs of inquiry, units of inquiry, governance guidelines, the structure of the school's board, and the role statement for the IBPYP coordinator. Local school newsletters were also examined as primary sources to place the research in a historical context and gives realistic insights as to the localized setting. Power relations and discourse omissions and biases were identified within each document. The information collected was added to each school profile developed.

We were also cognizant of the fact that it is as important to identify what is left out of documents is it is to identify their content (Bottery 2006; Fairclough 2003; Rizvi and Lingard 2010). Although a complete 'discourse analysis' was not engaged in, the documents under investigation at each level were viewed as information specific to each context and therefore were contextualized with other forms. On this, Tyson (2006, p. 4) highlights the power of the language of the written or spoken work by suggesting that "assumptions, whether stated or not, underlie every viewpoint".

4.5.5   Interviews

Interviews are one of the main data collecting tools in qualitative research and a good way of getting access to participants' perspectives, meanings, definitions of situations and constructions of reality (Patton 1987, 1990; Punch 2009). Therefore, interviews were a key element within the study. Two types of interviews were undertaken at the micro level in this study, namely, one focus group per school (whole staff from each site) and semi-structured individual interviews (three staff members from each site).

Interviewing as a method of social research was developed in the late nineteenth century predominately by social policy researchers and anthropologists (Travers 2009). Kvale (1996, pp. 126–127) located different kinds of interviews along a continuum, arguing that they differ in the openness of their purpose, their degree of structure, the extent to which they are exploratory or are hypothesis testing, and whether they are largely cognitive-focused or emotion-focused. Here arises the issue of 'fitness for purpose'. In the research reported here, the interview questions were framed in a semi-structured way so that the interviewer could rely on the uniqueness of the participants' responses to guide and inform the study.

It was necessary to construct an interview guide before conducting the interviews. The guide was structured around the research questions, highlighting the main topics or themes that needed to be addressed during the interview. These were based on the literature and the conceptual frame used for the policy analysis. The questions in the guide enabled the researcher to map results against the research questions. Each general interview question was subdivided into specific interview questions to help probe (Travers 2009) and highlight macro, meso and micro level foci. Each question was also structured to allow for open-ended responses.

The list of specific interview questions developed is as follows:

Interview Questions Used For Focus Group Interviews

Questions related to the context of influence

1. What do you see as the major influences in the adoption of the IBPYP in your school?
2. Who are the key decision makers in the development and production of the policy text and what influences do they bring? What influences do these decision makers bring?
3. What do you consider to be the prevailing ideological, economic and political conditions in your setting?
4. How does the 'remoteness' of your school influence the adoption and implementation of the IBO's PYP?
5. What do you consider makes Curriculum policy 'International'?

Questions related to the context of policy text production

6. What do you consider to be the essential characteristics of the IBO's PYP policy text?
7. How do local policies reflect the curriculum of the IBPYP?
8. What processes and personnel are used to build curriculum at your school?
9. How and who are involved in curriculum policy produced at your site?
10. How do you feel about the format and language of the policy?
11. Are the steps for 'implementation' set out as part of the policy text?
12. What mechanism is being used to evaluate the policy?

Questions related to the context of practice/effect

13. What is constitutes the 'whole curriculum' at your school?
14. How open is the policy to interpretation by practitioners?
15. To what extent do you feel familiar with and supportive of the IBPYP?
16. What effects has adopting the IBPYP had on your work?
17. How does 'remoteness' influence the implementation of the IBPYP?
18. What do you consider to be key features or characteristics of teachers to be recruited for international education and in particular for remote international schools?
19. What effect does the IBPYP have on students' learning?
20. Do you believe teachers in international schools are passive recipients or active constructors of policy?

Interview Questions Used for Semi-structured Individual Interviews

Questions related to big picture matters (influences and outcomes):

21. What do you see as the major influences in the adoption of the IBPYP program in your school?
22. How does the location of your school influence the adoption and implementation of the IBPYP program?
23. What is it that makes a policy or school 'international'?

Questions related to the curriculum (policy texts):

24. What do you believe to be the essential elements of the IBPYP material?
25. What processes do you believe to be key in developing the IBPYP at your school?
26. How are you involved in the curriculum policy production at your school?

Questions related to participants' practices:

27. How has adopting the IBPYP changed your teaching?
28. How does your geographical location influence the implementation of the IBPYP?
29. What characteristics would you consider teachers need to possess in order to be equipped to teach the IBPYP at your school location?

Questions related to outcomes:

30. What would you change about the IBPYP curriculum?
31. How would you define international mindedness?

Questions Used in Semi-structured Individual Interviews to Facilitate Further Exploration

1. Could you provide an overview of your background, schooling and international experience?
2. Why did you choose to teach in an international setting?
3. What qualities do you feel have enabled you to succeed in remote international settings?
4. What is your experience with the IBPYP curriculum?
5. What do you see as the major influences in the adoption of the IBPYP in your school/schools?
6. What do you consider makes IBO's PYP curriculum policy international?
7. What processes and/or personnel do you consider essential for the successful implementation and evaluation of the IBPYP?
8. What do you consider to be characteristics of international educators particularly those working in rural/remote centres?
9. How has the IBPYP changed your teaching practice?
10. Do you have a vignette/story/exemplar that best portrays the IBPYP in action in your class or school?

The intention of the interviews was to obtain data that could not otherwise be obtained using other means. Quality control in the form of technical checks, well-structured interview questions and piloted interview techniques and questions were put in place to ensure that the data obtained were useful and trustworthy (Patton 1987, 1990). The use of the group interviews could have presented a problem in that opinionated persons could have tried to take control of the groups (Rutter and Maugh 2002). To overcome this, the researchers countered with the strategy of redirecting the dominant participants' responses back to the focus group, particularly when longer responses were presented. Another concern was the possible influence of the group on the data collected, especially if there was a tendency for a 'polarisation' of views. This can be the case when participants express somewhat extreme views about the issue under discussion because of the group dynamic and power inequities experienced 'in situ' (Morgan 1997). This phenomenon can often be magnified in remote contexts, so that when and if noted, the researcher can redirect and restate specific issues and responses for group clarification. This approach was also adopted in the research.

The importance of meaning and subjectivity in interviews has been highlighted by Weber (1992), who has indicated that by focusing on the subjective there is likely to be variety and richness, possibly even conflicting accounts or versions in any set of interviews. Similarly, Travers (2009, p. 291) suggests that "a single interview might reveal multiple meanings or different meanings". The objective of interpretative enquiry is to address this level of subjective meaning and all its complexities. Therefore, the complexities of multiple meanings, multiple perspectives and multiple identities held by international educators were also explored.

It was essential that pseudonyms be used in transcriptions, particularly given the limited number of schools in Indonesia that fall under the categories required for the research. Whilst anonymity cannot be guaranteed in focus group sessions, confidentiality and anonymity were protected once the interview sessions had taken place. Neither the names of the participants nor of the schools were used in any transcripts or write-ups of the research data collected.

At the micro level, initial focus group interviews were undertaken to examine how the total population of each international school responded to the adoption, production and enactment of the IBPYP. Follow-up semi-structured individual interview schedules were used to probe themes that emerged from the focus groups. This process brought forth answers to the specific and general research questions. They were extracted carefully to facilitate later triangulation of data. The subsequent interviews were employed to elucidate how participants made meaning of key concepts. This included how their experiences and background reflected their ideologies and how they made meaning of such concepts as international mindedness. On this, Rubin and Rubin (2004, p. 129) state that an in-depth interview provides "depth and detail, vivid and nuanced answer, rich and thematic material". Interviews, accordingly, were selected for the research with this in mind.

Three teachers were selected from each site based on individual interest at the time. One of the researchers conducted all interviews and drew from a range of techniques to do so. The focus group interviews were between 40 and 60 min in duration, following suggestions by Vaughn et al. (1996). These interviews were conducted during time allocated for school staff meetings. This option was taken up positively by the teachers and administrators, as no 'out of school' time was required. This was significant in obtaining whole staff participation. The staff felt relaxed and comfortable in a common setting. The researcher outlined the use of the audio equipment at the start of the interview and reassured the staff that their comments would remain private and would not be used for any purpose other than the writing up of the research project. She then began with a preparatory period, chatting about recent events at each school to develop a relationship and help the participants feel more relaxed (Travers 2009). The staff quickly forgot the equipment was there once the questions began.

The development of a rapport with participants in the focus group interviews and in the in-depth interviews was essential (Lichtman 2010), particularly given that there were both first-language Indonesian-speakers and first-language English speakers in the groups. All of the Indonesian nationals who were teachers were confident English speakers and the interviewer is a confident speaker of Indonesian. Non-verbal cues from teachers from non-English speaking backgrounds were easy to pick up and simple clarification of the topic or issue, given through the use of Indonesian, was sometimes required.

Other techniques adopted in both the focus group interviews and in the in-depth interviews to draw out further information included asking relevant follow-up questions. These were directed by what Travers (2009, p. 161), refers to as an inner dialogue of "do I fully understand what the interview means or what is the central idea that is being conveyed here?" Travers also suggests that inner dialogue can help a researcher to retain concentration. Positive prompts such as 'I see' and 'tell me more' were used to show interest. Observations were also used within the focus group interviews. In particular, observations were made of body language and facial expression and tones of voice. These provided additional cues about participants' feelings in regard to the topic, or to other participant responses.

4.5.6   Data Analysis

Data analysis is an iterative process. It is also on-going, from the inception of the research at each case-study site (Ezzy 2002) to the conclusion. This pattern was followed in the research being reported here. Given the distance and difficulty of travelling in Indonesia at the time, the data were collected over a 3-year period and data reduction and analysis took place at times almost simultaneously with data collection. The data in relation to each case study were first of all analysed independently to respect the uniqueness of each case. Then, they were analysed sequentially for the purpose of cross case analysis (Vaughan 1992).

Contextual profiles, documents and interviews were analysed using two complementary approaches, namely, that of Miles and Huberman's (1994) interactive model for exploring qualitative data and Lichtman's (2010) three Cs of data analysis. Miles and Huberman's model of data analysis is referred to as analytical induction or as a process that supports the development of 'bottom up' theory. Bogdan and Biklen (1998, p. 157) suggest that this process "helps to systematically search and arrange one's data source". Miles and Huberman's three stages involving data reduction, data display and verifications, and drawing conclusions were specifically used to manage the data. This was in conjunction with Lichtman's (2010, p. 197) three Cs of analysis that takes data from coding, to categorizing, to identification of concepts. It involves what O'Toole and Beckett (2010) label as a process of 'distilling data'.

The complementary approaches outlined above required a continual sifting, filtering and redefining of data and relating it back to each dimension of the research aim and questions. To transform and analyse raw data to meaningful concepts, specific stages were employed. In the first stage of analysis, that of data reduction, the researchers became familiar with the range and diversity of the material collected (Punch 2000). All transcribed interview data and documentary data were read before data analysis in order to gain an overall impression of the material collected (Silverman 2000). Lichtman's coding approach was used as the primary means of data analysis. It involved using methods based on Berg's (1998) 'category development'. This enabled the researcher to build on concepts first identified from the literature review.

The first level of coding, or 'open coding', included generating concepts from the data through the use of the constant comparative method and the constant questioning method (Strauss and Corbin 1998). The next stage of analysis, 'data display' (Miles and Huberman 1994), involved the identification of "conceptualizations that encapsulate and represent diversity of experience, attitude, circumstance" (Ritchie and Spencer 1994, p. 180). The basic data coding that had occurred was revisited and data were rearranged thematically, as suggested by Ryan and Bernard (2000). Another level of coding, or higher level of processing, was also used. Berg (1998, p. 238) has referred to this as using 'coding frames'. It is akin to what Strauss and Corbin (1998) have termed 'axial coding'. Punch (2002, p. 215) describes this stage of coding as "putting the categories back together again" in conceptually different ways.

The next stage of data analysis yet again involved drawing and verifying conclusions (Miles and Huberman 1994). Associations, both implicit and explicit, were investigated and analyzed, and explanations were sought (Punch 1998). This stage of coding is what Punch (1998, p. 216) refers to as selective coding, "where the analyst deliberately selects one aspect as a core category and concentrates on that".

The study was aimed at investigating the research questions at the highest level of abstraction possible. The coding process facilitated this, allowing for moving from description to explanation as proposed, by Miles and Huberman (1994). It blended well with the approach to coding, categorizing and identification of concepts proposed by Lichtman (2010). The data reduction and displays that emerged from the process helped to identify regularities and patterns in the research data and assisted in the drawing of conclusions and the production of a set of propositions to be developed in relation to each of Ball's (1994, 2006) policy contexts.

Richardson (2000) uses the term 'crystallization' for a process which he compares to that whereby the final crystals emerge from an analysis of all of the data. Indeed, it may yield a category, or set of categories, that become the central pillars of the study. Lichtman (2010) refers to this as the phase in which there is an identification of key concepts. In this final phase the researcher chooses language structures that best articulate the conclusions and cognitive coherence of the research. The analytical tools involved include a process of writing that culminates in the final drafts of findings chapters. As Richardson (2000) sees it, this is an educative process of writing that involves producing revisions and drafts, adding clarity and insight to an analysis (Richardson 2000). Whilst attempting to retain 'neutrality' in the analysis, acknowledgement is made that the interpretations of the researchers may still be value-laden. The current authors were fully cognisant of this position when attempting to 'crystalize' their findings.

Finally, a meta-analysis was undertaken. This started out by again adopting a position that making meaning from qualitative data is a process that continually moves between the interconnected phases of reflecting on the research questions, data collection, analysis and writing. On this, Lichtman (2010, p. 200) suggests that the process is "iterative, circular and can be entered at any point". Also, critical analysis runs parallel to the process and is also entered at differing points.

The meta-analysis, conducted through a critical lens, was undertaken throughout each stage of the analysis process. Texts were viewed critically (Fairclough 2003). Data were triangulated through a process of cross case (horizontal) analysis at the micro level of the policy trajectory (Miles and Huberman 1994) and (vertical) analysis along the policy trajectory from macro to micro levels (Vidovich 2007). Each type of analysis informed the articulation of the findings and added method-ological rigour (DeCoster 2004). The meta-analysis also included triangulation of data. Attention was paid to Guion's (2002) five kinds of triangulation as means of adding credibility to an investigation: data triangulation, investigator triangulation, theory triangulation, methodological triangulation and environmental triangulation. This multi-method approach to analysis is what Denzin (1978, 2009) referred to as 'methodological triangulation'. At the same time, the limits to triangulation outlined by Silverman (2000, p. 99) who states "we cannot simply aggregate data in order to arrive at an overall truth", was accepted. Nevertheless, the present authors believe that, in this study, the empirical data revealed definite patterns in the policy processes along the policy trajectory from macro to micro levels.

Here it is apposite to consider Lichtman's (2010) suggestion that qualitative research is becoming more traditional in its approach and is led by a climate gener-ated by twenty-first century 'evidenced-based' researchers who value a more posi-tivist approach to research. We hold, however, that our use of several methods to gather and analyse data increased the credibility of our findings and provides a substantive view of how international policy (IBPYP) was interpreted and enacted in the remote Indonesian school settings we studied. The adoption of a multiple-site, case orientated study allowed us to "learn more about a little known or poorly understood situation" (Leedy and Ormrod 2001, p. 149). Our thick description of each of the three case studies, outlined in the next three chapters, highlights the importance of taking account of the settings of the schools when attempting to make sense of how the policy studied was understood. Finally, the cross case analysis, outlined in detail in Chapter 8, revealed both similarities and differences in the IBPYP policy processes at the three schools.

While there was no intention to generalize the findings of the three case studies and the IBPYP policy trajectory revealed in this study, the empirical research can be used as a springboard to engage with some meta-level conceptual themes around policy for internationalization of the curriculum (Vidovich 2002).

4.6   Trustworthiness

Appropriate methods were also chosen for the research project reported in this book to ensure the trustworthiness of the findings. It was recognized that meanings and interpretations are complex and are historically and socially located. To address this situation, a range of approaches, including thick description, a focus on process, possible reduction of subjective meanings and a tolerance for complex and nuanced explanations were employed (Ezzy 2002). Triangulation of complementary methods and data sources enriched data collection and analysis in addition to strengthening the dependability of the findings (Merriam 2009).

Due process and a systematic approach to data collection and analysis based on sound methodology and a theoretical framework ensured rigour and objectivity. Such canons of trustworthiness as honesty, depth of response, richness of response and commitment of the participant were taken on board when conducting the interviews. The interview process, as outlined earlier, provided the interviewer with a structured plan for implementation. Similarly, text analysis procedures were used to critique core IBPYP and school-based texts (Fairclough 2003). Trustworthiness was further enhanced through a sequential, transparent process of documentation that ensured a clear audit trail of the investigative process.

The essentially contested nature of education policy has been under investigation for years (Gallie 1955). More broadly, Boyd (1999) has drawn attention to the frequency of contradiction in virtually all aspects of education. This, he says, is because the field is "value-laden and debatable and many aspects have far reaching implications for the distribution of opportunity, social justice, and the shape and character of future society" (Boyd 1999, p. 239). It can be concluded that no matter how well designed, research can be neither value free nor conclusive for resolving value conflicts or the competing values and interests endemic in educational policy making. The present authors, far from seeking to contradict this view, embraced it fully through the conducting of the research.

4.7   Ethical Considerations

The research was undertaken in accordance with The University of Western Australia's (UWA) ethical code of conduct and guidelines. The researchers were aware of, and sensitive to, the ethical issues involved. As a result, they made sure they took heed of Miles and Huberman's (1994) list of thirteen ethical issues to be kept in mind whilst designing the research project. These issues are as follows: worthiness of the project; competence boundaries; informed consent; benefits; costs and reciprocity; harm and risk; honesty and trust; privacy; anonymity; research integrity and quality; ownership of data and conclusions; confidentiality of data; and the use and misuse of data, as its terms of reference. The normal protocols used for maintaining confidentiality, anonymity, informed consent and risk were followed to ensure that participants were treated ethically at all times.

To address Miles and Huberman's concern for research integrity the researchers made sure that when they embarked on the research they were aware they were doing so within a paradox of familiarity and possible bias. Having a well-structured, theoretical base with a specific framework for analysis can counter the possible bias or perspective of the researcher who has a strong IBPYP background, a strong sense of social justice and intimate knowledge of living and working in remote and international schools. The researcher who conducted the interviews made sure she was also well versed in Indonesian history, culture and language and was able to draw upon her experience of being heavily involved in local Non-government Organizations and community activities. She was an active participant in the PYP Indonesian teacher network and was an IBPYP coordinator. All of this was helpful to her in gaining access to a range of schools and enabled her to select those that were international schools, were in remote location, and were implementing the IBPYP. Her language skills also enabled her to liaise with Indonesian-only language speakers without having to rely on translators.

Throughout the research the position adopted with participants was one of honesty and trust, privacy and anonymity. The initial contact with case-study schools was made through each school's administration. Upon receiving authorization each potential participant was sent a letter seeking written consent to take part in the study. The letter clearly explained, in lay terms, the aims of the study, the interview procedure and the precautions taken to ensure each participant's anonymity throughout the research process. This was all undertaken in accord with principles laid down by Reynolds (1979), and Walter (2010). These principles also informed the focus group discussions. Several of the participants stated that the opportunity to express their views without reprise was appreciated. Similarly, email exchanges from teachers who wanted to add further to their discussions were very open and honest because of the anonymity and ease of the process.

Upon completion of the transcription of the focus group interviews and semi-structured individual interviews the digital files were transferred to a locked filing cabinet, with access restricted solely to the authors. Interviews were audio taped and transcribed in a manner that ensured that while the speakers' ownership of their statements could be traced by the authors, anonymity beyond them was protected. Transcripts were sent to participants taking part in individual interviews. Following UWA guidelines, recordings will be erased after being held in locked storage for a number of years.

Throughout the research, participants' welfare was deemed to be of utmost importance. Participants were made aware of the scope of the research and were informed that they had the right to withdraw from involvement at any time. None, interestingly, did choose to withdraw.

4.8 Conclusion

This chapter has outlined the research approach taken to explore the policy processes involved in enacting the International Baccalaureate's Primary Years Program (IBPYP) in select remote international schools in Indonesian. The policy trajectory study, the results of which are outlined in the next set of chapters, is based on Vidovich's (2007) conceptual framework for analysis derived from Ball's (1994, 2006) policy contexts: the context of influence, the context of policy text production, the context of practices, and the context of outcomes. The study encapsulates a global-local span along the policy trajectory (macro, meso and micro levels). It was also designed to capture the interconnectivity of the contexts and levels of the policy process along this trajectory.

The chapter described the research aim and questions, and detailed the theoretical framework that underpinned the research methods adopted. It was pointed out that qualitative research methods were adopted as they allowed for a systematic and integrated approach to data collection and analysis. Similarly, it was made clear that the use of a case study approach allowed for a close examination of the three remote IBPYP schools studied. The case was made that the interview data provided data on the perspectives of both individuals and members of focus groups perspectives on international education. The documents analysed, it was stated, enabled a critical review of the International Baccalaureate's PYP policy, related issues and school-based interpretation and production of policy to be undertaken. Also, the importance of ensuring that there would be thick description of each case to provide a rich depiction that would facilitate multiple levels of analysis and interpretation to take place, was highlighted.

The case for using both the interpretivist paradigm and the critical theory paradigm to inform the conceptualising of the study was also made. It was pointed out that an interpretive research approach was adopted for data collection and the early stages of analysis, and that a critical theory approach guided the meta-analysis to highlight 'bigger picture' patterns of power inequities and social justice across the policy trajectory. The latter was deemed to be important to take account of the multi-dimensional nature and the complexity of the curriculum policy phenomenon under investigation.

Chapters 5, 6 and 7 now follow. Each outlines the findings in relation to one of the three case studies. Each, also, is structured in the same way to facilitate cross-case analysis. It opens with a profile of the setting. This is followed by the findings, categorized according to Ball's (1994) contexts of influence, policy text production, practices and outcomes. Conclusions are then drawn, with core themes identified. This structure was adopted so that the reader can make judgments about the potential transferability and applicability of the research. Chapter 8 then goes on to present a horizontal analysis across the case study sites (micro level). The final chapter, Chapter 9 draws the book to a conclusion.

References

Agger, B. (1991). Critical theory, poststructuralism, postmodernism: Their sociological relevance. *Annual Review of Sociology, 17*, 105–131.

Aminzade, R., & Laslett, D. (2002). From race to citizenship: The indigenization debate in post-socialist Tanzania. *Studies in Comparative International Development, 38*(1), 43–63.

Anderson, C. W. (1986). Building theories from case study research. *Journal of Curriculum Studies, 19*(6), 201–222.

Audi, R. (1999). Self evidence. *Noûs, 33*(13), 205–228.

Babbie, E. R. (2002). *The basics of social research*. Independence: Wadsworth Publishing.

Bales, B. (2002, April 1–5). *Paradigm privilege: Determining the value of research in teacher education policy-making*. Paper presented at the annual meeting of the American Educational Research Association, New Orleans, LA.

Ball, S. J. (1990). *Politics and policy making in education: Explorations in policy sociology*. London/New York: Taylor & Francis.

Ball, S. J. (1994). *Education reform: A critical and post-structural approach*. Buckingham: Open University Press.

Ball, S. J. (2006). *Education policy and social class: The selected works of Stephen J. Ball*. Abingdon: Routledge.

Ball, S. J. (2007). *Education plc: Understanding private sector participation in public sector education*. Abingdon: Routledge.

Berg, B. (1998). *Qualitative research methods for the social sciences*. New York: Pearson.

Blase, J. (1991). *The politics of life in schools: Power, conflict, and cooperation*. Newbury Park: Corwin Press.

Bogdan, R., & Biklen, S. K. (1998). *Qualitative research for education: An introduction to theories and methods*. New York: Wiley.

Bottery, M. (2000). *Education, policy and ethics*. London: Continuum.

Bottery, M. (2006). Education and globalization: Redefining the role of the educational professional. *Educational Review, 58*(1), 95–113.

Bowe, R., Ball, S. J., & Gold, A. (1992). *Reforming education and changing schools: Case studies in policy sociology*. Abingdon: Routledge.

Boyd, W. L. (1999). Paradoxes of educational policy and productivity. *Educational Policy, 13*(2), 227–250.

Caffyn, R. (2010). "We are in Transylvania, and Transylvania is not England": Location as a significant factor in international school micropolitics. *Educational Management Administration & Leadership, 38*(3), 321–340.

Caffyn, R. (2011). International schools and micropolitics: Fear, vulnerability and identity in fragmented space. In R. Bates (Ed.), *Schooling internationally: Globalisation, internationalisation and the future for international schools* (pp. 59–82). Abingdon: Routledge.

Charon, J. (2009). *Ten questions: A sociological perspective*. Stamford: Cengage Learning.

Cibulka, J. G. (1994). Policy analysis and the study of the politics of education. *Journal of Education Policy, 9*(5), 105–125.

Coutas, P. (2008). Fame, fortune, fantasi: Indonesian idol and the new celebrity. In A. Heryanto (Ed.), *Popular culture in Indonesia: Fluid identities in Post-authoritarian politics* (pp. 111–129). New York: Routledge.

Creswell, J. W. (2005). *Educational research: Planning, conducting, and evaluating quantitative and qualitative research*. Columbus: Merrill.

Crotty, M. (1998). *The foundations of social research: Meaning and perspective in the research process*. St Leonards: Allen & Unwin.

Curry, C. E. (2006). Going international: Teaching and learning culture from the outside in. *The English Journal, 95*(6), 23–27.

DeCoster, J. (2004). *Meta-analysis notes*. Tuscaloosa: Department of Psychology, University of Alabama.

Denzin, N. K. (1978). *Sociological methods: A sourcebook* (2). New York: McGraw-Hill.

Denzin, N. K. (2009). *The research act: A theoretical introduction to sociological methods*. New Brunswick: Transaction Publishers.

Ezzy, D. (2002). *Qualitative analysis: Practice and innovation*. London: Routledge.

Fairclough, N. (2003). *Analysing discourse: Textual analysis for social research*. London: Routledge.

Fairclough, N. (2007). *Discourse and contemporary social change*. Bern: Peter Lang.

Gallie, W. B. (1955). Explanations in history and the genetic sciences. *Mind, 64*(254), 160–180.

Gomm, R., Hammersley, M., & Foster, P. (Eds.). (2000). *Case study method: Key issues, key texts*. Thousand Oaks, CA: Sage Publications Ltd.

Green, B. (Ed.). (2008). *Spaces and places: The NSW rural (teacher) education project*. Wagga Wagga, NSW: Charles Sturt University, Centre for Information Studies.

Guion, R. M. (2002). Validity and reliability. In S. G. Rogelberg (Ed.), *Handbook of research methods in industrial and organizational psychology* (pp. 57–76). Carlton: Blackwell Publishing Ltd.

Gunzenhauser, M. G. (2006). A moral epistemology of knowing subjects: Theorizing a relational turn for qualitative research. *Qualitative Inquiry, 12*(3), 621–647.

Habermas, J. (1972). *Knowledge and human interests*. (J. J. Shapiro, Trans.). Boston, MA: Beacon Press.

Harber, C. (1997). International developments and the rise of education for democracy. *Compare: A Journal of Comparative and International Education, 27*(2), 179–191.

Hargreaves, A., Lieberman, A., Fullan, M., & Hopkins, D. (Eds.). (1998). *International handbook of educational change*. Boston, Dordrecht, London: Springer.

Held, D., McGrew, A., Goldblatt, D., & Perryton, J. (1999). *Global transformations: Politics, economics and culture*. Cambridge: Polity Press.

Hitchcock, G., & Hughes, D. (1995). *Research and the teacher: A qualitative introduction to school-based research*. London: Routledge.

Horkheimer, M. (1972). *Critical theory: Selected essays*. New York: Continuum International Publishing Group.

IBO. (2003). *IB Learner Profile booklet*. Cardiff. IBO. www.ibo.org/ibla/conference/.../ TheLearnerProfileinActionFabian.ppt. Accessed 30 March 2006

IBO. (2004). *Making the PYP happen: A curriculum framework for international primary education*. Cardiff: IBO. www.ibo.org/documentlibrary/programmestandards/ Accessed 3 March 2006

IBO. (2005). *Programme standards and practices*. Cardiff: IBO. www.ibo.org/documentlibrary/ programmestandards. Accessed 4 Sept 2006

Jacobs, H. H. (2010). *Curriculum 21: Essential education for a changing world*. Alexandria, VA: Association for Supervision and Curriculum Development.

Kervin, L. (2006). *Research for educators*. Victoria, Australia: Thomson, Social Science Press.

Kvale, S. (1996). *Interviews: An introduction to qualitative research interviewing*. Thousand Oaks, CA: Sage Publications, Inc.

Leedy, P. D., & Ormrod, J. E. (2001). *Practical research: Planning and design*. Upper Saddle River, NJ: Pearson Education International.

Leonardo, Z. (2004). Critical social theory and transformative knowledge: The functions of criticism in quality education. *Educational Researcher, 33*(6), 11–18.

Lichtman, M. (2010). *Understanding and evaluating qualitative educational research*. Michigan: Sage Publications Ltd.

Mansfield, C. F., & Volet, S. E. (2010). Developing beliefs about classroom motivation: Journeys of preservice teachers. *Teaching and Teacher Education, 26*(7), 1404–1415.

Merriam, S. B. (2009). *Qualitative research: A guide to design and implementation*. San Francisco, CA: John Wiley & Sons.

Miles, M. B., & Huberman, A. M. (1994). *Qualitative data analysis: An expanded sourcebook*. Michigan: Sage Publications Ltd.

Milton-Smith, M. (2008). *A conversation on globalisation and digital art* (PhD). University of Western Australia. Retrieved from http://repository.uwa.edu.au:80/R

Moore, R. (2007). Going critical: the problem of problematizing knowledge in education studies. *Critical Studies in Education, 48*(1), 25–41.

Morgan, W. (1997). *Critical literacy in the classroom: The art of the possible*. London: Routledge.

Morrison, K. R. (2002). *School leadership and complexity theory*. London: Routledge-Falmer.

O'Donoghue, T. A. (2007). *Planning your qualitative research project: An introduction to interpretivist research in education*. Abingdon/Oxford: Routledge.

O'Toole, J., & Beckett, D. (2010). *Educational research: Creative thinking and doing*. Melbourne: Oxford University Press.

Ozga, J. (2001). Policy research in educational settings: contested terrain. *Journal of Education Policy, 16*(1), 85–87.

Patton, M. Q. (1987). *How to use qualitative methods in evaluation*. Newbury Park: Sage.

Patton, M. Q. (1990). *Qualitative education and research methods*. Newbury Park: Sage.

Peters, M. A., & Humes, W. (2003). Editorial. Education in the knowledge economy. *Policy Futures in Education, 1*(1), 1.

Pitman, T., & Vidovich, L. (2012). Recognition of prior learning (RPL) policy in Australian higher education: the dynamics of position taking. *Journal of Educational Policy, 27*(1), 761–774.

Polanyi, M. (1967). Sense-giving and sense-reading. *Philosophy, 42*(162), 301–325.

Pound, P., Britten, M., Morgan, L., Yardley, C., & Pope, P. (2005). *A synthesis of qualitative studies of medicine*. London: Elsevier.

Punch, K. (1998). *Developing effective research proposals*. London: SAGE.

Punch, K. F. (2000). *Developing effective research proposals*. London/Thousand Oaks/New Delhi: Sage.

Punch, S. (2002). Research with children: The same or different from research with adults? *Childhood, 9*(3), 321–341.

Punch, K. F. (2008). *Introduction to social research: Quantitative and qualitative approaches*. London: Sage.

Punch, K. F. (2009). *Introduction to research methods in education*. London: Sage.

Reynolds, P. D. (1979). *Ethical dilemmas and social science research*. San Francisco: Jossey-Bass.

Richardson, L. (2000). Writing: A method of inquiry. In N. K. Denzin & Y. S. Lincoln (Eds.), *Handbook of qualitative research* (pp. 923–948). Thousand Oaks: Sage.

Ritchie, J., & Spencer, L. (1994). Qualitative data analysis for applied policy research. In M. B. Miles & A. M. Huberman (Eds.), *Qualitative data analysis: An expanded sourcebook* (pp. 305–329). Newbury Park: Sage.

Rizvi, F., & Lingard, B. (2010). *Globalizing education policy*. London: Taylor & Francis.

Rosenmund, M. (2000). Approaches to international comparative research on curricula and curriculum-making processes. *Journal of Curriculum Studies, 32*(5), 599–606.

Rubin, H. J., & Rubin, I. S. (2004). *Qualitative interviewing: The art of hearing data* (2nd ed.). Thousand Oaks: Sage.

Rutter, M., & Maugh, B. (2002). School effectiveness findings 1979–2002. *Journal of School Psychology, 40*(6), 451–475.

Ryan, G. W., & Bernard, H. R. (2000). Data management and analysis methods. In N. K. Denzin & Y. S. Lincoln (Eds.), *Handbook of qualitative research* (pp. 769–802). Thousand Oaks: Sage.

Schwandt, T. A. (2001). *Dictionary of qualitative inquiry*. Thousand Oaks: Sage.

Silverman, D. (2000). *The neuro-genetic roots of organisational behaviour*. Lanham: University Press.

Stake, R. E. (1994). Case studies. In N. K. Denzin & Y. S. Lincoln (Eds.), *Handbook of qualitative research* (pp. 236–247). Thousand Oaks: Sage.

Stake, R. E. (1995). *The art of case study research*. Thousand Oaks: Sage.

Strauss, A. C., & Corbin, J. M. (1998). *Basics of qualitative research: Grounded theory procedures and techniques*. Thousand Oaks: Sage.

Travers, M. (2009). New methods, old problems: A sceptical view of innovation in qualitative research. *Qualitative Research, 9*(2), 161–179.

Tyson, L. (2006). *Critical theory today: A user-friendly guide*. New York: Routledge.

Vaughan, D. (1992). Theory elaboration: The heuristics of case analysis. In C. C. Ragin & H. S. Becker (Eds.), *What is a case? Exploring the foundations of social inquiry* (pp. 173–292). Cambridge: Cambridge University.

Vaughn, S. R., Schumm, J. S., & Sinagub, J. M. (1996). *Focus group interviews in education and psychology*. Thousand Oaks: Sage.

Vidovich, L. (2002). *Expanding the toolbox for policy analysis: Some conceptual and practical approaches*. Hong Kong: Comparative Education Policy Research Unit, Department of Public and Social Administration, City University of Hong Kong.

Vidovich, L. (2007). Removing policy from its pedestal: Some theoretical framings and practical possibilities. *Educational Review, 59*(3), 285–298.

Vidovich, L. (2013). Policy research in higher education: theories and methods for globalising times? In J. Huisman & M. Tight (Eds.), *Theory and method in higher education research*. London: Emerald Press.

Walford, G. (2001). Site selection within comparative case study and ethnographic research. *Compare, 31*(2), 151–164.

Walter, M. (2010). *Social research methods*. Melbourne: Oxford University Press.

Weber, M. C. (1992). *Special education law and litigation treatise*. Horsham: LPR Publications.

Woods, P. (1993). *Critical events in teaching and learning*. London: Falmer Press.

Yin, R. K. (1984). *Case study research: Design and methods*. Thousand Oaks: Sage.

Yin, R. K. (2011). *Applications of case study research*. Thousand Oaks: Sage.

Zhenhua, Y. (2004). Tacit knowledge/knowing and the problem of articulation. *Tradition and Discovery: The Polanyi Society Periodical, 30*(2), 11–23.

Chapter 5
Case Study One: Satu International School (SIS)

5.1 Introduction

This is the first of three chapters that map the policy terrain in relation to the adoption, production and enactment of the IBPYP curriculum policy reform in three remote international schools in Indonesia. Pseudonyms are used for all case study sites and for participants within the cases. The chapter opens by providing a profile of the particular case study setting. It then outlines the findings from policy analysis at the site. These findings are grouped with reference to the four contexts of the 'policy trajectory' framework, namely, the contexts of influences, policy text production, practices, and outcomes.

5.2 SIS International School Profile

Satu International School (SIS) is located in a small, remote site in the eastern archipelago of Indonesia. Living at SIS was described by one participant as "*like living in the pages of National Geographic*" (Fay, SIS). It operates for the expatriate employees of a large multi-national mining company and its associated contractors. It is the only school available for expatriate children at the jobsite.

At the time of data collection the school employed a principal, eight teaching staff and three ancillary staff. The teaching staff included four Australians, three Americans, one English and one Indonesian. The secretary was an Indonesian national from outside the area, while the gardeners and cleaner were both indigenous locals. In brief, expatriates held positions of power, Indonesian nationals who were not indigenous to the area were in mid-level management positions and local indigenous people were, for the most part, in unskilled labour positions.

© Springer International Publishing Switzerland 2014
S. Ledger et al., *Global to Local Curriculum Policy Processes*,
Policy Implications of Research in Education 4, DOI 10.1007/978-3-319-08762-7_5

This structural hierarchy between expatriates, Indonesian nationals from outside the area and local indigenous at the school level was replicated in the majority of workplaces within the closed mining community.

SIS lies 3° south of the Equator. It is surrounded by virtually untouched rainforest. The school is overlooked by one of the few equatorial glaciers left in the world and rests at the base of a large mountain range. A large percentage of the world's flora and fauna is found in this remote location, which still has a vibrant tribal hunter-gatherer and farming society, amongst whom a great variety of languages is spoken.

The local area is strategically positioned for mining in the region. It has the only port in the region capable of exporting minerals. Mining executives coordinate this process and make up a large percentage of the company employees in the town. One of the company's key strategies for enticing international teachers and Indonesian nationals not indigenous to the area to work in the remote location is to offer high salaries. It is listed as having one of the most generous financial teaching packages available in South East Asia.

The school caters for children of the mine-site executives as well as the children of sub-contractors. During a budget tightening exercise, the company moved from being a large, predominantly American mining operation in the early 2000s, to assuming a more international profile by the 2010s. During this time it recruited specialised mine workers, from Australia, New Zealand, Chile, Canada and South Africa. Spouses and children accompanied these miners. However, even with the diversity of staff, all senior positions within the mining company remained in the hands of Americans.

5.3   Findings

The impetus for curriculum policy change at SIS was the fatal shooting of two expatriate and one Indonesian teacher at a nearby school. The tragic event prompted SIS staff to reflect on the practices and priorities of the school. The reflective process highlighted a "*desire to be international and a dissatisfaction with the American based curriculum*" (Ken, SIS). SIS chose the IBPYP for implementation as part of the reform of the curriculum. The findings that follow are based largely on the perspectives of teachers and principal in relation to the policy processes that took place at SIS during the transition from the American curriculum policy to the adoption of the IBPYP. They are structured in relation to component parts of the 'policy trajectory'.

5.3.1   Context of Influence

Many influences had an impact on the initiation of curriculum policy reform at SIS. The ones that stimulated the decision to adopt the IBPYP can be outlined in relation to four broad themes: 'local politics', 'global branding', 'teachers' backgrounds', and the 'remote setting'. These themes highlight the common belief of participants that "*there wasn't one but probably a range of events that brought the school to adopting the International Baccalaureate as the international curriculum of choice*" (Anthony, SIS). Although the themes are considered in detail below as separate entities, all are interconnected and played a role in the decision for SIS to adopt the IBPYP.

5.3.1.1 Local Politics

The first and most common response to the question about what influenced SIS to adopt the IBPYP was the pressure of local politics. This pressure came to play in a range of situations. Two significant situations specific to SIS related to parental power and the changing face of the community.

Parental Power

Within the local setting, many power differentials, including those related to parental power, were revealed. Parents were a powerful influence on the decision for SIS to adopt the IBPYP as they played a significant role in the micro-political world of the SIS company-owned school community. The hierarchical structure found at SIS resembled other multi-national mining communities. Senior and middle management personnel were all American, with the remaining workforce being made up of workers from such recognized mining countries as Australia, South Africa, Chile and Canada.

The phenomenon of 'company couples' emerged in discussions with the participants. They were identified as being influential in school-based decision-making at SIS. Staff members at SIS painted a picture about how 'company couples' evolved in their unique company setting. Here, 'company couples' refers to a parent married to a person in senior or middle management in the company. In short, the large multi-national mining company executives brought their spouses and children to the remote job site. For many of these families it was the father's first promotion or executive role, and the partner and children's first venture overseas. On arrival, the couples benefited from the experienced 'company couples' introducing them to their new environment.

The new arrivals were quickly inducted into the hierarchical structure of the mining community through informal social processes. Because of their connections with senior company couples, the new arrivals received preferential treatment in the community and often they took up key roles as members of the school board. On this, one participant described the school board as "a quasi-community board made up of multiple *interconnecting* 'couples'" (Fay, SIS).

The principal from SIS highlighted the powerful influence company couples had enjoyed in the governance process at his school:

> Before anything can go ahead at school, approval by the school advisory board, and particularly their partners [company couples] is needed. They have to be consulted and must be convinced about any decision made here at school. (Anthony, SIS)

The following comment reflected a common view on the situation:

> The company that sponsors the school has the capacity to be the biggest influence at the school level. I don't know how much, but corporate human resources and their spouses would be first, principals second and teachers third. (Anne, SIS)

In addition to the school board, an external education advisor appointed by the company also supported this view:

> I require political astuteness, I need to be able to identify key players, set boundaries and realize and be happy with the freedom provided knowing that the executive and their spouses [company couples] have the power to veto any of my suggestions. (Bo, SIS)

There were some concerns expressed by the participants about the powerful influence the company-dominated school board had in school-based decision-making, including the decision to adopt the IBPYP. However, the general view was a more pragmatic one: "*We were driven by school administration and governed in all aspects by the company, but we were happy to adopt PYP*" (Barb, SIS). Another summed up this predicament with the comment that "*no one fought it because we know who pays us*" (Ken, SIS).

The term 'golden handcuff' was coined to describe Ken's response. Participants reported that a 'golden handcuff' was a lack of desire by staff to question those in power because of the financial security and benefits the company provide. In other words, workers were possessive of their high wages and were reluctant to leave, or to make trouble. An exception was one couple who questioned the overriding power of the company and were vocal in their opposition. As a consequence, their contracts were not renewed.

Changing Face of the Community

The changing face of the community also had an impact on the decision to adopt the IBPYP at SIS. The school's population represented a diverse range of western backgrounds other than that of the USA, while 30 % of pupils were children of expatriate miners married to Indonesian nationals. This contrasted with the situation when the school first opened in 1996, when the school population was made up of 80 % from the USA, with less than 20 % being from other cultures, and with only a few children being from intercultural marriages.

The participants commented that the most significant impact of the changing community at SIS related to curriculum and culture:

> Given the nationality mix of our student population the IBPYP seems like a policy that would fit all groups at the school. Traditionally the old policy was a good fit when everyone was American but now that the school population has changed it isn't a good fit. (Anne, SIS)

There was a general desire by staff to fill a void in the curriculum that would better cater for the changing population. However, the changing face of the school community was also mirrored in the changing face of the teaching cohort. On this, one participant commented: "*We aren't an American school anymore. It's time to change to one that is more international and better reflects the needs of the clientele*" (Fay, SIS). The population change had brought families from different cultures to SIS, many not having English.

5.3.1.2 Global Branding

The second theme identified as being influential in SIS adopting the IBPYP was global branding, or the desire of the staff and community to have a curriculum policy that would be internationally recognized and have global currency. A dominant view on this was that the IBPYP curriculum would legitimize the educational offering at the school. As one participant put it:

> The IB has a reputation, it is has been adopted in what is considered good schools, therefore we should choose a curriculum perceived and recognized to be the best international option available. (Ken, SIS)

In other words, the global status of the IB was a considerable draw card for adopting the IBPYP at SIS. Also, some staff were familiar with the programme and tried to influence others: "*It is the best international curriculum around. It has the reputation. Why wouldn't you adopt it*" (Anne, SIS).

Another view held by staff was that the global recognition of the IBPYP had the ability to remove the 'remoteness factor' associated with SIS. The principal suggested as follows:

> Part of the influence is that the IBPYP is recognized back home and that you are not going to be doing some kind of jungle Sanskrit but something that is widely recognized. (Anthony, SIS)

As well as legitimizing the education on offer at SIS, the IBPYP also provided benefits for the staff members in regard to their future employability. Teachers identified the IBPYP experience as a 'ticket' to join the international teaching 'circuit'. As one put it:

> I have a selfish reason for adopting the IBPYP... it gets us more qualified when we apply for future positions and makes us more employable. (Ken, SIS)

This participant's comment recognized the global branding of the IBPYP beyond curriculum outcomes for the school. In addition, many teachers at SIS saw the move to the IBPYP as an opportunity to "*connect to a larger organization in the same way that remote schools in other countries are connected to state departments of education. Being part of the IB gives you a sense of security*" (Ken, SIS).

5.3.1.3   Teachers' Backgrounds

The third theme to be revealed regarding the strong influences on the policy decision involved in adopting the IBPYP relates to the teaching cohort itself. The influence of teachers' backgrounds was felt at all levels of the policy trajectory. Participants described a combination of prior experience, attitude, attributes and character, as well as financial positioning, as key influences that had an impact on their involvement in policy processes. These influences are explicated separately below, but should be seen as interconnected.

Prior Experience

The majority of teachers at SIS were either from rural, remote or transient backgrounds. This, they believed influenced them in their engagement in the IBPYP policy process at the school. Many suggested that their background experiences allowed them to 'survive' the demands of remote living. Fay (SIS) outlined these demands, stating that "*a teacher's role in a remote location is all encompassing. You are everything to everybody, whether you like it or not*". Participants also commented that success in remote schools requires possession of a certain approach, or set of skills. Particularly highlighted was prior experience in remote locations. Anne (SIS) highlighted this thus:

> I grew up in such a small place like this so I knew what the deal was. You kind of have to get along with everyone and try to make sure that you have a work life and a personal life. I learnt this from growing up in small centres.

She suggested that her early life experience made it easy to adapt to the remote location.

Many, like Anne, believed their previous experiences built up their resilience to 'cope' with the demands of small communities. On this, the majority highlighted the need to divorce work from social life. However, they also said that within a small community, where schools are the 'quasi-community centre', this separation is not easy to accomplish; work and social life become intertwined, and are hard to compartmentalise. The prior experience of teachers was also considered by them to be an influential factor in how they adopted and enacted the IBPYP at SIS. Furthermore, they revealed that those who had limited background experience in remote areas found it difficult to adopt multiple roles and identities.

Attitude, Attributes and Character

The combination of attitude, personal attributes and character were identified by the teaching cohort at SIS as influences on the policy decision to adopt and engage with the IBPYP. These were also identified as influencing a teacher's decision to teach in remote areas such as SIS. Furthermore, they were able to identify key attributes that they considered to be essential for successful teaching in remote areas. These included being flexible, having a balanced lifestyle, being resourceful, having cultural awareness, and having a keen sense of humour. The following comment was made in relation to these basic attributes:

> After growing up and living in small communities, you learn to tolerate and accept differences and interact with a variety of people that you probably wouldn't normally get to interact with when you live in a larger setting. You rely on common courtesy, instinct and initiative. (Sandy, SIS)

On this, one teacher stated:

> I fluctuate between the 3Ms [*maverick, missionary and mercenary*], at the moment I think I am a bit of a maverick as I am keen to try new things and be adventurous with the IBPYP. Small schools allow you to be experimental. In my past I had missionary zeal. However I have become more of a realist now that I am older and hover between missionary and mercenary. (Em, SIS)

This was representative of the view of many staff, who commented on the dynamic movement between the roles represented by each of these labels and how it influenced their actions at school.

Teachers with experience in rural settings also tended to be those with experience in international settings. They were quite clear that what was required of them to be successful in these settings was flexibility, cultural adaptability, international mindedness and interpersonal relationship skills. They also spoke of the importance of being well-balanced, fair-minded and friendly. Some considered that a key factor which made them international teachers was the fact that they had worked in a number of countries, whilst others like Fay, at SIS, stated that it was the capacity to "*value and interact with locals*". All, however, held that one could not describe oneself as an 'international teacher' unless one was teaching, or had taught in, an international school.

Financial Positioning

The financial positioning of the company also played an important role in the adoption of the IBPYP. The principal talked about the wealth of the company and its ability to afford 'the best' curriculum package available. Financial incentive was also important to the SIS teachers, who were predominantly middle aged, heavily mortgaged and well-travelled. Two young staff members were of a different kind, spending most of their money on travelling. The overall belief was that teachers were enticed by the financial package offered at SIS. One of the participants enlarged on this 'mercenary' aspect of his appointment, stating "*I wouldn't be here and probably most of the others wouldn't be here too if it wasn't such a well-paid position*" (Ken, SIS).

In addition to base salary, staff members were provided with a travel allowance, a living-away-from-home allowance, a postal allowance, free rent and utilities, and access to free medical and dental treatment, either on-site, or in the form of medical evacuation to a major health centre. Family accommodation included a brick-and-tile, three bedroom, two bathroom, fully air-conditioned home, with access to a golf course. An Olympic-size swimming pool, medical centre, small shopping centre, and library and museum, all purpose-built by the mining company, were also available.

The principal explained that the company actively sought the employment of 'teaching couples'. They represented a financial saving for the company as it was cheaper 'per head' to bring a couple to a job site than a single person. Three teaching couples were employed at SIS and the remaining staff included a single pre-primary teacher, a local Indonesian language teacher and the wife of a company executive who took on the position as computer teacher. The 'couples' emerged as being significantly influential in the curriculum policy process. They were able to dominate the micro-political world of SIS curriculum reform and, in doing so, were influential in the decision to adopt and enact the IBPYP in the school. They considered that their decision to seek to be connected with the IBPYP would position them well for future employment.

5.3.1.4 Remote Setting

The fourth influence identified by participants in the decision to adopt the IBPYP was the remote setting of SIS. One of the staff commented that *"the remoteness of SIS and our starvation of professional development has made us very keen on taking on the IBPYP"* (Em, SIS). There was a general belief that an international curriculum would help provide a quality education in an isolated setting. The principal echoed staff perspectives on this:

> I believe our remoteness is one of the reasons for us adopting a curriculum that explores international issues. We lack a whole range of media that brings the world to us. We are in an isolated spot and in effect have only one stream of news into here, American. An internationally focused curriculum offsets the remoteness. (Anthony, SIS)

The majority of teachers at SIS were also parents of school-aged children themselves and expressed their concern about leaving the security of, for example, an American or Australian curriculum to come to a tiny, isolated location. They wanted the security of knowing their children would not be educationally disadvantaged. Adopting an internationally recognized curriculum was expressed as one way of allaying their concerns.

Although remotely located, the participants were impressed by the sophisticated digital connections to the 'outside world' provided by the mining company. The school and community had access to phones, computers and broadband television. The school also had continual access to technical support from the IT service department of the company. SIS staff considered this to be a significant benefit of working for a large company. The following comment outlines the pragmatics of the situation:

> We have the executive children at this school. If something breaks it is attended to as a priority, particularly anything to do with computers. (Ken, SIS)

Some IT issues, however, were simply beyond the control of the company. Due to the geographical location of SIS, an inordinate number of daily thunderstorms occurred. Power blackouts were frequent in the area and often took a long time to rectify.

Notwithstanding such obstacles, the staff felt well connected to the outside world. They had access to email and Skype to maintain personal connection to family and friends. At the same time, the company blocked access to Facebook and other social networking programmes, thus leaving staff with a feeling of being 'under surveillance'.

Staff at SIS were keen to discuss the importance of having access to technology for personal and professional reasons. On this, one commented thus: "*Without the link to the outside world to contact friends and family I wouldn't be here, it takes the edge off the remoteness and loneliness*" (Fay, SIS). While SIS had high levels of ICT resourcing, good access was offset by the irregular connections and company surveillance already mentioned. Nevertheless, there was general agreement with the view of one participant that adoption of the IBYP was not seriously affected. It, she stated, was valuable because it provided access to "*the technological world of the IB; its website, a network of international teachers, and a wide range of resources*" (Barb, SIS).

5.3.2 Context of Policy Text Production

The processes involved in policy text production at SIS focused on making meaning of the IBPYP global texts and translating them into IBPYP school-based policy text documents. Major differences in design and content were revealed when participants started to compare the previous American curriculum with that of the IBPYP. The distinguishing features of the American curriculum were its content driven, subject-based approach to delivery, with little reference to the needs of the students and the omission of an Arts, Health and Physical Education curriculum section. What they were now faced with in relation to the IBPYP was a trans-disciplinary, concept-driven, inquiry-based approach to learning and the notion of the centrality of the child in the learning process.

The SIS curriculum policy documents were described as being 'works in progress', rather than a complete policy. According to the principal, the record on the initial transition from the existing American curriculum was largely oral and fragmented. Whilst working through the IBPYP authorization process, however, the school curriculum policy started to be documented, guided by the IB *Programme Standards and Practices* (IBO 2003a) document. This document underpins the evaluation process across all four programmes and provides touchstones for accountability purposes. SIS was obligated to meet these requirements when engaged in policy production and design at the school level. The only additional policy components SIS had to produce that were not explicitly referred to in the *Programme Standards and Practices* document were those related to 'employment', 'security' and 'admissions'. These were produced to meet compliance requirements of the company and the Indonesian government.

Three distinct themes were generated in relation to the IBPYP policy text production at SIS. The first theme relates to the development of a 'shared vision' for the school using the IBPYP as a policy tool. The second theme relates to the importance of the 'IB *Learner Profile*' document. The third theme relates to IB school-based 'structural processes' involved in policy text production.

5.3.2.1 Shared Vision

The leadership team at SIS expressed support for the role of the IBPYP in developing a shared educational vision for the school. Traditionally, SIS relied on outside sources from the US for policy design and direction. Principals and teachers referred negatively to these sources as providing the 'grey policy file', as they termed it. The perceived lack of substance in the 'grey policy file' and a strong disconnect with the policy document suggested that a policy vacuum existed at the school. The following comment highlights some of the perceived reasons for this vacuum:

> Any policy that has existed in the past has been produced in isolation sometimes offsite, contextually irrelevant, forgotten in the transition or simply fallen between the gaps of staff transition. (Ken, SIS)

There was concern about a lack of professional dialogue and reflective practice at the site due partly to a lack of policy direction. Teachers suggested that, hitherto, they had been left to their own devices when it came to curriculum: "*We don't have any evidence of policy as it is inside people's heads and some key players aren't here anymore, so we do what we think is best*" (Barb, SIS). This generated openness amongst the school community to the development of a shared vision and a sense of policy ownership at the school level, and the IBPYP policy text production was seen as the first step in the process.

The IB authorization process promotes a shared vision approach by including opportunities for collaboration and reflective practice in all aspects of school operations. The professional shift that took place is reflected in the following comment:

> The best part now is that we meet and collaborate on the programme and planning it is challenging but rewarding. We are regularly involved in a lot of whole-school issues now it makes you feel like you are contributing. (Anne, SIS)

Teachers became more actively engaged in curriculum policy development at SIS than previously, and many participants suggested that they were being more accountable than before to management, parents and pupils.

Parents, like teachers and students, had to come to understand the IBPYP. During the authorization process, the IB authorization team initiated focus group discussions with teachers, principals and parents to gauge the extent to which all parties were familiar with the IB policy and the school curriculum. This process was seen as an accountability mechanism, or quality assurance strategy.

The leadership team recognized the importance of informing its community of learners about the IBPYP policy texts. The close-knit nature of the small community and the school's 'open door' policy had, as one teacher put it, already engaged support from the parent body:

> We have a strong three-way involvement between teachers, parents and children. All the groups need to be well informed feel comfortable and understand the IBPYP. (Fay, SIS)

Participants described how parents sat on the school board, supported co-curricular activities, and staffed the canteen. Friday canteen luncheons comprised a two-course sit-down meal for all students and parents, accompanied by an informal chat with the teachers about the events of the week.

5.3.2.2 The IB *Learner Profile*

Of all the IB policy documents used at the school level, teachers were most knowledgeable about the *Learner Profile* (IBO 2003b). They commented on its importance and saw it as an effective tool for establishing the core beliefs of the IB in the school and amongst the school community. The *Learner Profile* stimulated both informal and formal discussions about the IBPYP and 'internationally mindedness'. It was seen to provide a set of attributes to which students, teachers and parents should aspire.

Goal Two of the SIS, 'School Development Plan', highlighted the importance of the *Learner Profile* in the school to ensure all students gain success in their development of the *Learner Profile* and in the five essential elements of the written curriculum of the IBPYP. The following related view was shared by all staff:

> I think that the Learner Profile should be modelled in a PYP school ... those traits are certainly a strength of people's international character. The attributes should be embedded in teachers, students and parents in IB schools. (Anne, SIS)

At the same time, the IBPYP coordinator was also guided by the *Coordinators' Handbook* (IBO 2005). This handbook included the programme of inquiry, subject specific scope and sequence documents as well as sample programmes.

5.3.2.3 Structural Processes

The principal and the PYP coordinator put significant structural processes in place at the school to facilitate policy text production. The majority of staff commented on the success of the supportive administration, the encouragement of the PYP coordinator and the coordinated approach to timetabling, support staff, resources and relief time. The structural processes required to support the production of policy documents by the school can be classified into three broad categories. The first involved identifying systemic steps for implementation of the IBPYP. The second focused on providing teachers with opportunities for collaboration. The third incorporated mechanisms for programme evaluation and accountability.

Systemic Steps for Policy Design and Implementation

The challenge for SIS was to ensure that the IBPYP guided the policy reform at the school and that it wasn't relegated to the 'file', as were the previous American curriculum policy documents. The participants embraced the adoption of the IBPYP as an opportunity for SIS to develop a strategic approach to policy reform. The first strategic action was to appoint an IBPYP coordinator. This coordinator and the principal jointly constructed a policy implementation strategy in consultation with the staff. The IBPYP *Coordinators' Handbook* helped guide them. The emphasis was on access to, and provision of, IBPYP professional development at both the school and regional level. School level support included the provision of paedagogical focus sessions, dissemination of professional readings, and facilitating access to the IB 'Online Curriculum Centre'. The weekly staff meeting was described as providing the platform for many of these initiatives to be discussed and appraised.

The second strategy in the policy text production process related to scheduling and timetabling. According to the principal, the timetables had to meet IBO authorization requirements, including the provision of time for collaborative planning sessions for the staff and extended library and language schedules for the students. To assist, a teacher librarian was appointed to focus primarily on developing the research skills of the students to engage with the inquiry-based programme, as well as to build up an international collection of library materials, including second language texts.

The third strategy involved the production of policy texts specific to language acquisition. On this, the participants described how the development of a new language policy assisted in the promotion of the status of second language acquisition. A language teacher commented that it *"raised the profile of Indonesian within the school setting"* (Ria, SIS). SIS doubled the amount of class contact time for languages and for library-based work, and upgraded the language materials and library resources. However some staff questioned the importance of the school teaching Indonesian, seeing the extra time devoted to it as being unnecessary, particularly as it was not going to be spoken by the pupils when they returned to their 'home' countries.

Overall, the strategies combined to support the transition from the previous American curriculum through to the authorization process outlined in the IB *Standards and Practices* (IBO 2003a) document. Also, there was a redirection of funds in the school budget in order to facilitate their implementation. This latter development was uppermost in the minds of the participants, who agreed that the financial support that was forthcoming was significant in influencing policy text production and enactment.

Structural Opportunities for Collaboration

While a collaborative approach to policy text production and enactment underpins IBPYP paedagogy, it was not common practice at SIS when it was initially decided to adopt the IBPYP. Soon, however, the school schedules were changed to provide time for policy text production in collaborative groups. The IBPYP requirements for authorization, as one teacher recalled, forced the hand of SIS in this regard:

> The school's physical isolation does not lend itself to school mentoring, planning or networking opportunities. However, with IBPYP, it is a requirement so we all have to work together to come up with ideas. (Brian, SIS)

The SIS leadership team set up a range of opportunities for staff collaboration. Each Wednesday school classes finished early and staff worked in small collaborative groups to either plan, or review, a 'unit of inquiry'. These sessions were known as 'collaborative Wednesdays'. A common perspective amongst the teachers on this development was along the following lines

> Collaboration and the strength of team teaching, planning and sharing of activities and topics that allowed interaction with specialty teachers made the school more cohesive. (Anne, SIS)

In similar vein, the leadership team considered that this formal approach to promoting collaboration was very significant in the ensuring successful and sustainable policy text production.

The school also offered timetabled sessions for teachers to engage in collaborative planning with the PYP coordinator. These sessions were described as *"professionally engaging and powerful"* (Fay, SIS). They involved on-going interaction, with support for all staff, and provided opportunities for the IBPYP coordinator to offer her support based on the needs of each teacher. Also, access to the IB global network and the Indonesian PYP Network entitled the 'PYP Dunia (World)' was sought and provided.

One of the most influential strategies adopted to support policy text production, as identified by participants, was attendance at IBPYP workshops and conferences. The Asia Pacific Regional Office provided all IBPYP regional professional development and conferences in Singapore. The principal explained that staff members were happy to go there as Singapore was considered a safe and neutral meeting place in South-East Asia. Also, while the trips were costly, SIS was financially capable of sending all staff to the IBPYP annual conference in Singapore. Teachers mentioned how they enjoyed the opportunity to collaborate and be involved in IBPYP discussions outside of their remote school setting. On this, one teacher stated:

> The professional development in Singapore gave us opportunities to talk professionally about global issues rather than being caught up in insignificant issues that become major issues in a small community. (Ria, SIS)

The provision of professional development and collaborative planning time provided SIS staff with opportunities for engaging in IBPYP professional dialogue. Teachers, in turn, took ownership of, and developed confidence in, the programme and the curriculum policy texts produced.

Setting Up Mechanisms for Evaluation

The final policy strategy employed during policy text production was to develop mechanisms to evaluate the education programme on offer at SIS. Following its inception, SIS had sought accreditation from the Western Association of Schools and Colleges (WASC). The external accreditation process with WASC continued after the adoption of the IBPYP and is still in place. In conjunction with WASC, the school utilizes the annual IOWA State testing regime as an external auditing tool. SIS has continued to administer the IOWA tests of proficiency to provide itself with longitudinal data on performance.

Given the changing nature of the school's population, the principal searched for an external test that would be perceived by the staff as being appropriate for students. One staff member recalls reflecting as follows:

> We can devise wonderful inquiry based teaching programmes but in regards to bench-marking them we don't have anything. I know we are stuck in the remote wilds but we think you are working at this level which will be commensurate with your peers elsewhere. (Anthony, SIS)

In response to such concerns, the school decided to trial the International Schools Association (ISA) test for International Schools, launched in 2006. This is a test designed originally for international schools and developed by the Australian Council of Educational Research (ACER). The families were able to choose between IOWA or ISA testing, but many families wanted their children to sit both tests. This they did, with the parents bearing the additional cost.

To support the external auditing and testing regime, internal structures were put in place. Parents were involved in three-way conferences and portfolios of learning were produced each term to reflect the inquiry-based, concept-driven approach embedded in IBPYP. One teacher referred to these developments as the "*IBPYP windows to parents*" (Barb, SIS)

SIS also developed a range of mechanisms for evaluating school-based policy documents. All policy documents were re-designed and aligned with the IBPYP *Programme Standards and Practices* (IBO 2003a) so that they met the essential criteria laid down by the IBPYP. The process was contentious for some staff, who considered it too demanding. One suggested that the "*policy jargon bogged us down and clouded what the programme stands for*" (Brian, SIS).

The procedure of aligning all strategies and processes with the *Programme Standards and Practices* (IBO 2003a) document was established early in the implementation process at SIS and guided the structural changes outlined above. Many saw the whole school approach to policy text construction as a positive strategy. Some found the level of active policy involvement difficult because of a lack of common understanding or personal interest. Others, however, saw the production of IBPYP school-based curriculum policy texts, particularly the 'units of inquiry' as unnecessary extra work.

5.3.3 Context of Practices

The adoption of the IBPYP coupled with the changing nature of the school's population, saw notable changes in practice at the school administrative and classroom level at SIS. Four main themes, all related to change, capture this. These are: 'changes to policy documentation and dissemination practices'; 'changes to teacher practices, paedagogy, and professional networking'; 'changes to school resourcing and procedures'; and 'changes to interaction with the local setting'. Each of these changes is now outlined below.

5.3.3.1 Changes to Policy Documentation and Dissemination Practices

Documentation on previous policies at SIS was hard to locate, and what was located omitted certain curriculum areas and lacked an outline of strategies to guide policy enactment. SIS relied heavily on the individual experience of the principal and teachers, rather than on whole school policy. The majority of staff alluded to relegating the SIS 'grey policy file' to their bottom drawers. This was also an issue of concern for the school principal. He commented on how *"our old policies aren't as transparent as we would like them"* (Anthony, SIS). He saw the adoption of the IBPYP as an opportunity to promote policy, rather than hide it.

Engagement in policy development and curriculum design were essential requirements for the IBPYP authorization process. The principal suggested he had to include structural processes such as school timetabling and resourcing in the school strategic plan to help enact the policy documents. Teachers had the opportunity to work together in pairs and groups to develop class and school-based curriculum policy texts. They commented that throughout the early IBPYP implementation phase they became familiar with the programme vernacular and the content of the policies, due primarily to receiving an on-going deluge of information from the school's administration teams.

However, there were significant differences in the familiarity of the participants with the policy documents during this time, and particularly so between classroom teachers and specialist teachers. Subject specialist teachers felt isolated and had limited access to personnel, or policy, documentation in their field. Concerns related to their sense of isolation were expressed by one of them as follows:

> We have department and faculties that consist of one person, so the need for written policy has been superfluous. Teachers had it in their heads and left us with nothing. So now we have to start from scratch. (Anne, SIS)

While the IBPYP planning requirements placed a heavy workload on all teachers, the lack of policy documentation available in the specialist areas made it particularly hard for the specialist teachers. During this stage they had to generate policy and practices out of their own initiative and link them to the IBPYP *Programme Standards and Practices*. This included determining the scope and sequences for their subject areas and 'units of inquiry' that were cohesive and consistent.

To disseminate and promote the IBPYP policy, a range of approaches was identified as effective in the school's weekly newsletter and monthly parent evenings. Participants also constructed a large painted wall mural in the breezeway at the entrance to the school. This depicted the SIS journey toward IBPYP authorization as a train journey, highlighting milestones, key documents and events. It was designed by staff and painted by the students. Units of inquiry for each year level were located on separate passenger carriages of the train. The backdrop for the IBPYP train journey was the geographical image from port to the mountaintop. The mural became a meeting place for parents to observe curriculum policy changes, discuss events and provide feedback.

5.3.3.2   Changes to Teacher Practices, Paedagogy and Professional Networking

Changes to teacher practices, paedagogy and professional networking were linked to the adoption of the IBPYP at SIS. A visual representation of the school-based sequence of events allocated to these matters was displayed in the SIS staffroom. Significant policy events were embedded in the associated timeline, including those related to professional development, visitors, collaborative planning sessions, parent evenings, conferences, whole school planning days and excursions.

The usefulness of the visual timeline was captured by one of the teachers, who stated,

> It is great to sit here when you are struggling with the demands of teaching in a remote location and just reflect on the mural as it shows us how far the staff and school have come in regard PYP. The learning journey and our adjustments need to be valued and viewed. (Fay, SIS).

Teachers also considered that the most profound change to their practices at SIS was their increased involvement in professional discussion and policy text production. This was followed by the usefulness of the IB *Learner Profile*. The former involved the development of more collaborative practices, while the latter emerged as a tool for individual and school reflective practice.

The active involvement of teachers in curriculum policy development, as required by the IBPYP *Programme Standards and Practices* (IBO 2003a), resulted in their engagement in conversations and debate about their practices. As one of them said, it forced "*real conversations about real issues*" (Brian, SIS). Another significant development was the adoption by the teachers of a more reflective approach to their planning, teaching and assessment than had been the case up to then.

The adoption of the IBPYP also resulted in changed classroom practices. These varied from teacher to teacher. Some, who thought they were already 'doing' IBPYP, believed they only had to "*tweak it a little*" (Barb, SIS). Others could identify the key elements of IBPYP and spent time trying to implement these in their programmes. A few, like Brian, not only embedded IBPYP core beliefs within their practices but continually sought ways of refining them: "*I am practicing trans-disciplinary skills while developing an understanding of the key concepts- so that children can try to improve the state of the world and accept the responsibility to take action to do so"* (Brian, SIS).

The most difficult change related to inquiry-based and conceptual-based teaching and learning. Many of the participants commented on a lack of confidence in both of these areas. However, there was mention of how much easier it was for early childhood teachers to adopt the IBPYP because they already embraced a concept-driven curriculum and inquiry-based programmes. Furthermore, they were familiar with holistic teaching styles. By contrast, teachers who taught content-driven subjects seemed to find it more difficult to grasp the key concept-based approach of the IBPYP. For many staff, a view prevailed that *"the more you think you know about IBPYP the more you realize you don't know about it!"* (Ria, SIS). Many also commented in positive fashion on the role played by the IBPYP coordinator during the process. As one participant stated: *"without the support of the IBPYP coordinator working in partnership with the principal changes in curriculum policy practices would not be as smooth or as effective"* (Barb, SIS).

5.3.3.3 Changes to School Resourcing and Procedures

As a result of implementing the IBPYP curriculum policy, the SIS leadership team made several internal changes to the way it allocated school resources. These were directed at supporting the professional growth of teachers and the provision of support materials. They were outlined in the SIS strategic plan and were considered to have been influential in supporting change in both paedagogical practice and outcomes at the school.

The principal reported that SIS found itself in a quandary as to how to effectively utilize the generous funding made available by the mining company to promote and support the adoption of the IBPYP policy. Traditionally, each teacher had been provided with a large amount of funds to purchase class materials and resources, but there was no system-level method in place to monitor these purchases. In many instances, teachers would order highly specific and costly resources (including kilns, art easels, and electronic Lego sets), but due to a range of logistical reasons, including delays in arrival, many of the resources remained untouched in storerooms. Indeed, with the transient nature of the remote school staff, there were occasions when items ordered would not arrive until after a teacher had moved to take up a position at another school. This practice resulted in resource wastage and often also in a doubling up of resources across the school.

The principal also reported a change in financial practices as the mining company put a spotlight on the financial wastage in each of its departments, including the school. A new whole-school approach to resource allocation focused on accountability was adopted. Now, all purchasing of resources became more strategic in terms of the needs of the school. This included resourcing newly formed 'units of inquiry' and providing curriculum support. The school also upgraded teacher support materials for inquiry-based and concept-driven teaching approaches, as well as providing second language learning material.

The school budget included provision for the professional development for all staff. The nature of such development, as pointed out by the participants, had traditionally been left up to the individual choice of a teacher, and large amounts of money had been assigned for him, or her. Teachers planned international trips to anywhere in the world as long as they could find a suitable conference to attend. Accordingly, it is not surprising that the principal stated that the push for a whole-school coordinated approach to conference attendance "*met with a large amount of resistance from some of the teachers*" (Anthony, SIS). A bi-annual approach to funding conferences was introduced. Additional support was provided for the ICT teacher and the librarian, with the library and attached computer centre becoming the central hub of the school. Also, the employment of the PYP coordinator was planned for within the SIS budget, with resourcing to help him to work collaboratively with teachers in their class.

5.3.3.4 Changes to Interaction with the Local Setting

Although the teachers at SIS had drawn upon experiences related to the unique setting and local indigenous community in their teaching prior to the introduction of the IBPYP, the principal reported that it had been very limited. Goal Two of the SIS strategic plan, developed as part of the policy text production process, addressed this concern, stating that SIS would build better relationships with the school's Indonesian national and indigenous community as well as the unique setting in which it was placed. The principal noted that staff changed the way they interacted with the local environment once the core IBPYP concepts, principles and standards were better understood. Principally, the major shift meant taking on a more sustainable and focused connection with the surrounding resources, rather than the previous tokenistic and often *ad hoc* approach to the interaction. The following represented a view held by most staff:

> We do a lot of outreach programmes that take advantage of our setting. Local tribes come in, we do the valley walk, and we have sessions with the local Indonesian school, but they really rely on the interest of the teachers and there seems to be little continuity. (Anne, SIS)

The dilemma the school faced, however, according to the principal, was how it would utilize the social, geographic and economic resources of the area in a sustainable and effective way. The staff considered that the development of 'units of inquiry' and a whole-school 'programme of inquiry' provided a sustainable backdrop. Staff members were able to identify key personnel and locations within the community that could link to a particular 'unit'.

A specific example of the latter related to a world-renowned anthropologist who lived with the locals in the area. Once approached, he was delighted to be involved in the IBPYP units. He gave the school access to thousands of photographs and artefacts. In addition, local indigenous group leaders were consulted and information was sought concerning significant events that were to be held throughout the year. Also, the mine-site opened up its facilities and resources for the school and set up a rotation of events. This strategic approach to community engagement as outlined by one of the participants, *"was embedded into the yearly calendar and became part of everyday practice"* (Brian, SIS). The following description by one teacher is a good example of how SIS reconsidered and changed the way it interacted with the local context:

> A small but poor village on the outskirts of the community was struggling to raise enough money to buy a generator but was too proud to ask for money. Originally the school would have simply raised the funds or donated money. After a series of discussions a cultural visit was planned and costs associated were given to the community (at an inflated cost). The excursion lasted for a whole day in the jungle and mangroves guided by local elders. The children watched the process of cutting sago and the traditional methods of draining and filtering within the process. The school returned to the village for a sago meal. Dances were performed and handicrafts were on display for sale. The cultural experience was a memorable one for both parties. The community and school benefitted enormously, no-one lost face and a generator was bought. (Anthony, SIS)

This highlights the three-way benefits to the school, company and village from interacting together. The school identified the issue, the company provided the financial resources and the needs of the small community were met.

5.3.4 Context of Outcomes

The curriculum policy processes involved in the adoption and enactment of the IBPYP at SIS resulted in a range of policy outcomes. These included the production of new school-based IBPYP curriculum policy texts, changes in school-based policies, practices and procedures, and a school and teaching cohort that had IB 'brand' recognition and experience. However, there was also a number of unplanned outcomes that revealed a range of issues relating to relationships, power, social justice and local politics. These can be considered in relation to three themes: 'international mindedness and expat-mindedness'; the link between 'finance and power' and 'the impact of remoteness'.

5.3.4.1 International Mindedness and Expat-Mindedness

Issues of power and inequity at the school surrounded the terms 'international mindedness' and 'expat-mindedness'. The conceptualization of the term 'international mindedness' invoked discussion, confusion and debate for staff. Many teachers included the term in their responses to the interviews, yet when questioned about it, found it difficult to define. They tended to respond with questions such as *"Who judges what constitutes international mindedness?" "Can only international travellers be internationally minded?"* (Barb, SIS) and *"Are expatriate workers internationally minded?"* (Ria, SIS). At the same time, there clearly was a desire to promote an international outlook, rather than a nationalistic one, amongst the children. Some also spoke about developing a global outlook, rather than a local one, while one of the few experienced IBPYP teachers in the group discussed the need to develop "*a set of trans-disciplinary skills, attitudes and international ideals that are transferrable*'" (Ria, SIS).

Teachers discussed the increased international mobility of the teaching staff and students, and the experiences gained from this. Yet, they also talked about their concern for what they saw as problems associated with what they termed the 'expat-mindedness' that pervaded this new internationally mobile group. One of the teachers explained as follows:

> We'd been doing energy conservation and one of the kids came in and told the class that last night when he was playing on the computer he reminded his maid to turn off her TV and radio to save energy while he kept on playing his computer. He was so delighted that he had saved energy for the family. To me that sums up the life of an expat brat! (Brian, SIS)

The power inequity displayed by this expatriate child could reflect socio-cultural attitudes towards ethnic diversity.

The power differential between expatriate children, their support staff at home, and even service providers within the community, including teachers, was obvious across the school. The term 'expat-mindedness' was also used to describe the parent body within the hierarchical structure of the SIS company-owned setting. The participants clearly saw the parent body at SIS as privileged, and with privilege came perceived and actual power. Yet, they themselves were also products of the 'expat-mindedness' enclave at SIS and faced the same challenges.

The irony of teaching an 'expat-minded' community about 'international mindedness' was not lost on the principal at SIS. He indicated that he had been active in developing the service and action component of the IBPYP to help counter the 'expat-mindedness' phenomenon. He designed activities to improve the capabilities of local indigenous groups and provided opportunities for the children at SIS to understand their privileged lifestyle. The premise behind his actions was that "*with privilege there is responsibility*" (Anthony, SIS).

A power differential between the IB head office, regional office and schools was also revealed in relation to whose knowledge was privileged in the construction of IBPYP curriculum policy texts. At the local level, power was expressed in the construction of school-based curriculum policy and practices. It was, however, constrained by what was a compliance document, the IB *Programme Standards and Practices* (IBO 2003a) produced by head office, and directed and influenced by regional office. Variations in interpretations often led to tension.

5.3.4.2 Finance and Power

In all aspects of life in the closed mining community, financial and power differentials were evident. The company manager, a self-confessed multi-billionaire, used to drive through one of the poorest villages to get to his workplace. The international school had air-conditioning, yet the neighbouring national school did not.

The financial enticement for teachers to move to the remote area was extremely generous, yet some frustration was expressed at the subservience of the school to the mining company. One teacher claimed:

> It is a company town, so they have the right to have a lot of influence in school decision-making. We have to learn to do as we are told or else we won't have a job. (Ken, SIS)

The term 'golden handcuffs' was again used by participants to explain how they dealt with this. As one teacher put it: "*the money is too good to go, so you put up with things you wouldn't necessarily agree with until it gets too hard*" (Em, SIS). Teachers deferred to the decisions and views held by the company, and more importantly, the decisions made by 'company couples'. Unless teachers were connected to the company couples, their voices, they felt, often went unheard or were not considered.

The power differentials noted above emphasize the significant impact power can have on the IBPYP policy process. It was apparent that the company had the 'final say' in all major policy decisions at SIS. As one teacher stated: "*Approval by the school advisory board, and particularly their partners* [company couples] *have to be consulted and must be convinced about any decision made here at school*" (Anthony (SIS)). The principal also reported that the autocratic leadership and decision-making style of the company overrode his own more democratic style in certain instances, while stating that he felt he had had some, albeit limited, success with some decision-making involved in the IBPYP policy reform.

5.3.4.3 The Impact of Remoteness

The 'remote' factor was regularly noted by participants as being a significant influence in the decision to adopt and enact IBPYP curriculum policy processes. Many policy outcomes were attributed by them to the fact that they lived and worked in the remote setting of SIS. Also, they held, remoteness had an impact on the practices that occurred at the school and on the teachers' autonomy within the school.

The attitude and interpersonal relationship skills of the teaching cohort at SIS were considered by participants to be one of the most significant influences on the IBPYP across the policy trajectory. Indeed, a teacher's commitment to the IBPYP was seen as key in determining the successful outcome of IBPYP enactment. On this, teachers felt like they had to be counsellors, community organisers, surrogate parents, sports coaches, confidants and friends in the small community. As one of them put it, as teachers in remote locations, they were "*required to wear multiple hats for multiple roles*" (Fay, SIS) and another stated that they were "*judged vigorously by members of the small mining community depending on how they embraced these various roles*" (Ria, SIS). To this, they added that they were required to be ambassadors of the IBPYP 'brand' and, in some cases, be sales persons for it.

Professional and personal isolation, however, had to be contended with. Ken expressed the view of many staff when he stated: "*We are stranded professionally and socially*" (Ken, SIS). Others reported that family and friends acted as support mechanisms when they felt personally aggrieved by decisions, or events, at school, or in the community. On a professional level, isolation also meant limited access to professional development and discourses. At the same time, remoteness could have a positive impact. Fay gave voice to this: "*Because we are so remote and small we have freedom to make our own decisions and be involved in all facets of school and community life*". This comment highlights a common refrain of the participants, namely, that working in a remote location can give teachers a sense of professional autonomy and empowerment, which in this case was important for the successful introduction of the IBPYP. It was a policy enabler for teacher involvement in policy development and curriculum design; they were actively engaged in curriculum policy decisions in all areas of schooling. On the other hand, it was recognized that there was also a downside to professional autonomy, namely, a sense of being "*overwhelmed by the local demands of parents*" (Fay, SIS). Once again, one is brought face-to-face with the complexities of policy reform in a company-owned school, a dominant theme throughout this chapter and relating to power inequities and social justice issues including in international mindedness, finance and power, and the impact of 'remoteness' on school and teacher outcomes.

5.4   Conclusion

This chapter presented findings from the first of three case study schools adopting the International Baccalaureate Primary Years Program (IBPYP) in remote international schools in Indonesia. The analysis captured the relevant curriculum policy processes, and it highlighted the dynamic nature of international education in practice, including the micro-politics evident at the school site. The policy processes involved in initiating, producing and enacting the IBPYP in the remote company-owned school are summarized here.

Analysis of the 'context of influences' revealed the powerful role of local politics, global branding, teachers' backgrounds and remote settings in the adoption of IBPYP at the company-owned, remote SIS. Concepts such as 'company couples', 'golden handcuffs' and teachers as 'missionaries, misfits, mercenaries and mavericks' provided insights into the curriculum policy processes involved at the school. The concept of 'expat-mindedness' was introduced in characterizing the internationally mobile teaching workforce in the school, and it was presented in potential contradistinction to the core IB concept of 'international mindedness'.

In regard to the 'context of policy text production', three themes emerged, namely the need to develop a shared vision; the significance of the IBPYP *Learner Profile*; and the structural processes employed to facilitate the production of IBPYP policy texts and collaborative practices. The transition from the previous American curriculum to IBPYP policy text was guided by key IB documents. The role of the leadership team, particularly the IBPYP coordinator, was identified as being significant during these curriculum policy transformations.

The curriculum policy processes involved in the 'context of practices' all related to change: changes in policy documents and dissemination; changes in school practices; changes in teacher practices; and changes in interactions with the local setting. The teachers' engagement in policy text production helped direct and change school and classroom practices as the IB's trans-disciplinary, concept driven and inquiry based approach to teaching and learning evolved within a collaborative framework.

The findings relating to the 'context of outcomes' highlighted the complexities of implementing curriculum policy reform in a company-owned school in a remote location in Indonesia. Many planned and unplanned outcomes of the curriculum policy processes were revealed. These related to international mindedness, finance and power inequalities, and the impact of remoteness. The analysis of outcomes focused on personal and professional power inequities and relationships.

In all, the adoption of IBPYP at SIS transformed a wealthy, individual-focused American school that hid its 'grey policy file' in the drawer, into a school with a renewed whole-school focus on curriculum policy text production, paedagogy, collaboration, budgeting and accountability. The staff believed that IBPYP developed SIS into an 'international school' rather than a nationally affiliated one.

References

IBO. (2003a). *Programme standards and practices*. Cardiff: IBO. www.ibo.org/documentlibrary/ programmestandards. Accessed 30 Mar 2006.

IBO. (2003b). *IB learner profile booklet*. Cardiff: IBO. www.ibo.org/ibla/conference/.../ TheLearnerProfileinActionFabian.ppt. Accessed 30 Mar 2006.

IBO. (2005). *Programme standards and practices*. Cardiff: IBO. Retrieved from www.ibo.org/ documentlibrary/programmestandards/documents/progstandards.pdf

Chapter 6
Dua International School (DIS)

6.1 Introduction

This is the second of the three case studies. It relates to Dua International School (DIS). To help facilitate the cross-case analysis presented in Chap. 8 the organizational structure replicates that used in Chap. 5.

6.2 DIS International School Profile

DIS is perched high on a large mountain range. The setting was described by one of the participants as "*like living on top of the world*" (Viv, DIS). Access to the school and community site is by means of a dirt road that winds its way from the regional airport, up a steep incline and through a mountain tunnel constructed in the early 1950s. When the road is blocked, access to DIS can be gained only by helicopter because of the impenetrable terrain that surrounds it. It is also the only school available for expatriate children on the job site.

At the time the study was conducted, the school employed expatriates in the role of principal and deputy principal. The majority of teaching staff were also expatriates. The teacher of Indonesian, the secretary of the school and the head cleaner were all Indonesian nationals. One local who was indigenous to the area was also employed as a cleaner. This reflected the general pattern across the various occupations in which the 18,000 strong mine workforce were engaged. In other words, expatriates held the positions of greatest power, non-indigenous Indonesian nationals were in clerical to mid-level management positions, and members of the local indigenous populations were, for the most part, employed in unskilled labour positions.

From a geographic, environmental and engineering perspective, DIS is located in a challenging location. It is positioned just south of the Equator at 6,500 ft above

© Springer International Publishing Switzerland 2014
S. Ledger et al., *Global to Local Curriculum Policy Processes*,
Policy Implications of Research in Education 4, DOI 10.1007/978-3-319-08762-7_6

sea level and is surrounded by untouched mountain forest. The mountain range dominates over a vast lowland of rainforest. The area is rich and diverse in both geological and biological resources, but earthquakes, mudslides and food shortages are frequent events in the community.

The local area is resource and mineral rich, but the local residents are income poor. The multi-national mining company that funds the school pays a very large mining tax annually to the Indonesian government. It is able to attract international teachers and Indonesian nationals not indigenous to the area to work there by offering generous salary packages. However, at the time the study was conducted teachers were at considerable risk as civil unrest was frequent in the surrounding community.

DIS was established to cater for the expatriate employees of the large American mining company and associated sub-contractors. The jobsite workforce consisted predominately of middle management personnel and blue-collar mine workers. While the company recruited specialized miners from around the globe, all senior positions at the jobsite were occupied by employees recruited from America. DIS was the only school option for expatriate English-speaking children of parents at the site.

Due to limited living space on the mountainous terrain, blocks of flats provided the majority of housing options on the jobsite. Company executives were provided with houses on the hill, middle management had large town houses midway up the hill, and teachers and other service providers were provided with one and two bedroom apartments. The majority of blue-collar miners were housed in 'dongas', a one bedroom shared bathroom facility. Located just outside the town-site are small communities and villages. These villages are home to a large section of the local indigenous workforce.

6.3   Findings

The capacity of civil unrest to disrupt life in the DIS community was highlighted in the mid-2000s, when a car carrying DIS teachers was caught up in an incident. A rogue group of locals, disappointed with company contract negotiations, went on a shooting rampage that targeted company vehicles. It resulted in three teacher fatalities. The remaining teachers escaped with bullet wounds. All teachers at the school were evacuated at this time and never returned.

The shooting provided the impetus for curriculum reform at DIS. It triggered concern about links to the American mining company (the target of the attack) and resulted in a desire by the school to "*remove itself from perceived American attachments*" (Sofie, DIS). The eventual outcome was that the school moved from using an American curriculum to using the IBPYP.

6.3.1 Context of Influence

Although policy change was triggered by the fatal shootings, the rationale and processes involved in choosing to adopt the IBPYP as the curriculum of choice were diverse. Five influences can be identified: 'global branding'; 'the IBPYP acting as a unifying package'; 'local politics'; 'teachers' backgrounds'; and 'the remote setting'. These influences, while interconnected, are considered as separate entities below.

6.3.1.1 Global Branding

The first influence leading to the adoption of the IBPYP was the global cache of its brand. The desire of the staff was to have a curriculum policy that would be internationally recognized. The participants reported that the IBPYP would elevate the quality of education on offer at DIS and, at the same time, distance the school from its American national ties. These sentiments are reflected in the following comment by a teacher at the school:

> We needed a programme that was going to be rigorous, that was going to develop skill rather than content because kids had to repatriate and you can't repatriate from one country to another with just a knowledgeable content-based programme. The IBPYP has an international skills base that is transferrable. And it also has international recognition, so when the students do repatriate it has status. (Mon, DIS)

Participants identified the IBPYP experience as invaluable for their own future employment opportunities, as outlined by one of them:

> I am in heaven. I have a great paying job, small class sizes and now I will be considered an experienced IB teacher. I can get a job anywhere in the world! (Viv, DIS)

Such comments highlight the 'global currency' the participants felt the IBPYP had for them.

The principal reported that having the IBPYP at the school also proved beneficial for recruitment. He pointed out that it "*started to become a recruitment tool – being linked to the IB and its website – gives us more exposure.*" (Sol, DIS). Over a two-year period the number of teaching applications at DIS rose three-fold. One new recruit stated his motivation in simple terms: "*I found the school to have the best package in Asia and I applied for it. I didn't even know where DIS was, but it was doing the IBPYP, so I was comfortable that it would be a good school*" (Pat, DIS). A general view of the participants also was that the high wages constituted an attractive compensation for having to live in crowded conditions, having to cope with mining camp restrictions and having to negotiate inhospitable terrain. In all, the participants agreed that IBPYP global brand became an influential marketing and recruitment tool for DIS.

6.3.1.2 The IBPYP as a Unifying Package

The second influence leading to the adoption of the IBPYP was the perceived role it would play as a unifying package for policy reform. Prior to the adoption of the IBPYP at the school, very few whole-school curriculum policy decisions were made involving the largely American teaching cohort. Rather, most of the experienced staff, as they reported themselves, 'did their own thing' in the classroom. Yet, with the changing situation, a new approach was sought. One participant hoped that the IBPYP *"would remove curriculum parochialism and elevate the status of the educational package on offer"* (Mike, DIS). It was also recalled that there was a general consensus that it would lead to curriculum stability, sustainability and global recognition at DIS. One participant put this succinctly:

> The IBPYP will provide our students with a coherent, cohesive, developmental programme of learning from three year olds to fifteen year olds. When you have people coming out of so many different systems, we had to choose a curriculum that would unify everybody. We couldn't choose a curriculum that was nationally based, it had to be international and the IBPYP has the best reputation. (Sol, DIS)

The principal, referring to the frequent destabilizing events, such as the tragic shooting, civil unrest, and natural disasters, said that he felt that *"the school leadership team needed a solid curriculum and philosophy so that the school could weather future changes with little disruption"* (Sol, DIS). Partly, he was referring to the possibility that there might be a repeat of such destabilizing events as shootings in the area, civil unrest and natural disasters.

6.3.1.3 Local Politics

The third influence leading to the adoption of IBPYP at DIS involved local politics. The participants identified power plays within and between personnel in the small school community as being disruptive for the school. The following comment provides insight into what life at a school such as DIS can be like:

> Confidentiality exists less in a small school because everybody is living so close to each other. This is exaggerated at DIS because of the high-density living. Everyone knows or wants to know everything that is happening, particularly at school. Decision-making becomes difficult because of the lack of confidentiality and lack of discreteness. The IBPYP moved school discussions to education rather than local social issues. (Viv, DIS)

The findings show that local politics, including the lack of confidentiality, had an impact on decision-making, the adoption of IBPYP, and other curriculum policy processes. On this, local politics can be sub-divided into two influences, namely, that of 'company couples' and that of the changing face of the community. Both local influences are now considered.

Company Couples

Participants reported that people living and working in the DIS community were inextricably linked to the company. Those who lived in the DIS community worked for the company, were married to someone in the company, had children in the company-owned school, or provided services to the company. Within this close-knit community setting, the phenomenon of the 'company couple' emerged. According to the participants, it manifested itself in two ways. First, it referred to "*married employees who saw the remote posting as a stepping-stone for future promotion and power*" (*Mick*, DIS). It also referred to "*parents of school-aged children married to someone in senior management within the company*" (Viv, DIS).

The principal reported that the 'company couple' phenomenon dominated school decision-making and had an impact on school and community relationships:

> The school had to 'sell' the IBPYP to the company and their spouses as well as the teachers and their spouses. Economics didn't come into it the school is extremely well funded. It is the support from the company couples and teaching couples that is essential for the success of any programme here at DIS. These are the powerful voices in the community. (Sol, DIS)

Participants considered 'company couples' and also 'teaching couples' as social constructs specific to remote mining towns. They highlighted both as powerful players in the IBPYP curriculum policy process at the school. Their opinions were reported to be influential at the local level because they had a voice on the school board as well as in the community.

Accordingly, it is not surprising that the administration team at DIS reported that they had to target this group for support during considerations on the introduction of the IBPYP. As one of the teachers put it:

> The school board, or should I say company board has the capacity to be the biggest influence at the school level because they are our bosses and we have to do as they and their wives say. (Olga, DIS)

The DIS school board consisted of the principal, two human resource personnel, two parents and two teachers. It was structured to be inclusive. However, during the time of data collection the principal noted that no Indonesian parent or teacher was appointed, even though Indonesians made up approximately a third of the school parent population. 'Company couples', as well as teachers, wore multiple hats within the community. Participants reported that this allowed cross-fertilization of ideas, beliefs and opinions into the school arena. The following comment explains how values and opinions were intertwined:

> You can't just step away from work and have a separate life here. Everything and everybody is interlinked somehow. You see parents, teachers and students everywhere in all facets of community life and can't escape. The strong, confident voices of the community influence the weaker ones. So sometimes you don't know whose voice is actually being represented when decisions are made. (Pat, DIS)

The findings revealed concern by participants about the powerful influence the company had on the school board, however, the general view was a more pragmatic one as outlined below:

> We have to have a school board, but we know it is the voice of the powerful couples in the community that will get what they want! This is a company town and we are providing a service for them. (Sol, DIS)

It was inevitable that 'company couples' could wield power within a closed company town. Participants reported that company couples had financial security, status and positions of power. As a result of their seniority in the company and length of stay in the community participants considered them "*a formidable force in school decision-making*" (Olga, DIS). The administrative team at DIS reported that they had to target this group for support during IBPYP curriculum policy reform.

Changing Face of the Community

The changing face of the community was also recognized as a powerful influence in seeking curriculum policy change at DIS. The participants commented that it had a strong impact on local politics. The nature of the school population of parents and students was in stark contrast to the rather homogenous face of the teaching workforce. The principal outlined the differences between the two groups:

> Of the 12 staff at DIS we have a significant portion of American teachers who have not taught outside of America whereas the student body is from around the globe, many of them have been to other international schools. This is an issue for us here at DIS. American students are the minority but American teachers are the majority. (Sol, DIS)

This contrast resulted in a range of socio-cultural and curriculum policy issues, particularly in relation to teaching English as a second language and to the notion of international mindedness. Also, the administration team reported that they faced concern from a few of the teachers who were reluctant to change to the IBPYP because of their "*loyalty to the American curriculum*" (Olga, DIS).

The IBPYP, however, was chosen to counter this national parochialism. Local political pressure from the parent and teaching bodies revealed a desire to "*find a curriculum that was able to transcend all nationalities and enable seamless repatriation of students to their country of origin*" (Viv, DIS). There was overwhelming support to "*better cater for the changing population at DIS*" (Mon, DIS).

6.3.1.4 Teachers' Backgrounds

The fourth influence leading to the introduction of the IBPYP at DIS relates to teachers' backgrounds. The principal believed that the background of the cohort of teachers determined how they engaged with the policy processes at the school level. Many of the staff at DIS considered themselves international teachers because they "*were teaching outside of their home country*" (Mon, DIS) For most teachers, it was their first overseas appointment, yet all were experienced teachers within their home countries, and many had taught for over 20 years.

The personal and professional background of teachers influenced the policy decision to adopt the IBPYP at DIS. The teachers wanted 'to become' international teachers and the IBPYP helped facilitate this. Many of the American teachers had limited experience teaching overseas. The majority of them were either from rural or remote backgrounds. Most were practicing Christians and the majority commented on having a strong sense of belonging and connection to their home community.

The participants reported that their own prior experiences, including living in small communities, allowed them to 'survive' the demands of living and teaching at DIS. They stated that their *"previous experiences provided them with a range of transferable skills"* (Viv, DIS). One commented on the relationship between these skills and the attributes required by the IB *Learner Profile*:

> Well I think a great characteristic of an international educator is someone who has taken risks and travelled, been places. Often they are from small places and have had to move for higher education, so they are independent quite early. You know I think in so many ways it comes back down to the IB Learner Profile, you know, they're risk takers, they're willing to go places and do things. They're open-minded to other ideas, other cultures, and other languages. (Pat, DIS)

They also reflected on the role of the IB *Learner Profile* as a tool that explicitly describes a set of attributes for 'international teachers'. One of the staff explained the consequences for small communities in having teachers who did not embody these attributes:

> The ability to cope in small communities and on the international circuit boils down to a teacher being adaptable and personable. If they aren't they can make life very difficult for those around them. (Viv, DIS)

In addition to this, teachers talked in general about the importance of balancing their life between work and home.

School policies also reflected the interconnectedness between the school and the company. The principal reported that 'teaching couples', rather than single teachers, were employed because they represented significant financial and logistical savings for the company. Wives of company executives were used to fill positions as education support officers and relief teachers in the school. The presence of company wives in the school staffroom provided grounds for cross-fertilisation of ideas, interaction and influence between school and the company. However according to the participants, it also *"blurred the lines between professional and social interaction"* (Sol, DIS).

6.3.1.5 Remote Setting

The fifth influence leading to the decision to adopt the IBPYP was the remote setting of DIS. There was a general belief by participants that an international curriculum would help offset issues to do with isolation, access, and the quality of education. The participants noted that the families did not want their children to be educationally disadvantaged whilst at DIS. The idea of adopting an internationally recognized curriculum was expressed as one way of allaying parental concerns:

> Adopting a recognized international curriculum means that we can offer a world-class education no matter how remote we are. We become part of an international community of learners that has access to a wide range of resources. We remain physically isolated but not professionally isolated with IBPYP. (Sol, DIS)

The principal commented on the need for remote schools to hear 'outside voices' as a way of addressing professional isolation of the staff. The PYP coordinator supported this view, stating: "*I can say things lots of times, yet when they hear the same thing at a conference or from a visitor they take it on board straight away*" (Pat, DIS).

The principal put systems in place to connect staff to 'outside voices'. Professional development took the form of conference attendance and in-house workshops. The former was expensive and the latter logistically difficult. The principal explained how difficult it was to get workshop presenters to the job-site because DIS was a closed mining community. Visitors had to apply for approval from the company and the Indonesian Immigration Department before entering. A seat on the company plane had to be allocated and accommodation found in a setting where only a small number of rooms were available. Also, visitors could find themselves being removed from a flight because mine workers were given preference to visitors in the allocation of seats. Whilst it was an arduous and expensive process to bring presenters to the jobsite, the principal outlined its importance, stating that it was "*an essential tool to help overcome professional isolation*" (Sol, DIS).

The participants reported that the "*remoteness of DIS was offset by the large amount of resources in the school*" (Mick, DIS). The principal, however, explained that the logistics involved in ordering resources was as problematic as getting visitors onto the job-site. The funds were available, but the company processes, permissions and systems were not always supportive. Large items had to be shipped into the area and brought to the job-site via truck, or helicopter. There were times when goods would sit in the lowlands for a month or two before they were transported up the hill. School resources were not considered essential items; mine machinery and supplies were always given priority.

Another issue specific to DIS that influenced the adoption of the IBPYP was the "*interpersonal relationships between staff members and the leadership role of the principal*" (Mon, DIS). Some of the teachers suggested staff management was more difficult in remote centres because of the familiarity that develops between staff members. The principal supported this view. He explained how staff became very close with each other and found it hard to divorce personal issues from professional ones. He added that "*professional disputes, or disagreement, would often become personalized*" (Sol, DIS). Sol believed that adopting the IBPYP and its strict authorization processes would keep the school focused on education, rather than on personality clashes and local politics.

6.3.2 Context of Policy Text Production

The changeover from the American curriculum policy documents to the IBPYP curriculum policy documents was primarily guided by the IB *Programme Standards and Practices* (IBO 2003a, 2005a) text, in conjunction with the *Coordinator's Handbook* (IBO 2005b). Both documents steered the school through the candidacy phase and directed the structure of the school-based policy documents produced. The principal outlined how this process embedded the IBPYP philosophy, paedagogy and assessment within school-based policy texts.

The processes employed at DIS to enact the IBPYP policy text production can be considered in relation to three themes. First, there was a desire to have a 'shared vision and policy ownership' of the IBPYP policy text. Secondly, the importance of the 'IB *Learner Profile*' (IBO 2003b) was highlighted. Thirdly, there were 'structural processes and planning opportunities' employed to facilitate the IBPYP collaborative practice in the development of school-based curriculum policy texts.

6.3.2.1 Shared Vision and Policy Ownership

The principal and curriculum leaders at DIS expressed united support for developing a shared vision of the IBPYP. They recognized its capacity to promote policy ownership by the staff. However, they commented on the difficultly of the task given the somewhat parochial nature of the American staff who made up the majority of the teaching cohort. The principal talked about the need to:

> ...merge the staff together to work as a cohesive team for the benefit of the kids. Relationship management and asking people to make paradigm leaps to shift their thinking is difficult. The need to work as a collective is a big part of the leadership role here. (Sol, DIS)

He was also influenced by the mandatory requirements of the IBPYP authorization process.

The *Programme Standards and Practices* (IBO 2003a) document outlines the criteria needing to be addressed for authorization. The authorization process demands engagement with collaborative and reflective practices in all aspects of school operations. However, some staff expressed concern about the amount of professional time and work required to achieve these criteria. The following comment was indicative of many staff at DIS on this:

> I feel like a beginning teacher again with the amount of time I am putting into my planning but I must admit working with others does make it more palatable and dare I say better. (Jack, DIS)

The administration team noted that teachers soon became actively engaged in curriculum policy development. However, they also admitted that the fact that it was mandated and thus a forced collaboration, often resulted in power struggles and pedagogical differences of opinion. Often this resulted, in the words of the IBPYP coordinator, in "*compromise and conflict during collaborative planning and assessment sessions*" (Anna, DIS), especially in relation to paedagogical issues.

6.3.2.2 The IB *Learner Profile*

The participants identified the *IB Learner Profile Booklet* (IBO 2003b) as the most recognized policy document at the school level. Staff commented on its importance in curriculum policy design and practice. They saw it as an effective tool for establishing the core beliefs of the IBPYP. The booklet was espoused as a set of attributes for students as well as for teachers and parents. One participant's view on this resonated across staff:

> Teachers should readily model the attributes of the Learner Profile and attitudes of the IBPYP in all that they do. People who comfortably and naturally exhibit the attributes of the Learner profile are considered international-minded. (Anna, DIS)

The principal discussed the impact of such a view, stating that *"if the teachers don't exercise all of the characteristics of the learner profile, then their students aren't going to learn the attributes as well as they ought to"* (Sol, DIS). According to the participants the *Learner Profile's* set of attributes emerged as a symbolic representation of what defined an IBPYP student, teacher and parent. To highlight its importance the principal at DIS included the *Learner Profile* as one of the school's teacher-appraisal policy documents.

The following description about an ex-Science teacher from DIS was used to promote the attributes of the *IB Learner Profile Booklet* amongst the students:

> Our science teacher was a dedicated, knowledgeable scientist who loved 'space'. He exhibited all the qualities of the IB Learner Profile. He captured the hearts of the children by introducing them to the world of space exploration. He talked to the children about reaching their goals and following their dreams. He had always wanted to be an astronaut. He began his teaching career in America then went on the teaching circuit to gain an international perspective. During this time he spent a couple of years at DIS then two years later, after teaching in Eastern Europe, he rang to say that he had finally achieved his dream and had become an astronaut. The school tuned into the NASA website to view his induction. He kept in contact with the school throughout his training and even emailed the school from the space station. He was a great role model for the school and the epitome of the IB Learner Profile. (Lou, DIS)

The participants commented on how the *IB Learner Profile Booklet* became embedded in curriculum policy documents as well as in policy practices in all aspects of schooling at DIS. This, however, was not perceived as being positive in every respect. For example, there was concern by some of the subject-specific teachers that the *"Learner Profile and its affective focus took the emphasis away from curriculum pedagogy and practices"* (Mon, DIS).

6.3.2.3 Structural Processes and Planning Opportunities

The principal made key structural changes to facilitate the IBPYP school-based policy text production at DIS. The most significant decision, according to the participants, was the creation of the PYP coordinator role and the development of a school plan. The majority of staff commented on the success of the principal's role in facilitating the IBPYP processes at DIS. They also commented on the role of the PYP coordinator who "*is a leader and understands paedagogy, she leads by example on a day-to-day basis*" (Viv, DIS). Furthermore, the principal recognized the important role of the PYP coordinator, and he described her style of leading as being "*on the factory floor rather than from an office*" (Sol, DIS).

A coordinated approach was planned to facilitate the transfer to the IBPYP. The development of a school plan was described as the starting point for IBPYP policy text production at DIS. The structural processes that emerged as a result of considering this document fell predominantly into three categories. The first involved identifying and timetabling milestones for policy design and implementation. The second focused on providing teachers with opportunities for collaboration. The third involved setting up mechanisms for evaluation. These three approaches are now considered.

Milestones for Policy Design and Implementation

Participants revealed that the first structural process employed at DIS for policy text production was to develop milestones for the IBPYP policy design and implementation for the whole school. These were outlined in the DIS school plan. The implementation process focused on the provision of professional development, timetabling to provide support staff in classrooms, and allocation of resources and release time.

The first milestone related to providing learning opportunities for teachers and parents. The PYP coordinator reported that she "*offered in-school professional development and joined collaborative planning sessions for teachers*" (Anna, DIS). She explained that teachers had the opportunity to visit other IBPYP schools in the region and all teachers were sent to the IB regional conferences held in Singapore. Teachers also had access to the IBPYP Online Curriculum Centre and website. The PYP coordinator explained how the parents were also involved in the process: "*parent development at the school level included parent evenings, coordinated workshop sessions and open classrooms*" (Anna, DIS). The workshop sessions introduced the school community to the essential elements of the IBPYP policy and programme, with the *IB Learner Profile Booklet* (IBO 2003b), sample 'units of inquiry' and 'programmes of inquiry' being the starting points for parent information sessions.

The second milestone involved restructuring the timetable to support the policy text production. The principal stated that a "*new timetable offered release time for teachers to work on collaborative planning sessions with the PYP coordinator*" (Sol, DIS). Also, additional library sessions were provided to develop research skills to "*suit the inquiry-based orientation of the IBPYP*" (Mike, DIS). The new timetable included an increase in time allocated to second-language learning. The principal noted that it had to "*reflect the IBPYP commitment to second-language acquisition*" (Sol, DIS).

The third milestone related to the school budget. The administration team considered the budget as significant in facilitating policy text production: "*Policy related to resource allocation and funding had a direct impact on the classroom teachers*" (Anna, DIS). The school employed extra support staff in classes so that release time was available for collaborative planning sessions. The budget also included funding to internationalize resources for the library. Participants identified the financial support offered during this stage as the "*lifeline for developing IBPYP policy texts*" (Sol, DIS).

The final milestone involved in policy text production related to the procedure of aligning all policy text and structural changes with the IB *Programme Standards and Practices* (IBO 2003a) document. This process was established early in the implementation process. Participants commented on the strengths and weaknesses of the initiative. Many saw the 'whole-school' approach to policy text production as a positive strategy. Some, on the other hand, saw it as "*extra work and time consuming*" (Lou, DIS).

The findings related to 'structural processes' employed to support policy text production indicate the importance which was attached to the IB *Programme Standards and Practices* (IBO 2003a) document. The principal stated that "*DIS teachers were forced to become active participants in policy text production in order to meet the demands of the IBPYP authorization process*" (Sol, DIS). One teacher associated the professional shift that took place with his colleagues, stating:

> During the authorization period there was a lot of immersion straight into IBPYP, it was quite intense preparation but we were all involved and are pretty proud of our results. It became our policy and our curriculum! (Mick, DIS)

Overall, the IBPYP authorization process, particularly regarding policy text production, was, as another teacher put it, viewed as "*a time of steep learning, paedagogical reflection and philosophical transformation*" (Sol, DIS).

Opportunities for Collaboration

The professional shift that took place across the school was considered by the administration team as a direct consequence of teachers becoming very much involved in the curriculum policy process. According to the team members, DIS invested a lot of time and money and initiated a lot of structural changes to develop a collaborative culture at the school. Collaboration underpins the IBPYP philosophy and paedagogy, and, according to the principal, "*had to be reflected in DIS policies and practices*" (Sol, DIS).

The participants reported that the language of collaboration became embedded in discourses and texts at DIS. This, as illustrated in the following comment, was acknowledged by the staff as being a significant factor in successful and sustainable curriculum policy:

> My planning is definitely different and I love working collaboratively. I prefer to plan with others or at least talk with someone about what I'm doing. I like the backwards by design

idea working out the assessment and then going backwards. When you work with others
ideas become more focused particularly when you are continually questioning and focusing
on the central idea and core concepts. (Viv, DIS)

However, some staff found collaboration difficult. In this regard, a few staff
members at DIS were reported to be "*strong minded and inflexible*" (Anna, DIS).
At times, these key players led the collaborative planning sessions, and debate often
resulted in conflict. One participant stated that "*sometimes it is easier to agree with
them and just change the planner when I get back to my class. It saves the hassle*"
(Mick, DIS). The PYP coordinator explained how she worked with collaborative
teaching pairs each week to help overcome the problem of 'professional bullying'
felt by some teachers. She was released to provide assistance to individual teachers.
She also led collaborative reflection sessions at weekly staff meetings. The principal
considered this strategy to be an effective vehicle for keeping PYP curriculum policy
texts and practices on the school agenda.

Setting up Mechanisms for Evaluation

The final structural process employed to facilitate policy text production at DIS
related to the development of mechanisms for evaluation of the new curriculum reform. The principal noted that DIS traditionally relied on outside sources
for accountability purposes, including external accreditation from the Western
Association of Schools and Colleges (WASC) and IOWA (USA) State testing.
However, with the adoption of the IBPYP, the administration team investigated
new mechanisms for evaluating school-based policy documents and programmes.
The principal outlined the role of the IB *Programme Standards and Practices*
(IBO 2003a) to guide and evaluate text production, practices and programme
evaluation at DIS:

> We used Wiggen's and McTighe's 'backward by design' assessment model to guide us. We
> have to meet the requirements of IB Programme Standards and Practices so we used these
> to frame our whole school planning process and worked backward from that. (Sol, DIS)

The ICT teacher developed an electronic recording and filing system that was
directly linked to the IB *Programme Standards and Practices* document. All IBPYP
policy texts, including the school's 'programme of inquiry', were located on the
school network.

One of the participants commented on how IBPYP 'units of inquiry' were
easily accessed and could be edited easily during collaborative planning sessions,
because "*we did all our planning and assessment of the units directly on the
interactive whiteboard and on the share drive*" (Mike, DIS). The computer teacher
explained that "*all planning and reviewing as well as resource lists went into the
system and were easy to view, edit or print*" (Lou, DIS). The system also provided
student record-keeping facilities. This included collating results using such external
testing bodies as IOWA State testing and the more recent 'International Schools
Assessment' testing regime designed by the Australian Council for Educational
Research specifically for the international school market.

In summary, the administrative team utilised the ISD *School Plan* document to identify a set of milestones for the enactment of IBPYP. The policy texts produced at the school outlined opportunities for teacher professional development, collaborative planning and specific mechanisms for programme evaluation. The participants reported that these strategies, as Mon put it, *"helped them become familiar with the requirements of the IBPYP"* (Mon, DIS). At the same time, there were times of conflict and compromise at all stages of policy text production. This was reflected in the following comment:

> There are some staff members who want to revert back to the American model as it is much easier, it tells them what to do and they can teach from a text for each subject. IBPYP demands teachers take a bigger role in policy development. But not all want to! (Anna, DIS)

Also, the IB coordinator stated that while she spent a lot of time trying to encourage and support teachers, this often resulted in frustration for her as she had to spend a lot of time *"juggling personalities and manoeuvring so that the difficult ones felt as if things were their idea and that they were in control. (Anna, DIS)*

6.3.3   Context of Practices

The adoption of the IBPYP resulted in many practical changes taking place at the school site. The context of practices witnessed 'changes to policy documentation'; 'changes to teaching practice'; 'changes to school practices'; and 'changes to connections with the local community'. Each of these changes is now outlined below.

6.3.3.1   Changes to Policy Documentation

The principal emphasised that the production of the new IBPYP policy documents at the school level aligned to the *Programme Standards and Practices* (IBO 2003a) document to guide change at DIS. He stated that the *"explicit nature of the IB document ensured that IBPYP policy development remained a dynamic process at the class and administrative level"* (Sol, DIS). The administration team ensured the IBPYP was embedded in everyday practice by developing organizational and structural processes to facilitate the change.

There were significant differences between general classroom teachers and specialist teachers in their familiarity with the policy documents. Subject specialist teachers at DIS felt isolated and believed they had limited access to policy documentation and policy collaboration in their field. The principal expressed his response to their concerns as follows: *"I recognize the Issues faced by specialist teachers and try to develop ways around this professional isolation"* (Sol, DIS). He provided release time for the specialist teachers to meet as a group on a regular basis. The PYP coordinator also commented that *"at least one specialist teacher was included in the collaborative planning sessions for each grade level*" (Anna, DIS). She outlined how she guided staff through the specialist resources on the IB online curriculum centre. In the eyes of the PYP coordinator:

> The specialist teachers can be very demanding of your time. They are so entrenched in their subject that the move to an inquiry and concept-based approach to learning is really difficult. You have to guide them through the process step by step and at times show them how it can be done. The best approach has been to link them with someone from their specialist area who is successfully implementing IBPYP. I think they have to see it to believe it by one of their own. (Anna, DIS)

The principal also stated that he "*connected the specialists with specialists from other IB schools*" (Sol, DIS).

Participants outlined how policy documents were made visible at DIS through updates in the weekly school newsletter and monthly parent information sessions. The majority of staff agreed that "*the most visual means of promoting DIS policy and practices were the large displays along the indoor corridor*" (Mon, DIS). 'Units of inquiry' were displayed on each classroom door. The IBPYP essential elements, namely, the *IB Learner Profile Booklet* and the trans-discipline model, were displayed outside of the front office for easy reference. Staff explained how these displays constituted an effective tool for promoting the IBPYP to the school community.

6.3.3.2 Changes to Teaching Practice

According to the principal at DIS, adopting the IBPYP required that specific changes be made to teacher practice. These changes related to developing an understanding of the essential elements of the IBPYP, particularly its trans-discipline, concept-driven and inquiry-based approach. The key changes that occurred at DIS and the strategies that supported them are now detailed.

The administration team commented on how the adoption of the IBPYP was an opportunity to share a common educational vision and unify the teaching cohort. In doing so, however, the principal also recognized the following difficulty:

> People can learn curriculum and curriculum requirements. They can learn scope and sequences and syllabus, they can learn how to use a planner and all those things and the mechanical easy to learn processes. They can go off to a course, learn how to do it, come back and apply it. But, to inherently understand the process of learning to acquire knowledge, skills and attitudes and to guide a group of young minds towards inquiry is a whole lot more difficult especially if you haven't got it embedded in your current paedagogy. The IBPYP requires a paradigm shift for many of our teachers. (Sol, DIS)

The PYP coordinator also stated that "*the most profound paradigm shift and change to teaching practice was the level of active involvement in policy development by the staff*" (Anna, DIS). The active involvement in policy development and curriculum design resulted in teachers engaging in conversations related to their practice.

Another paedagogical shift reported by the participants was the adoption by them of a more reflective approach to the planning, teaching and assessment cycle than had previously been the case. One participant, reflecting on her own professional growth and development during IBPYP curriculum policy reform, explained as follows her understanding of why reflection is important:

> We have to encourage people to read, to reflect, to have critical friends, to foster and improve their teaching. IBPYP is international, innovative and current practice. You don't go to a doctor that's still using leaches and you don't want to see a teacher that's still using textbooks for everything. (Sheri, DIS)

Another described his experience of reflection as follows: "*I have become really critical of my practices. I keep asking myself, why I am doing things and what action can occur?*" (Ken, DIS) More specifically, some teachers reflected on the difficulty of understanding a 'concept driven curriculum' and many struggled with the notion of 'inquiry based' learning. Teachers who taught content-driven subjects, mainly specialist teachers, agreed that they "*found it very difficult to grasp the key concepts of the IBPYP, particularly its trans-disciplinary nature*" (Sheri, DIS). Early childhood teachers, by contrast, said that they found it easy to adopt the PYP because they "*already embraced concept-driven curriculum and inquiry-based teaching approaches*" (Mon, DIS). Furthermore, they stated that they were they were familiar with a teaching style that is "*holistic rather than content-driven*" (Viv, DIS).

Another change in teaching practice identified by participants related to the process of translating knowledge and learning into action. The 'action' component of the IBPYP was an area that participants considered to be an IBPYP 'point of difference' from other curricula. On this, one teacher stated:

> For me, it's difficult at times, I try and avoid the tokenism type of action and avoid the contradiction of planning the student-initiated actions. You want them to initiate it you shouldn't force it. Recently one of the mums told me that their little girl had decided that she was going to write up some bedroom central agreements and stick it on her door. It said 'Brothers aren't allowed here after 5 pm'. This is a great example of a child taking her learning home to use in her own life. I thought it was quite funny. (Sheri, DIS)

Some, however, recognized that engaging in authentic action based on reflection can be difficult. One teacher commented on this, stating:

> It is hard to pull away from a token charity approach to the action component. I am still trying to force what I think the action should be but I know it has to be an action that is generated by the children. I have to get more comfortable with post planning and let the children lead in this area. (Mon, DIS)

Participants also mentioned two strategies as being significant in supporting their developmental knowledge of the IBPYP and triggering change in practices. The first strategy related to the school-based professional development offered by the PYP coordinator. This individual was mentioned by most of the participants as being a key player in the process of curriculum development, in networking and in promoting change. He was reported as having guided staff to "*set goals, support the collaborative planning sessions and target the needs of each teacher*" (Sofie, DIS). Such action led to one teacher summarising as follows her appreciation of the importance of his role:

> Philosophically you have to know why you are doing it. Then you need to have somebody who is going to drive that. So you need somebody who is going to guide, drive and lead the process. It requires someone who's passionate about IB, who models the IB Learner Profile and finally someone who is professionally respected. (Sophie, DIS)

She finished by stating that *"the quality of the PYP coordinator determines the quality and success of the implementation"*.

The second strategy involved facilitating DIS teachers to be active participants in, rather than passive recipients of, policy text production and practice during the authorization phase. Engagement with policy was recognized as being the most powerful strategy for change. Indeed, the principal reported it as being an essential part of the curriculum policy process because *"it kept policy at the forefront of teacher practice"* (Sol, ISD). Also, some participants considered it to be the most demanding of the strategies.

6.3.3.3 Changes to School Practices

The administration team noted that they made several internal changes to school practices and procedures at DIS to support the adoption of the IBPYP. The major changes in school practice were in the areas of professional development, timetable changes, and school resource allocation, including staffing. Many of the changes were outlined as 'structural processes' in the 'context of policy text production'.

A major change to school practices noted by the administration team was the development of a 'whole-school' approach to resource management in facilitating IBPYP policy reform. The principal said that this *"triggered some strong resistance from the longer serving teachers at DIS"* (Sol, DIS). Previously, many of the staff had had access to thousands of dollars of what they considered to be 'their' money to buy classroom resources. One of the participants expressed their concern about a change in policy in this regard:

> It is as though they don't trust us to make appropriate decisions. I know what my class needs and I am the best person to decide where the money goes. (Mon, DIS)

The change in school practice from an individual, class-based approach in resource allocation to a 'whole-school 'approach to budgeting was considered an *"essential transitioning strategy"* (Sol, DIS). The IBPYP coordinator stated that the change in practice facilitated a *"whole school approach to IBPYP and streamlined finances so that the administration team could target specific teacher needs"* (Anna, DIS).

A related change involved human resource allocation. An increase in time at work was allocated to the librarian, the technology teacher, the language teacher and also the academic support teacher. The librarian stated her response to this as follows:

> Now I feel like a true resource person I am involved with all classroom teachers and have contact with all the students in the school. This has provided me an opportunity for the library and myself to bring the IBPYP alive. But, I would like to have more time with the collaborative teams so that I am not considered an add-on in the planning process. (Mike, DIS)

Similar positive comments were made by others. Overall, what took place in this regard was recognized as a significant change by all. As one participant put it, there was great appreciation of the fact that "*support was now readily on hand to help in our transition to PYP practices*" (Viv, DIS).

6.3.3.4   Changes to Connections with the Local Community

The participants commented that they changed how they connected with the local community. They discussed being more strategic about long term, sustainable connections, rather than continuing with the often *ad hoc* approach previously employed by DIS. They commented on the unique area in which they lived. They described how they were surrounded by a remarkable landscape, they had access to local indigenous communities, they could also gain access to one of the world's largest open-pit mining operations, they were protected by a large military and security force, and they had some of the most enviable mountain views in the world. For many, the unique environment provided a wealth of learning experiences for the school. On this, one participant stated that he was "*overwhelmed with choice*" (Mike, DIS).

With such an array of choice it was hard for staff to identify or prioritize what they considered to be the most appropriate connections to make with the local community. This problem was described by Mon when he stated that "any golden opportunities were overlooked because the staff had not engaged with the local community other than superficially (Mon, DIS).

Another teacher commented in similar fashion:

> Yes we connect with the wider community, but some school projects and community links are very superficial in nature usually made by some-ones contact in the community. It seems very ad-hoc. (Sheri, DIS)

Also, some of the previous connections with the community were seen as being "*gratuitous handouts delivered with missionary zeal*" (Anna, DIS). The principal explained this situation by referring to the "*itinerancy of staff, the porous nature of the curriculum and a lack of local knowledge*" (Sol, DIS).A major issue identified by the administration team was that of how to utilize the surrounding social, geographic and economic resources in an effective sustainable way. The development of the IBPYP mandated 'units of inquiry' and a whole school 'programme of inquiry' provided what one participant referred to as the "*perfect backdrop for teachers to reflect on the possibilities*" (Mick, DIS). One participant recounted his experience of connecting with a local third generation missionary. The missionary connected the school with one of the most remote communities in the area and then set about teaching the expatriate students how to live sustainably. The organising teacher described this unique connection in the following words:

> When it did happen it had quite an impact on everyone, it was a moment that was quite powerful for both groups of children. Out of the experience came empathy and also admiration for each other. Our kids saw the skills and values and the environmentally

based way that the locals lived day by day. Our children came back hugely impressed with what the locals could do. They had a high level of respect for the local people after the experience – something that they, and probably their parents, did not appreciate prior to going. (Mon, DIS)

Not all were as enthused, however, by such developments, with some staff reporting that connecting with the local community necessitated that they commit to additional work and time.

Another shift did take place in the way teachers started to use local situations to help students think about global issues. They would take a local issue such as illegal logging or mining, explore the local consequences and then transfer this knowledge to regional and global experiences. However, staff suggested that they still had to 'tread lightly' when they looked at certain topics, particularly if they were connected with the mine, or its operations. They couldn't and didn't want to get the company 'off side'.

Participants reported that making stronger connections to the local area provided more opportunities for staff to teach comparative studies. An example provided by one of the participants was the juxtaposition of the school being located directly below one of the world's largest 'state of the art' open cut mining facilities, against the illegal gold-panning camps operating down river. Such socio-cultural and economic contrasts were found in various aspects of living and working at DIS. As the principal reported, there was evidence of extreme wealth and abject poverty, access to technologies yet lack of access to fresh water. The librarian provided another insight on this:

In regard to illegal mining the local indigenous groups could make more money in one day collecting tiny grains of gold from the slurry waste that went into the rivers than they could by growing sweet potatoes in a year. (Mike, DIS)

The DIS school plan specified the need to for teachers to cooperate, utilise and work with appropriate personnel who could assist with developing students' understanding of such issues, of the local culture and of the various Indonesian cultures more broadly. One participant elaborated on why this was important, arguing that it would be educationally remiss of the school to ignore the local socio-cultural and economic issues that surrounded DIS, and would be tantamount to "*putting blinkers on the children*" (Lou, DIS). Overall, however, participants suggested that they found it more helpful to connect with the local environment rather than with people because it was easier and less problematic.

6.3.4 Context of Outcomes

The analysis of the curriculum policy processes at DIS provided insight into 'bigger picture' issues of inequalities and social justice at the site. These issues have been categorized into three groupings. First, there were issues surrounding 'power inequities related to company ownership of the school'. Secondly, there were issues concerning 'staff difficulties with the concept of international-mindedness'. Thirdly, there were issues surrounding the 'remote setting' of the school. These themes are considered in detail below.

6.3.4.1 Power Inequities Related to Company Ownership of the School

DIS is a company owned and operated school. These factors automatically imply a significant power bias for the company. The DIS school plan identifies the power inequity, thus:

> DIS must ensure all school policies are cross referenced to applicable company policies as well as creating new school policies and procedures to comply with company requirements, Issues or directives. DIS policies are overridden by company policy.

A range of outcomes was revealed during the transition to the IBPYP that relate to company ownership. They involved gender, racial, financial and social inequities.

Gender Inequity

The nature of the relationship between the company and the surrounding community was described by participants as being 'patriarchal'. DIS is a company school located centrally in a 'closed' company town. Access to the area is restricted. Participants reported that American 'culture' influenced all facets of daily life, whilst the Indonesian 'culture' was minimized on the job site. They also commented that *"males dominated every facet of the workplace except for the school"* (Sheri, DIS).

The school was unique in the community because it had a balanced workforce of half male and half female. The female participants reported that they felt professionally isolated because of the lack of working women in the wider community. There were only two middle management female employees at the mine-site. On this, one of the female participants expressed her concern that *"the only women you have to talk to are inevitably parents. It makes for social rather than professional relationships to develop."* She also commented on the powerful female voice of the community:

> The female voice within the company was dominated by the wives of the company executives and because many of them had children in the school it had certain ramifications. (Anna, DIS)

The comment links to the perceived power of 'company couples' already referred to.

Racial Inequity

In addition to gender inequity, participants commented on 'racial' inequity in the company workforce. They noted that, in general terms, Americans held all senior management positions and other expatriates held middle management positions. Skilled miners were predominately Indonesian nationals and the majority of unskilled workers were local indigenous-nationals.

During the time of data collection the Indonesian government legislated that all foreign companies had to employ Indonesian nationals at equal level and status to senior management positions and a percentage of these appointments had to be local indigenous nationals. DIS was exempt from this legislation. The company had negotiated with the government and had established a neighbouring Indonesian school that catered for the children of its Indonesian national employees and the small number of local indigenous national families. The principal commented that the location of expatriate and Indonesians in separate schools situated next door to each other highlighted the 'segregated culture' of the company.

Financial Inequity

Participants discussed the financial inequity evident in all aspects of their lives at DIS. They reported extreme inequity between the expatriate workforce and local indigenous groups. They also noted that there were significant financial differences in wages within the expatriate community. Some senior managers received seven-figure salaries, with additional benefits. Middle level wages were in the six-figure category. Teachers were amongst the lowest paid expatriates at the job site, with wages in the five-figure range. They did report, however, that their financial package was generous in comparison to teacher wages in Australia, America, New Zealand and Indonesia at the time.

The principal complained that while the school budget was generous, financial decision-making had to follow certain company accounting protocols and procedures. There were times when he found the situation frustrating and time-consuming because "*educational purchases and needs do not fit easily into the mine-site budget boxes*" (Sol, DIS). Often, significant creativity was required by the administration team to 'fit' the budgetary framework of the company. The principal explained how the school budget was ratified by the school board and authorized by the company accountants, a process that the principal considered "*lengthy and problematic because you had accountants continually questioning and blocking orders.*" The impact on the school was significant and the administration team knew that they had limited power to rectify the situation other than "*sweet talk the accountant and his wife*" (Sol, DIS).

Social Inequity

The participants reported that social inequity was also evident within the local community. They explained that within the expatriate community, the top-down autocratic nature of life in a mining community generally made "*teachers feel lower down the structural hierarchy*" (Anna, DIS). Constant reminders of this structural divide included the allocation of housing, access to a range of services, and wages. The participants commented that a similar disparity was found between the Indonesian nationals and the indigenous Indonesians within the community. The golf course, swimming pool and country club were 'closed' to non-mine workers.

The principal outlined how the company had the final decision on everything in the community. Many teachers were reluctant to speak up about issues because "*they didn't want to lose their jobs*" (Sheri, DIS). On this, participants spoke of the 'golden handcuff syndrome'. One participant explained the term as a situation where "*the money is too good to leave so you put up with certain things*" (Mike DIS). Teachers were limited in objecting to the decisions and views held by the company and the decisions made by 'company couples'.

6.3.4.2   Difficulties with the Concept of 'International Mindedness'

Some staff had difficulties with the concept of 'international mindedness'. The term invokes questions about power and inequity. One participant asked, "*Who determines if you are international minded?*" (Viv, DIS). In an environment where staff members were developing a shared vision of the IBPYP, the principal explained that the concept of what constitutes international education and 'international mind-edness', caused confusion. The majority of teachers included the term international mindedness in their descriptions of how curriculum policy changed at DIS. Yet, when questioned about it, participants found it difficult to define. There were con-tradictions and concerned comments from participants. A few identified the desire to develop internationally transferable skills for the students and teachers, while the principal commented on "*respect for the host country and others*" (Sol, DIS).

Although definitions were diverse, the common response related to "*a desire to have a more international perspective at the DIS*" (Mon, DIS). Many teachers found the IBPYP *Learner Profile* (IBO 2003a) the easiest tool to use to explain 'international mindedness' to their students and parents. They commented on how the ten attributes in the *IB Learner Profile Booklet* encompass the IBPYP mission statement and the IB vision of 'internationally minded' students.

The participants also spoke of 'expat mindedness'. They reported that 'expat mindedness', like 'international mindedness', was difficult to define. Some also referred to the term 'expat-brats', saying that they were a product of the "*new mobile middle-class workforce who were financially privileged but culturally impoverished*" (Sofie, DIS). Others referred to 'cashed up bogans', a colloquial term used to describe mobile miners and their families and the changing socio-cultural and economic culture that they represent.

There were comments also that the social construct of 'expat mindedness' was a direct but negative outcome of international education in general. The term was used to describe expatriates who remained in the social bubble of their 'home' culture, rather than engaging with the 'host or local' culture. In many instances the participants made comments similar to that of Anna when she said that it referred to those that "*felt superior and didn't want to engage with, or respect, the local community*" (Anna, DIS).

6.3.4.3 The Remote Setting

Nearly all of the teachers at DIS stated that they had previously lived or worked in remote, rural or small communities in their home countries. Teachers said that their prior experiences had prepared them well for the demands of DIS, but not necessarily for the 'company town' scenario. They reported that issues of power inequalities within the school population related to the influential voices of 'type A' characters, 'teaching couples' and 'company couples'. On this, one teacher stated

> The strong, confident voices of the community influence the weaker ones. So sometimes you don't know whose voice is actually being represented when decisions are made. (Pat, DIS)

This was a common response from participants. Some suggested that curriculum policy outcomes were informed more by the more powerful voices on the staff, than by their common view.

The remote context, it was argued, also created certain difficulties in terms of negotiation and collaboration in remote contexts. This arose partly out of the extent to which all the members of the school community were regularly in contact with each other, not only in school but outside of school also. The principal commented that this led to he having to spend an inordinate amount of time managing staff interpersonal relationships. On this, he stated,

> Relationship management becomes a very big part of your leadership role, because you have got a diverse group of people. The school becomes their home away from home and the staff form part of a family. When you have a disagreement or professional discussion it is often taken to heart and can upset people. You have to continually tread a fine line. We know how to manage people but managing a surrogate family can be problematic. (Sol, DIS)

The PYP coordinator reflected on her role in similar fashion, in this case drawing attention to difficulties arising out of the school being small. She summarised her view on this as follows:

> In a small school sometimes it is more difficult to guide people, because in a small school if people aren't doing what you think they should be doing, or what is required, it becomes difficult. You can't push it because then it creates too much trouble. If you work in a big school you can kind of run away and hide for a while. (Anna, DIS)

Personnel management in a smaller setting, she concluded, "is probably a bit tougher than in a big school".

Finally, the participants explained how teachers living and working in remote centres were often the 'social threads' that kept small communities connected. At the same time, they felt as though they were under a microscope, with one saying that "*we often face judgment on too many levels in a small community*" (Viv, DIS). Also, participants like Mon, commented on having to "*take on multiple roles both inside the school and outside in the community*" (Mon, DIS). It was also reported as being necessary, with staff stating that if teachers embraced the multiple roles, then, the community would embrace the teacher.

6.4   Conclusion

This chapter presented findings from the second of three case study schools adopting the International Baccalaureate Primary Years Program (IBPYP) in remote international schools in Indonesia. The analysis captured the relevant curriculum policy processes, and it highlighted the dynamic nature of international education in practice, including the micro-politics evident at the school site. The policy processes involved in initiating, producing and enacting the IBPYP in the remote company-owned school are summarized here.

The 'context of influences' involved in the adoption of IBPYP at DIS were identified as: the power of global branding; the role of IBPYP as a unifying package for staff; the impact of local politics; the influence of teachers' backgrounds; and the effects of living and working in remote settings. Examining the 'context of influences' also exposed issues surrounding a company owned school and highlighted the tensions that occurred between economic and educational decision-making. As with the first case-study school, the concept of 'expat-mindedness' was useful in characterizing the internationally mobile teaching workforce in the company owned school, and it was contrasted with the core IB concept of 'international mindedness'. Other concepts useful in analysing influences on the adoption and enactment of IBPYP in this company owned mining community and school were 'company couples' and 'golden handcuffs'.

IBPYP documents, especially the *Standards and Practices* (IBO 2003a) document, guided the 'context of policy text production' at the school. These documents were particularly important during policy text production at the school as they ensured the IBPYP vernacular, philosophy, paedagogy and assessment were embedded in the process of curriculum policy changes. The findings highlighted three core themes that impacted policy text production at DIS: the desire for a shared curriculum policy vision and policy ownership by staff; the importance of the IB *Learner Profile*; and structural processes to facilitate a whole-school approach to IBPYP. During this process teachers became active participants in IBPYP policy text production.

Analysis of the 'context of practices' revealed that the curriculum policy processes involved in transitioning from an American national curriculum to that of IBPYP authorization were complex. The findings revealed four key themes related to changes in curriculum policy practices, namely, changes in: policy documentation; teaching practices; school practices and procedures; and the nature of connections with the local setting. The changes along the policy trajectory at DIS occurred as a result of ongoing negotiation, compromise and often conflict, both personally and professionally, for the staff involved.

Planned and unplanned outcomes occurred during the policy process of initiating, producing and enacting IBPYP at DIS. Key themes related to the 'contexts of outcomes' were power inequalities; difficulties with the construct of internationalization; and issues with the remote location. Power inequities within the local school community were exacerbated with company ownership of the school; in particular issues of gender, race, financial and social inequities were highlighted. Teachers had difficulty making meaning of IBPYP and 'international mindedness' as well as 'becoming' international teachers. Issues surrounding living and working in remote locations were exposed. Those who lived and worked at DIS indicated new outcomes, in both professional and personal terms, during IBPYP curriculum policy processes.

In all, IBPYP policy processes were employed at DIS to develop structural, pedagogical and attitudinal change. This curriculum policy reform highlighted the interconnectivity of issues faced by small remote schools in company owned school communities, and power relationships were the threads weaving together many facets of the local curriculum policy dynamics.

References

IBO. (2003a). *Programme standards and practices*. Cardiff: IBO. www.ibo.org/documentlibrary/programmestandards. Accessed 30 Mar 2006.

IBO. (2003b). *IB learner profile booklet*. Cardiff: IBO. www.ibo.org/ibla/conference/.../TheLearnerProfileinActionFabian.ppt. Accessed 30 Mar 2006.

IBO. (2005a). *Programme standards and practices*. Cardiff: IBO. www.ibo.org/documentlibrary/programmestandards/documents/progstandards.pdf. Accessed 4 Sept 2006.

IBO. (2005b). *Coordinator's handbook*. Cardiff: IBO. www.ibo.org/product_info.php?products_id=1626. Accessed 8 Oct 2007.

Chapter 7
Case Study Three: Tiga International School (TIS)

7.1 Introduction

All staff members at Tiga International School (TIS) were participants in the study. The first section of this chapter provides a profile of TIS. The chapter then goes on to outline the findings from the policy analysis regarding the introduction of the IBPYP at this site. As with the previous two chapters, they are considered in terms of the four contexts of the 'policy trajectory' framework, namely, the contexts of influences, policy text production, practices, and outcomes.

7.2 TIS International School Profile

TIS was established in 1974 as a non-profit organization to cater for the schooling of English-speaking expatriates in a rural hillside region in central Indonesia. It was described by one of the teachers as *"like living in an old black and white Dutch East Indies film"* (Lea, TIS). For years it was the only school available for expatriate English-speaking children in the district. In the mid-2000s a number of independent schools, including another international school, opened in the area. This thrust TIS into the competitive world of international education. Soon it was to become an IBPYP candidate school. The staff members working there at the time produced curriculum policy texts and documentation that addressed the IBPYP requirements and the result was authorization. Later on, at the time the study was conducted, the school was going through a re-authorization process. Thus, it was different from the other two schools, which were studied during a period when they were adopting the IBPYP for the first time.

© Springer International Publishing Switzerland 2014
S. Ledger et al., *Global to Local Curriculum Policy Processes*,
Policy Implications of Research in Education 4, DOI 10.1007/978-3-319-08762-7__7

At the time of data collection the school employed 20 staff members. The ten teachers at the school included eight expatriates and two Indonesians. The principal was an Australian female and half of the teaching staff was male. The PYP coordinator was a female teacher from England. The remainder of the teaching staff originated from the Philippines, America, Australia, New Zealand and Germany, and many were in intercultural marriages. All teaching assistants were female and all auxiliary staff members were male.

The school sits on fertile land between two large rivers. Volcanoes and a small escarpment overlook the school. The once agriculturally rich and biologically diverse area close by has become a haven of zoos, museums and botanical gardens. These serve to remind visitors of the scientific and biological origins of the district.

The scientific and environmental profile of the region attracts multi-national organizations and international non-government organizations. It is also a regional government centre. The availability of personnel in the fields of agricultural science, biology, veterinary, ichthyology and dendrology provide export opportunities for the area. The region is also renowned for its production capabilities and manufacturing.

The school caters for children of highly qualified parents. The area holds the population with the highest number of doctorates in the country. The parent population is multi-national and multi-cultural. Many parents hold senior positions in their organizations related to the fields of science, biological, chemical and environmental endeavours. Enrolment at TIS is not, however, limited to expatriate children. While tuition costs are prohibitive for many Indonesians, wealthy national citizens are attracted to the school.

7.3   Findings

The impetus for curriculum policy change at TIS, one participant claimed, was "*the fact that it was thrust into competitiveness and needed to reinvent itself*" (Lea, TIS) when English-speaking schools with international student populations began to appear in the region. The school responded to the competition by adopting the 'globally recognized brand' of international education. The perspectives of teachers and principals at TIS in regard to the curriculum policy processes and changes that took place to obtain IBPYP authorization status are now considered in relation to the four contexts of the 'policy trajectory' framework.

7.3.1   The Context of Influence

During the early 2000s when it began to feel the impact of local competition, TIS decided to adopt the IBPYP. It gained IBPYP authorization and increased school enrolments. The principal reported that the "*decision for TIS to become an IBPYP school was innovative for schools in the region at the time*" (Trish, TIS). There were few experienced IBPYP teachers and schools at the time, particularly in Indonesia. A group of new teachers, along with a new principal arrived in the mid-2000s, with minimal IBPYP experience. It became necessary to make a decision about whether to continue with the IBPYP, or replace it.

The findings revealed that the eventual decision for TIS to continue with the IBPYP was a result of four influences. First, there was the importance of retaining the IBPYP for 'global branding' for the school. Secondly, the IBPYP was seen as having value as a 'professional tool for unifying staff'. Thirdly, the offering of an international education with a focus on 'international mindedness' was seen as having qualities to add value to the curriculum. The fourth impact was 'the impact of the teachers' because of their commitment to the programme. Each of these will now be considered in turn.

7.3.1.1 Global Branding

The staff and community at TIS desired a curriculum that would be internationally recognized and have 'global branding'. The IB was seen to be an appropriate vehicle. As one participant put it:

> The management wanted more credibility for the school, a higher status in order to keep the school going. IBPYP is growing in prestige within Indonesia so it is something that parents are looking for. As a marketing tool it's a way of ensuring that we are competitive and we could keep our numbers up. It is all about marketing now. (Mark, TIS)

The participants also identified involvement in the IBPYP as providing them with invaluable experience for their own future employment. They spoke of how an experience in an IBPYP school would provide them with 'global currency' on the international teaching circuit.

The participants reported that the school board also played a pivotal role in the continuation of the IBPYP at TIS. On this, one of them stated that *"parents and students are more aware of the skills and attitudes that make a global citizen than some of the teachers"* (Lars, TIS). Other staff members agreed, and suggested that the IBPYP suited the international background of the parent population. At the same time, they were also clear that while parents were more than happy to have their children enrolled in what was perceived to be a very prestigious programme, most parents had little desire to become more informed about it through attendance at workshops. On this, one of the teachers paraphrased as follows what he considered to be typical of the attitude of the parents of the pupils in his class:

> I don't want to be ear-bashed about IBPYP in a parent workshop. It is a great program. We are happy with what happens at school we trust you! (Mark, TIS).

Others agreed that this view was representative of the TIS parent body. Some saw this in a positive light, commenting that the diverse multi-national highly educated parents *"trusted educators to do their job and were a valuable resource for the school"* (Jo, IST). Another staff member gave voice to a more cynical view when she stated that *"they trust us because they are just too busy to get involved"* (Lea, TIS).

The principal explained that since adopting the IBPYP a certain sense of global market demand and business acumen had come to permeate the school. For example she reported that the school board offered a 'bonus payment' to the principal if she was able to increase enrolment numbers. She was helped in achieving this aim by an Indonesian policy decision made by the Ministry of Education to allow Indonesian nationals to attend international schools. Notwithstanding the rise in student numbers, however, the teachers said that they constantly felt as if they had to 'sell and promote' the school and the IBPYP global brand in order to attract ever more students.

The principal also stated that *"small IB schools are the training ground for future IB school leaders particularly in the primary years"* (Trish, TIS). Many principals of IB schools in international settings, she argued progressed through a set of stages, starting out in a small school and moving to various levels of responsibility there, before progressing to a large school, and then back to small school as a deputy principal or principal. On this, she noted that both herself and the previous principal had been deputies in large schools prior to arriving at TIS and both aspired to be principals in large international schools. She went on as follows:

> I knew I had to start my international career as either a curriculum leader in a large school or a principal of a small school, I had already been a deputy and wanted to run my own school so I applied for the principal position at TIS. (Trish, TIS)

The same pattern of progression was evident at the other two schools reported on in the previous chapters.

7.3.1.2 Professional Tool for Unifying Staff

The IBPYP provided TIS with international recognition and, according to the principal, with a *"professional tool for unifying staff"* (Trish, TIS). She deemed this to be important for the school because after the adoption of the programme she had to employ an almost totally new group of teachers, most of whom were unfamiliar with the IBPYP. The principal and the TIS board held the view that the IBPYP would unify them because of the requirement that collaboration be embraced and a common curriculum provided. As the PYP coordinator put it:

> IBPYP encourages collaboration and working together. You are forced to have systems in place that allow for a lot of collaboration, a lot of input, a lot of professional sharing (Lea, TIS).

There was also a general consensus that the existence of the programme was successful in this regard, and that engagement in it this, in fact, result in professional discussion and debate occurring.

The principal heralded the role of the IBPYP as a unifying tool for the staff. She used the IB *Programme Standards and Practices* (IBO 2003a) document and the recommendations from the IBPYP authorization process to guide decision-making and policy direction at the school. She gave responsibility to the mentoring staff to help colleagues make meaning of IBPYP curriculum policy. Also, she gave responsibility to the IBPYP coordinator to set up procedures that would support its embracement.

7.3.1.3 International Mindedness

The principal commented on how she highlighted the 'international mindedness' espoused by the IBPYP as having the potential to add value to the educational offerings at TIS. She stated that this involved utilizing the diverse origins of the school population as a strength in 'selling' it to the education market within the region. The parents and teachers at TIS, she said, were *"multi-cultural in construct, cosmopolitan in approach and international in outlook"* (Trish, TIS). The teaching cohort was equally diverse. On this, she stated:

> All expatriate staff at TIS had international experience. Many have had international experience in Indonesia and can speak the language. Most of the married teachers have culturally mixed marriages, for example Philippine and Thai, German and Indonesian, Australian and Indonesian, American and Spanish. The single teachers have travelled extensively and are internationally minded. The Indonesian teaching staff members have travelled extensively throughout Indonesia with work and leisure (Trish, TIS)

Of the ten expatriate teachers employed at TIS, three originated from New Zealand and Australia and the remaining staff originated from the USA, The Philippines, Germany, Spain, England and Indonesia.

The participants were unanimous in their opinion that the diverse teaching force, student population and community body of TIS promoted a strong multi-cultural and international perspective amongst all. They highlighted what they saw as the nexus between the IBPYP philosophical underpinnings and the profile of the school community. In short, as one participant claimed, *"the IBPYP epitomised the 'type' of student that the school and community desired"* (Lars, TIS).

7.3.1.4 The Impact of Teachers

The participants recognized that the background experience of teachers, their personal attributes and their connections to the 'outside' world were influential factors on the persistence of the IBPYP at the school. Each of these influences is now considered.

Background of Teachers

The majority of teachers at TIS were from rural backgrounds in their home countries. They expressed a belief that this influenced the way they connected with the IBPYP policy process at TIS. They mentioned that they had a strong sense of belonging and a sense of place in their home towns and that they tried to replicate this at TIS.

The participants also considered that their early life experiences, particularly those in their small home communities, made it relatively easy for them to adapt to the demands of TIS and the rigour of the IBPYP in a remote setting. In particular, they held that their previous experiences had provided them with a range of relevant transferable skills, including self-management and interpersonal skills, for working at TIS and on the IBPYP. Their perceived value was stated by one participant as follows:

> Teachers in rural and remote areas have to be resilient and have a strong paedagogical core so that they can hold firm in any situation particularly when various community pressures are placed on them. (Lea, TIS)

They also expressed a belief that their early-life experiences had prepared them appropriately for the uncertainty of life at TIS.

Personal Attributes of Teachers

The school administration team identified the personality and character of the teaching cohort as strong influences on the adoption of the IBPYP at TIS. According to the IBPYP coordinator *"the teachers' interpersonal relationship skills and personality traits had a strong positive impact on discussions, collaborations and negotiations in all aspects of schooling"* (Lea, TIS). The principal reinforced this view and added as follows:

> I think you have to be open to a whole variety of perspectives whilst also having a strong knowledge base in education. Without the core IBPYP attributes it is difficult teaching successfully in small communities. (Trish, TIS)

The teachers concurred. On this, they referred to the *IB Learner Profile Booklet* (IBO 2003b) as providing them with a key point of reference for desirable teacher behaviour. In particular, they emphasised the positive impact on them of the stress placed on the adoption of an 'international mindedness' view.

The principal was also well aware that she needed to exercise careful leadership in order to maintain the positive atmosphere that prevailed in the school. In particular, she expressed cognisance that teachers' personal self-interests and biases in micro-political worlds evident at schools like TIS had the potential to be very destructive. She stated, for example, that if a disagreement occurred in the staffroom it could often be taken personally rather than professionally and could have lasting negative effects within the school. She also stated that she sometimes had to head off such situations developing, a task that *"made leadership more difficult"* (Trish, TIS).

Connections to the Outside World

Almost all of the staff at TIS discussed the importance of being connected to the outside world. It was also suggested by them that their particular connections to family, friends and professional organizations allowed them to develop a balanced view of the isolated situation in which they found themselves. On this, one participant commented that relationships with people outside of the school provided *"access to an external sounding board for personal and professional issues helped take the pressure off colleagues"* (Lars, TIS). The staff also valued the connections they were obliged to make with the local community and the importance of developing a capacity to move freely between it and the wider world. One participant put this view succinctly:

> You need to be able to stay calm and mange yourself in an isolated area and have the ability to stay connected, not isolated. I think especially in this day and age you can be in a remote area and still remain very connected with the outside world. Teachers need to be able to switch between worlds in small centre; the world of school, the outside world, the social world, the professional world, and the community. (Mark, TIS)

The principal also highlighted what she saw as the value in being able to enrol the children of Indonesian nationals in the IBPYP at TIS. This added yet another 'world' to enhance the educational experience of all at the school.

7.3.2 Context of Policy Text Production

Policy text production regarding the IBPYP at TIS was guided by the requirements of the IBO authorization and re-authorization process. The IBPYP coordinator explained how this was conducted through reflective self-study framed around the IBO's *Programme Standards and Practices* (IBO 2003a) document, resulting in TIS policy texts being modified and changed. Two key themes were identified in relation to the process. The first theme relates to the 'reinforcement of the basic tenets of the IBPYP' that took place in relation to the new policy texts produced, while the second relates to the 'roles, procedures and structural processes' employed to encourage a sense of ownership of the policy texts amongst the staff. An exposition of these two themes is now presented.

7.3.2.1 Reinforcement of the Basic Tenets of the IBPYP

The participants identified the principal characteristics of the IBPYP as being trans-disciplinary, concept driven, inquiry based. The principal insisted that the TIS policy documents developed reflected these characteristics and that their meaning was well understood by all of the staff. The PYP coordinator commented that use of the IB *Programme Standards and Practices* (IBO 2003a) document and the *Making the PYP Happen* (2004) documents were crucial resources in bringing about this situation. She was given the task by the principal of ensuring that *"all staff members were confident with each of the IBPYP basic tenets"* (Trish, TIS). The coordinator indicated that her job was not an easy one, stating that many new teachers found it difficult to come to *"a solid understanding of the core principles of the IBPYP"* (Lea, TIS). Teachers also commented on how they struggled with one or more of these basic elements, particularly with the notion of 'concept-based learning' and 'inquiry'.

At the same time, teachers stated that the *Learner Profile* (IBO 2003a) was an effective tool in bringing them to understand the core beliefs of the IBPYP and that they eventually came to be able to produce 'unit of inquiry' planning documents that were trans-disciplinary, concept driven, and inquiry based. The principal and the IBPYP coordinator concurred. They also stated that the nature of the 'units of inquiry' produced by each collaborating pair of teachers provided them with 'professional windows' into how the teachers were making meaning of the basic tenets of the IBPYP. These 'professional windows', in turn, provided them with starting points for offering targeted support.

7.3.2.2 Roles, Procedures and Structural Processes

The principal stated that the roles of key players were made explicit, procedures were documented and structural processes were put in place to ensure that the IBPYP central tenets remained the focus during all policy text development at TIS. However, having people, procedures and processes in place, as the PYP coordinator identified, *"did not necessarily mean that understanding was uniform"* (Lea, TIS). Rather, as the participants, indicated, four key factors contributed to the successful adoption and persistence of the IBPYP in the school, namely, 'leadership', 'professional development', 'timetabling' and 'resource allocation'.

Leadership

The participants commented that the role of the principal was significant in the policy text production. They considered it crucial that the principal had a voice on the school board and represented their views. They identified her leadership style as being firm but supportive, highlighting her approach for 'shared responsibility' of the curriculum.

The principal and staff also highlighted the important role of the IBPYP coordinator. The principal said that the coordinator *"provided professional support and on-going leadership in the area of paedagogy"* (Trish, TIS). An associated key core role was to ensure that the teachers constructed the policy texts collaboratively. She said that this process helped *"teachers take ownership of the policy documents because they were active participants in policy design, enactment and review rather than passive recipients"* (Lea, TIS). Guided by the IBPYP's curriculum documents and with allocated release time from classroom demands, she confidently led collaborative planning and assessment sessions.

The IBPYP coordinator, reflecting on her first year in the position, stated:

On reflection the first year I was in survival mode, I had no induction as a PYP coordinator only the booklet and my experience as an IBPYP teacher. The second year I trialled a range of collaborative approaches and reviewed all previous documents with the staff. But, I really learnt a lot through the evaluation visit. It improved my understanding of the process and I became a lot more knowledgeable about the expectations. I had to be very systematic and tighten my understanding about what we were actually doing at school. I will take the concept of a self-study to new schools in the future. (Lea, TIS)

The principal did, however, add that the actions of the IBPYP coordinator in trying to empower staff, was not without its challenges. She noted that while the coordinator did an excellent job, she had the disadvantage of being "*a self-proclaimed perfectionist*" (Lea, TIS). While, in the view of the principal, she was a reflective practitioner who had a desire to continually improve her knowledge about the IBPYP and impart this onto others, her enthusiasm was often misread by some the staff. One staff member commented on this, saying: "*she is so enthusiastic and continually pushing us, sometimes it's good to have a break*" (Mark, TIS).

Professional Development

According to the principal, teachers were provided with access to a range of professional development opportunities to help them make sense of the basic tenets of the IBPYP. She explained that "*all 'in-school' professional development was organised by the PYP coordinator during her class release time and also during collaborative planning sessions*" (Trish, TIS). Teachers were given opportunities to visit other IBPYP schools in the region either before, or after, a school vacation. Some attended IBO regional conferences and the East Asia Region Council of Schools' conferences. Also, the location of TIS, 2 h away from a large city, allowed staff to gain access to workshops offered by the regional networks. The principal maintained that this also gave regional workshop leaders the chance to deliver in-school workshops for all members of TIS.

As part of the self-study process, it was decided to include parents in discussions on the curriculum policy texts. To this end, participants conducted workshop sessions to introduce parents to the essential elements of IB policy and the structure of the IBPYP programme. Related parent-teacher evenings were also conducted and parents were invited into classrooms by teachers.

Timetabling

The principal noted that restructuring the timetable was another key strategy used to support the policy production and enactment processes. There was flexibility in timetabling as each class teacher had a teacher assistant to substitute for them if absent, or there was a need to engage in extra planning or review time. The principal explained that this was possible as "*the school was not legally bound to have 'qualified' teachers in the classroom at all times*" (Trish, TIS). Therefore, from time to time, and particularly on Wednesday afternoons, teachers were able to work on collaborative planning sessions with the IBPYP coordinator to plan, produce and assess policy texts during 'normal' classroom time. The teachers were all positive about this experience, characterising it as invaluable for engaging in effective collaboration and professional development.

Conversely, the IBPYP coordinator mentioned that she was provided with only limited time-release to successfully complete her duties, or engage in her own professional development. She maintained a full teaching load in a multi-aged classroom while providing support for others during her student-free time. Her frustration with this situation is evident in the following statement:

> We have tried all sorts of approaches and I believe we haven't hit on the right formulae yet for this staff. The Wednesday sessions are great as it allows the classroom teachers and the specialist teachers to collaboratively plan but it isn't quite right. We have planned as a whole group; it was great but very slow. I give up lunch and afterschool time to help those in need but it is not sustainable. We have tried working in different groups from across the school rather than grade level counterparts. I am always looking at how to best use the limited time I have knowing that I still can't please everyone. (Lea, TIS)

Her situation was not helped by the fact that most of the teachers, while very appreciative of her efforts, were not willing to invest their own time into the process.

Resource Allocation

The participants outlined how resource allocation was another area that helped facilitate policy text production. Decisions were made by the leadership team that saw increased funding channelled into the employment of teacher assistants in every classroom. A small proportion of the building funds for a new multipurpose sports hall was channelled to help fund library resources and purchase support materials for the 'units of inquiry' developed by staff. This financial support was considered a significant step in supporting policy text production and in the adoption of the IBPYP.

The school board offered the leadership team a yearly stipend of $3,000 and a bonus for the principal if she could increase the number of students at the school. The basic wage at TIS was not high compared to other international schools. It included a housing allowance, a flight home at the end of every year and a small holiday or well-being allowance. Although the financial incentives were not particularly competitive, the big attraction as expressed by the participants was its geographical location and the family-friendly lifestyle provided by the hillside community.

In brief, these findings outline the complexities of policy text production at TIS. The importance of key players and documents were highlighted in the curriculum policy process. The principal and the IBPYP coordinator were identified as key players whilst the *Programme Standards and Practices* (IBO 2003a), *IB Learner Profile Booklet* (IBO 2003b) and *Making the PYP Happen* (IBO 2004) documents had a significant influence.

7.3.3 Context of Practices

Three key themes were generated from the data in relation to the 'context of practices'. The first is concerned with 'changes to ownership of policy documents'. The second relates to 'changes to procedures at TIS'. The third is focused on 'changes to teaching practices'. These themes are now considered.

7.3.3.1 Changes to Ownership of Policy Documents

The teachers considered that taking ownership of the policy documents was a significant change in practice. The recommendations provided by the IB regional office in response to the IBPYP authorization process at the school provided the starting point for change. These recommendations, as one participant stated, "*helped the teachers fill the gaps in the curriculum and identified areas of need within the policy texts*" (Trish, TIS). Areas of strength were commended and areas of weakness were targeted.

Various changes in policy and curriculum documentation at TIS followed during the re-authorization phase. One such change was the production of a new collaborative planning sheet that was adapted for use on the computer. This allowed all teachers and specialists to get access to, change and review 'units of inquiry' online. The computer teacher took the initiative on this. Participants also commented that much time was spent on addressing identified gaps in the Mathematics and Language curricula. Curriculum leaders in these areas took ownership of reworking the associated documents. As a result, the school produced a scope and sequence document from kindergarten through to grade seven for each subject area. The PYP coordinator explained that these were then cross-referenced to the school's 'programme of inquiry'.

The IBPYP coordinator remarked that there was significant variation in familiarity with the policy documents between general classroom teachers and specialist teachers. Subject specialist teachers at TIS, she stated, were reported to have felt isolated and to have had limited access to policy documentation and policy collaboration in their field. In response, the principal restructured the timetable to include specialists in the Wednesday collaborative planning sessions.

IBPYP planning requirements placed a heavy workload on teachers but participants stated that they believed the process enabled them to take ownership of the new policies. In relation to this, there were suggestions by some staff that it was a real challenge to ensure that there was a balance between open-ended inquiry and the demands of curriculum benchmarking. The following comment reflected the systematic approach to the workload issue:

> To help the implementation of our scope and sequence documents specific teaching recommendations were included. Teachers can use these as well as their own ideas. Planning is done collaboratively so other teachers can contribute. We have a long-term plan and continually review our policies. It is a thorough and sustainable approach to policy and curriculum renewal. (Trish, TIS)

The principal remarked that she also wanted the parents to understand the policy documents. To this end, the school adopted a range of methods to disseminate the documents to the wider community. Classroom teachers described how they also displayed planning documents on their classroom doors for the parents to view.

Sometimes teachers invited parents to comment on the units at the start, or conclusion, of the term in which it was taught. IBPYP updates were provided in the weekly newsletter and at monthly parent evenings to cover different aspects of policy documents. All agreed, however, that the most visual and effective means of promoting IST policy and practices was through providing a large display in the front foyer of the school where the school 'programme of inquiry' could be viewed. This display generated discussion and feedback for the school, while teachers got great satisfaction out of seeing their plans in public view. As one of them put it, "*I am proud when I see my planning documents on display for everyone, they have to be good*" (Jo, TIS).

7.3.3.2   Changes to Procedures

The TIS administration team made many procedural changes to support the adoption of the IBPYP policy. In particular, they articulated, illustrated and embedded the central pillars of the IBPYP into the daily routine of the school in a systematic manner. The IBPYP coordinator stated that these changes began with the holding of collaborative planning sessions. The outcome was changes to resource budgeting and changes to professional development approaches, both aimed, as one teacher put it, at "*supporting the professional growth of the teacher*" (Trish, TIS).

Changes to Resource Budgeting

Purchasing of resources became transparent and was targeted to meeting the IBPYP needs during the re-authorization process. The principal highlighted the need for procedural change in budgeting practices, stating that "*money was tight so we had to make sure the school benefited from every dollar spent, with the IBPYP being our priority*" (Trish, TIS). The administration team believed they could provide local support to meet the specific needs of the teachers and to help reduce resource costs. Budget allocation was directed towards professional development, teacher relief, timetabling and resources.

Participants identified the budget changes and associated procedures as being significant in ensuring the policy process at TIS was conducted smoothly. A particular initiative that was appreciated was the allocation of funds for additional teacher assistants. The principal stated that she wanted *"every class to have a qualified teacher as well as a teacher assistant because it gives the school flexibility"* (Trish, TIS). Teachers commented that the adoption of this strategy was helpful. This was expressed by one of them when he stated that it *"helped relieve the workload and allowed them to address the difficulties of catering for specific needs in the classroom including students with English as a second language"* (Jo, TIS). The IBPYP coordinator added that an extra person in the classroom enabled the teachers to trial such specific IBPYP teaching approaches as inquiry based learning, which many found difficult. The additional support provided opportunities for on-going professional dialogue to occur between teacher, teacher assistant and the coordinator. This also allowed those who initially were uncomfortable with working with someone else in their class to make a positive transition in their practice.

Changes to Professional Development

The new policies at TIS provided a more strategic approach to professional development than had previously existed. The IBPYP coordinator provided in-school workshops on an on-going basis and, according to the principal, attended to the prioritized school needs. One participant described how visitors were called upon to develop *"culturally specific awareness of life in an Indonesian setting"* (Louise, TIS). Associated professional development that targeted cultural awareness was considered important. It was also appreciated. On this, one participant commented: *"I thought I knew a lot about Indonesia and Islam but after only one cultural session I realised how stereotypical and limited my views were"* (Ria, TIS). As already indicated, money was also allocated so that staff would be able to attend regional conferences.

7.3.3.3 Changes to Teaching Practices

Teachers identified a number of influences that supported paedagogical change in their classrooms at TIS. The majority identified key people and policy documents as being significant change agents in this regard. The principal and the IBPYP coordinator were particularly influential, especially in their harnessing of the IBO *Programme Standards and Practices* and *Making the PYP Happen* documents. These documents not only helped guide participants' curriculum and lesson planning, as noted already, but also helped guide their teaching practices. On this, one participant referred to the *Making the PYP Happen* (IBO 2004) as *"my IBPYP bible, with all the answers"* (Jo, TIS).

The principal commented that the most recognized paradigm shift and change to teaching practice took place at the level of active involvement in policy development. This resulted in teachers engaging in conversations and debating issues related to their classroom practice. Teachers also began to adopt a more reflective approach to the planning, teaching and assessment cycle than they had previously done. This, along with the collaborative planning sessions, professional development workshops and staff meetings, helped them to arrive at a common understanding, or whole school vision.

7.3.4   Context of Outcomes

The final context in the policy trajectory framework is the 'context of outcomes'. Considering this context allows one to come to appreciate the impact of policies on existing social inequalities. Three themes will be considered in this regard, namely, the 'marketization of education', 'international mindedness' and 'remoteness'.

7.3.4.1   Marketization of Education

The principal commented that TIS found itself thrust into an era of competition and had to reinvent itself in order to remain the 'school of choice' for expatriates living in the region. TIS went from being the only English-speaking school for the children to expatriate parents, to being one of many. The principal stated that the "*forced competitive paradigm in which TIS found itself resulted in a business- like approach to its operation being adopted and directed by the school board*" (Trish, TIS).

The school board gave the principal an annual bonus payment if she enrolled additional students at the school. Initially, this was seen by some teachers as being somewhat at odds with the school's mission statement that promoted small class sizes. Staff wanted TIS to remain small and intimate but, as one participant stated, "*this was in direct contrast to the new business model being embraced by the school*" (Louise, TIS). The board had the final decision and many staff members were reluctant to speak up about their concerns. Consequently, they argued, there was constant pressure to remain committed to the IBPYP because so much money had already been invested in its development.

7.3.4.2   International Mindedness

At first glance, TIS appeared to be an internationally minded, multicultural community involved in environmental and scientific programmes addressing local and global issues. For example, teachers used the term 'international mindedness' to describe the student and parent population at TIS. Yet, when questioned about it, many found the concept difficult to define.

The principal also drew attention to the extent to which the well-educated, multicultural parent body was involved in social and environmental work with large companies and non-government organizations in the region. The school expected this cohort to be proactive and involved in the 'units of inquiry' and school outreach programmes. The IBPYP coordinator, however, highlighted the following incident that arose during the middle of the 2000s, indicating how such involvement could sometimes lead to problems:

> At the start of second term we aimed to revise our mission statement. We called for input from students, parents, board members and external community groups. We really wanted to go down an eco-friendly environmental focus. However the parents didn't actually want it. They worked for large organizations like the Wildlife Conservation group, but feedback was that they didn't want to shove it down kids throats. I was gob-smacked, particularly given the background of the parent body. It could have been a cutting edge school – similar to Bali's Green school. However the strong parent body pushed us toward a performing arts and music focus rather than a science one. (Lea, TIS)

This lack of desire by the parents to re-invent TIS as an eco-friendly environmental school surprised many of the staff. Teachers expressed concern that the focus on international mindedness was actually developing into 'rural-mindedness' and *"single-mindedness of some parents"* (Lea, TIS).

7.3.4.3 Remoteness

The staff at TIS claimed to be intimately linked within the community. They described the role of a teacher in a small community such as TIS as being full of complexity. They shared the responsibility of educating the children and acted as a conduit between the school and family. One participant summarised the situation thus: *"In many instances we are connected to the socio-cultural environment that surrounds the school whether we like it or not"* (Lars, TIS).

Another outcome of living in a remote area identified by the participants was the lack of anonymity that prevailed. At times teachers at TIS felt as if they lived in a goldfish bowl. One participant described how *"everyone and everything is observed by the close-knit community"* (Jo, TIS). This was reported as having a negative impact on the participants' sense of belonging. While teachers were housed in private properties in the area, some responded by choosing to live further afield. This strategy, as one put it, *"enabled them to divorce their school life from their work lives"* (Lea, TIS). Others, however, considered that those who took such action really did so to avoid extra-curricular activities, or out-of-school functions.

The principal argued quite strongly that forced change and mandated collaboration, such as that which took place at TIS on the adoption of the IBPYP, can be difficult and cause tension. On this, she provided the following example of an event that took place at the school prior to her arrival; one which also had unpredictable consequences:

> One incident triggered an unplanned chain of events and policy changes at TIS. The principal was disappointed with the collaborative commitment of two staff members. So,

after a series of warnings, she reprimanded them and told them their contracts would not
be renewed. One of the affected staff members rallied support and turned the community
against the principal. The teacher's partner, who was also on staff and socially popular,
supported his wife. The rest of the year proved to be difficult for all parties. The situation
resulted in the principal being offered a less than adequate teaching package for the
following year that in turn forced her to move. (Lea, TIS)

Remote international schools such as TIS tend to attract teaching couples and most
schools are happy with this because certain economies of scale ensue. But in this
instance the dynamics of a small setting and a less-than-committed teaching couple
influenced the employment policy at TIS. Participants indicated that the unease
and discomfort identified by the staff, parents and community during this time was
influential enough for the school board to change the school policy. Ever since the
incident occurred, the TIS employment policy favours single teachers in preference
to teaching couples.

Finally, the remoteness of TIS was considered both an advantage and a disadvantage by the staff. One of the perceived advantages of living in a remote location
was stated as follows: *"At TIS you have the best of both worlds – the comfort of a
small school in a beautiful green environment and good access to the outside world*
(Louise, TIS). Conversely, remoteness was also considered to be a real disadvantage,
especially because, as one teacher stated: *"The local politics in small schools is
overpowering"* (Trish, TIS).

7.4   Conclusion

This chapter presented findings from TIS as the final of three case studies of
curriculum policy development undertaken in remote international schools in
Indonesia. It tracked the re-authorization process involved in continuing with the
enactment of the International Baccalaureate Primary Years Program (IBPYP) at
the school. The findings captured the dynamic nature of IBPYP policy processes and
identified the micro-politics that prevailed at the school. The conclusion summarizes
the findings and key themes for each of the contexts along the curriculum policy
trajectory.

In terms of the 'context of influences', TIS decided to re-commit to IBPYP
(and thus seek IB re-authorisation) because of its 'global brand' and international
recognition. However the curriculum policy processes involved in the decision
to be re-authorized were not smooth. Four influences were significant. The first
was recognizing the importance of IBPYP as a global marketing tool for the
school to attract and retain staff. The second was the value of IBPYP as a
professional unifying tool for staff. The third related to the 'value adding' element
of international mindedness. The fourth factor recognized teachers as influential in
the policy process, including the power of 'teaching couples'.

In regard to 'policy text production', TIS reviewed its curriculum policy during
the self-study component of the IBPYP re-authorization process. Policy texts

were modified during this process. Two key themes emerged. The first was the importance of recognizing and reinforcing the basic tenets of the IBPYP within the new curriculum policy texts at the school. The second was the recognition of the roles, procedures and structural processes which would encourage 'a sense of ownership' of the school-based policy texts. The characteristics of the policy texts were changed so as to highlight the IB vernacular, philosophy, paedagogy, assessment components, collaborative practices and assessment procedures inherent in IBPYP. All policy texts were aligned with the IB re-authorization requirements and the IB *Standards and Practices* (IBO 2003a) document.

Three core themes emerged from the findings in regard to the 'context of practices' and each related to change. At IST, there was a change of ownership of policy documentation; change in procedural practices; and changes in teaching paedagogy. Each of these changes was interconnected with the others during the enactment of IBPYP. Key players and documents drove these changes, namely, the principal and IB coordinator as well as key IBPYP policy documents.

The 'contexts of outcomes' highlighted a range of 'bigger picture' issues relating to power inequities and social justice. Three main themes to emerge included, the marketization of education, 'international mindedness', and issues surrounding 'remoteness'. These outcomes were both planned and unplanned and many of them were specific to living in the remote setting of TIS, including the 'disconnect' between the well-educated parent body and the school.

In all, the findings at this case study site revealed that the small, financially struggling school used IBPYP curriculum policy and processes to promote structural, pedagogical and attitudinal change as it transitioned into a competitive school in the education market place. A more corporate approach to education permeated the school during this period. This process of change brought with it much debate and discussion.

References

IBO. (2003a). *Programme standards and practices*. Cardiff: IBO. www.ibo.org/documentlibrary/ programmestandards/. Accessed 30 Mar 2006.

IBO. (2003b). *IB learner profile booklet*. Cardiff: IBO. www.ibo.org/ibla/conference/.../ TheLearnerProfileinActionFabian.ppt. Accessed 30 Mar 2006.

IBO. (2004). *Making the PYP happen: A curriculum framework for international primary education*. Cardiff: IBO. www.ibo.org/documentlibrary/programmestandards/. Accessed 3 Mar 2006.

Chapter 8
Discussion

8.1 Introduction

The three case studies reported in Chaps. 4, 5 and 6 presented an analysis of policy regarding the International Baccalaureate Primary Years Programme (IBPYP) in particular remote Indonesian school settings. This chapter now presents the results of an analysis undertaken across the three cases. It is a cross-case analysis framed by the conceptualization of the policy trajectory consisting of the contexts of influences, policy text production, practices, and outcomes (Ball 1994, 2006; Rizvi and Lingard 2010; Vidovich 2007). Each of these four policy contexts is used as a heading in organising the presentation below. In reality, however, they are multi-faceted, multi-dimensional and inherently interrelated contexts. This becomes evident on considering the themes generated in relation to the different contexts. Also it is important to highlight that in undertaking this analysis, account was taken of Vidovich's (2007) position on the importance of considering the global, national and local aspects of each context; a position akin to Marginson and Rhoades' (2002) 'glo-na-cal' (global-national-local) agency heuristic which is relevant to the policy analysis conducted here. At the local level, the setting of each case study was attributed an importance beyond being merely a descriptive backdrop to the policy (Green 2008). That is, it was seen as being an integral part of the policy process.

The adoption of the latter stance in relation to foregrounding setting is supported by a number of authorities engaged in policy research in recent years in international, rural and higher education (Azano 2011; Fail 2011; Gruenewald 2003; Marginson and Rhoades 2002; Reid et al. 2008; Wylie 2011). At the same time, sight was not lost of the fact that each of the case studies particularly targeted the local level and was informed by typologies, categories and classifiers related to people and places (Roberts 2003; Wylie 2006). Consequently, both convergence

© Springer International Publishing Switzerland 2014   153
S. Ledger et al., *Global to Local Curriculum Policy Processes*,
Policy Implications of Research in Education 4, DOI 10.1007/978-3-319-08762-7_8

and divergence across the three case study sites were identified, with cognizance being taken of Stake's advice not to lose a sense of the fact that each case has "its unique character" (Stake 1995, p. 41).

8.2   Context of Influences

This section provides an exposition of those influences that led to the adoption of the IBPYP in the selected remote international schools within Indonesia. The analysis upon which the exposition is based recognized that policy actors and settings at different levels of the policy trajectory are central to, and influenced by, a variety of interconnected and multi-layered influences (Vidovich 2007). These include those of a geographic, demographic, economic, socio-cultural, technological, political, paedagogical and ideological nature, that have been identified by educational policy analysts as being embedded in discourses surrounding international curriculum policy in general (Marshall 2011; Rizvi and Lingard 2010).

Five major inter-connected themes were identified in regard to the context of influences. These include 'globalization', 'global branding', 'the IBPYP as a unifying package', 'local politics and practices', and 'teachers' backgrounds and characteristics'. Each of these themes is now considered in turn.

8.2.1   Globalization

The twenty-first century wave of globalization is often presented in the literature as a multi-faceted phenomenon influenced by profound technological advances and policy decisions (Giddens 1994; Held et al. 1999; Rizvi and Lingard 2010, Sklair 2001; Spring 2009; Zhao 2010). Furthermore, its interconnected and transformative effects are demonstrated as having an impact across the globe on both individuals and systems (Dyer 2010; Kenway et al. 2005; Steiner-Khamsi 2004). Specifically in relation to education, it has led to an expansion in international schools. As Bates (2011a), Hill (2007), Vidovich (2013) and Wylie (2011) have pointed out, this has been facilitated, to some extent, by increasing advances in technology and ease of mobility, what Zhao (2009) has termed 'the death of distance'. It has also been characterised by the international ideology that it transmits; as Bates (2011a, p. 2) has put it, "the expansion of international schooling is not simply numerical, it is also ideological".

The general international patterns identified so far were evident in the specific cases from Indonesia analysed in the study. Under the influence of globalization, the number of international schools in the country increased greatly from the time of the establishment of the Jakarta International School in 1976. Furthermore, they now include a range of different international school types, including 36 authorized IB schools. The study indicated various ways in which forces of globalization facilitated ideological transference of the IBPYP policy into practice across three of these schools and, in the process, accommodating Western social norms. These methods of policy transfer are identified as three subthemes which are considered below. They refer to the effects of globalization forces on the IB organization and regional offices, to globalization and the nature of Indonesian national governance, and to globalization and its impact on local politics and practices.

8.2.1.1 The Effects of Globalization Forces on IB Organization and Regional Offices

As mentioned in Chap. 3, a change in the Director of the International Baccalaureate Organization during the time the study was conducted led to structural and ideological developments consistent with a global trend of corporatization of education. The new director moved away from an educational leadership style and moved towards a more corporate leadership one characterized by forging a corporate image, a global market strategy, organizational change, economic rationality, and measurable outcomes to manage the IB's exponential growth. This, in turn, had a significant influence on management, on policy text production and on governance.

The corporatisation of the IB organization was most evident in its emphasis on branding, such as the introduction of a revamped logo. It also included modifying policy texts, developing consistency in terminology across texts and programmes, outlining promotional pathways, improving website accessibility, developing ICT partnerships, and the initiation of a range of quality assurance processes. Concurrently, the re-location of the IB head office and the regional offices reflected the growing geographic spread of the organization. It was during this time that the IBPYP 'student profile', introduced in 1994, was changed to become the *IB Learner Profile Booklet* (IBO 2003b), now embedded in all IB global programmes and documents. The 'learner profile' has become the central tenet of the IB as it embodies the IB mission statement and its international-minded focus.

A significant outcome of the global restructure of the IBPYP was the establishment of regional offices in the Asia Pacific, The Hague, and America and, consistent with the global education trend of decentralization, the transfer of power to the regional level. Thus, in terms of Marginson and Rhoades' (2002) 'glonacal' agency heuristic, the incorporation of a regional-level construct became important. The devolution of power to the regional offices was a response to the contextual and cultural nuances of each region. Within this structure, the IB Asia Pacific regional office played an influential role as a conduit for the transmission of macro level IBPYP ideologies and standards to micro level IBPYP practices at the case study schools.

The new regional structure, including the Asia Pacific regional office based in Singapore, also provided a strategic management base to help increase the number of IB schools within its sphere. Staff members at the regional offices supported, promoted and guided schools through the IB authorization and re-authorization process. The team members also managed and delivered IB professional development throughout the region. Their personal contact with schools made them 'the face' of the IB. Referring to the Singapore office, one participant in the study commented that it provided a "*professional link to the world of the IB*" (Anne, STI). Regional office personnel became especially involved in working collaboratively with school-based IBPYP coordinators and were guided in the policy process by the *Programme Standards and Practices* (IBO 2003a) document. This development serves to illustrate the view that while regionality (an influential, yet often-omitted layer in analyses of policy processes) is usually positioned between a national and local construct (glo-na-re-cal), it can also be positioned between a global and national construct (glo-re-na-cal).

8.2.1.2 Globalization and the Nature of Indonesian National Governance

At a national level, both Indonesian government legislation and the Indonesian Ministry of Education were influential in the IBPYP policy process, especially in relation to employment, education, and customs that had a direct impact on the case study schools and the teachers. The Ministry began 'internationalizing' their national curriculum to reflect the global educational discourses of the time. The number and structure of international schools in Indonesia grew rapidly from the turn of the millennium and brought with it associated pressures and benefits. Once only available to students who held foreign passports, international schools now cater for the rising number of wealthy and middle class Indonesian students. During the period in which the study was undertaken, a policy decision was made that allowed Indonesian nationals to enrol their children in international schools if they obtained a letter of support from the Ministry of Education.

8.2.1.3 Globalization and Local Politics and Practices

The impact of globalization also filtered through to the local level. Workers from a wide variety of backgrounds came to the school sites that were the focus of the study. These miners, and their families, displayed a mixture of religions, values and beliefs, thus reflecting a general pattern internationally as a result of the global movement of workers that is accompanying the current international resource boom. Cultural differences influenced group interaction and interpersonal relationships within the local community and at times led to conflict and other tensions related to intercultural marriages and language barriers.

On the other hand, cultural differences at the mine sites also contributed to the embracement of difference. On this, the merging of cultures was at times forced on groups of people who would not necessarily choose to interact in a larger setting. Reflecting on this, one participant stated:

> You learn to interact with the people who are there and you may not necessarily be the sort of people you would choose to interact with . . . you learn to accept differences . . . it prepares you well to mix in multicultural settings. (Sophie, DIS)

Thus, while remote centres had the capacity to magnify differences, they could also serve to break down personal, professional and cultural barriers. In this regard, Hayden (2006) has commented, albeit in relation to the IBPYP beyond the specific Indonesian setting, that affiliated schools can act as agents of cultural exchange for parents and students.

Finally, while globalization can bring many benefits, these may be "uneven, creating greater social stratification and inequality" (Rizvi and Lingard 2005, p. 419). For example, specifically focusing on education in nine different societies in the Asia Pacific region, Mok and Welch (2003) found that the globalization process "intensified education disparities between the poor and the rich" (p. xi). This finding was also clearly reflected in the specific case studies in the research project.

To summarise so far, the major theme of globalization was identified as a key influence in adopting the IBPYP in each of the case study schools, thus echoing the findings of other studies (Caffyn 2011; Hayden 2006). The schools were influenced by economic, cultural, paedagogical and ideological rationales for adopting the IBPYP. On this, the corporatization of the IB and the marketization of international education in general contributed to the decision. Globalization forces also provided opportunities for 'expat mindedness' to develop. The tension between international-mindedness and expat mindedness influenced the ways teachers tried to deal with issues of privilege and power embedded in each international school setting. The IB *Learner Profile* helped mitigate the struggle by providing schools with a list of ten attributes to which children, teachers and parents should aspire.

8.2.2 *Global Branding*

The second major theme related to the 'context of influences' is the importance of global branding. The International Baccalaureate is one of the most recognized international curriculums around the world (Bagnall 2008; Bates 2011a; Bunnell 2011; Luke 2010). Regarding the three schools in the study, one of the main reasons why they adopted the IBPYP was because of its global currency. One participant expressed this as follows: "*Part of the influence is that the IBPYP is recognized back home and that you are not teaching some kind of jungle Sanskrit but something that is globally recognized*" (Anthony, SIS). This view reflects a global push for schools to internationalize (Wylie 2011), an impetus that has contributed to the exponential growth of international schools in the South East Asia region (Bates 2011b; Bunnell 2007). To put it another way, the policy reform adopted by the case study schools positioned them, as Apple (2004) and Bottery (2006) would see it, in a global knowledge economy.

A heavy emphasis was placed within the schools on reputation-building by adopting the IBPYP and by aligning themselves with the creation of a transnational ruling class of privileged students. One of the participants in the study put this bluntly when he stated: "*We want the most prestigious and recognized international curriculum available*". (Ken, SIS) Cambridge (2002) referred to this mind-set and associated developments as the franchising of brand positioning in high profile international schools and argued, like others, that it is a process that represents what some commentators call a contamination of education by a profit-driven, neo-liberal agenda (Bates 2011b; Bunnell 2011).

At the same time, not all of the participants were accepting of the status quo. On the contentious debate about international education becoming an industry (Brown and Lauder 2011; MacDonald 2006; Wylie 2011), one participant spoke about the need for a mutually beneficial relationship between profit and paedagogy, stating: "*Although the corporate ethos and goals are the driving force behind all that happens here we actually all benefit greatly both professionally and personally*". (Lea, IST) This participant provided a micro-level example of how time and money invested in the IBPYP brand gave the schools a perceived competitive edge and enhanced their already-established international experience. In particular, adopting the IBPYP brand as a marketing tool was beneficial, attracting teachers to remote areas and retaining them, thus overcoming what can be a major problem for remote schools in other spheres.

At the same time, negative undercurrents and resistance did manifest themselves at the three schools. This was mainly due to tensions surrounding nationalistic ideologies and internationalization. Subtle comments and withdrawal from tasks reflected Walker's (2011, p. 210) findings that "there are still those who wish to maintain the mythology of nation-state self-sufficiency". Furthermore, strong paedagogical and personal beliefs offered barriers to IBPYP curriculum change at all three case study schools and provided teachers with justifications for their resistance. These findings resonate with views held by Walker (2004), who suggests that barriers accompany reform because teachers' ideas, values, actions and even emotions are challenged. They both suggest that teachers are cultural products related to where they have been prepared as teachers, and where they have been brought up.

8.2.3   The IBPYP as a Unifying Package

The third major theme that emerged in relation to the 'context of influences' is the desire the schools had to utilize the IBPYP as a unifying package for curriculum reform. Administrators and curriculum leaders, including the IBPYP co-ordinators at the case study schools, cited the importance of having a shared vision as one of the most influential factors in their decision to adopt the IBPYP. As one administrator put it:

> The predominant factor was to try to unify the teaching staff into a paedagogy that was going to provide our students a coherent, cohesive, developmental programme of learning ... a curriculum that would unite everyone. (Anthony, SIS)

The adoption of this position by various participants reflected their experiences, often in a range of countries (Walker 2004), including New Zealand, England and Australia, that have a long history of valuing a 'whole school', or a 'shared vision', approach to school planning, policy-making, curriculum development and enactment (Grundy 2002; Marshall 2011; Pinar 2004).

One of the perceived benefits of developing a unified approach to curriculum policy, including through 'educational policy borrowing' (Phillips and Ochs 2004; Steiner-Khamsi 2004) by the case study schools, was the assumption that it would improve professional responsibility and accountability, and overcome dissatisfaction with the previous national-based curriculum. The IBPYP was seen to offer direction, stability and sustainability within each setting. There was, however, a personal and professional cost for some. These included additional demands on their time, extra workload, increased financial commitments, forced collaboration and, at times, personal and paedagogical conflict. One participant summed up this situation, stating: *"The IBPYP makes teachers think about what and how they teach and for some of us this was neither easy nor wanted"* (Pat, DIS).

Conversely, one of the concerns about developing a unified curriculum policy centred on the role that international schools can play in transmitting the globalization of neo-liberal ideologies and social norms (Bates 2011b). Since its inception, the IB has been under regular scrutiny for its perceived Western orientation and world-view (Quist 2005; Walker 2011). Developments in other contexts have sought to address this. For example, a recent joint venture between the Aga Khan Development Network and the IBO produced a series of units entitled *Intercultural Understandings: Muslim Contexts* (IBO 2010). While there is no evidence to suggest that participants at the case study sites were cognisant of such developments, there were some indications that they would be favourably disposed towards them.

To observe that the IBPYP curriculum was adopted at the case study schools to assist in unifying staff is not to observe a new phenomenon. As far back as 1987, Grundy (1987) was recommending the adoption of policy reform as a means of leading schools toward a shared vision of policy, practice and improved outcomes. In the specific instance of the case study schools, the reform process revealed issues related to the internationalization and marketization of education, fractionalisation of staff, and a misinterpretation of culture and curriculum policy. These features have also been noted by Zhao (2009) regarding other contexts. At the same time, the policy reform in which the schools were engaged led to the development of friendships, changes of alliance, the inclusion of marginalised individuals and cultural groups, and the cross-fertilisation of ideas, beliefs and values. This gives some credence to Zhao's (2009, p. 158) view that a truly global mind-set about international education can lead to "tolerance for multiple perspectives, different talents and a respect for diversity in a globalised world".

8.2.4 Local Politics and Practices

The fourth theme that emerged related to the 'context of influences' is that local politics and practices, within a globalized setting, had an influence at each case study school. This can be considered under the two sub-themes of informal and formal group structures, and the changing face of the community.

8.2.4.1   Formal and Informal Group Structures

At each of the case study schools, the organizational infrastructure consisted of the administration team, the IBPYP coordinator, curriculum leaders, the school board and the parent committee. They were informed in their actions by a myriad of school policies, practices, timelines and goals. What was then translated into curriculum practice was influenced by relationships between, and interpretations by, key players within these formal structures.

The small, remote locations investigated were places of social intrigue that had an impact on curriculum policy processes. When there was debate, conflict and possible misinterpretation in these settings, teachers found it hard to be objective. One of the reasons offered was that *"powerful emotional ties"* (Rose, DIS) existed within the groups. Pearce (2011) highlighted this phenomenon in the case of large international schools, but this study indicates it can be equally present in small ones.

A powerful key player, or subgroup, emerged at each case study school to influence curriculum policy processes. Payne (2005) describes this kind of development as the rise of the 'de facto executives'. Within the schools, friendships and connections between groups of couples developed and resulted in power being wielded at times to further their own interests. Their actions were often fuelled by emotions, conflict of opinion, manipulation, and control. This corresponds to Caffyn's (2007) finding that self-interest can be a powerful force in international schools and that clientele power can manipulate and control school agendas.

At TIS, a 'teaching couple', about to be removed by the principal for being incompetent, had their contract renewed because their friend, also a board member, attacked the professional competence of the principal, who was then removed. At SIS, one of the most experienced teachers was pressured into leaving because a disgruntled parent married to a senior mining executive didn't agree with the structured programme of her junior primary classroom. In both cases the result was fragmentation and demoralization of staff, a phenomenon identified in similar settings elsewhere by James et al. (2005).

8.2.4.2   The Changing Face of International School Communities

The multiple identities and changing face of the staff and the community had an influence on curriculum policy processes in each of the case study schools. The Anglo-American mix of the executives within two mining communities (SIS, DIS) contrasted with the multicultural, multi-experiential and multi-occupational nature of the parent body of IST. This diversity reflects the diversity within global migrating workforces (Banks 2008; Beck 2006; Marshall 2011), bringing with it the "proliferation of difference accompanying globalization" (Pinar 2003, p. 5). The changing face of each setting included a rise in the number of intercultural marriages between foreigners and Indonesians. There was also an increase in the number of lower-skilled workers in the workforce as a whole.

While some groups were marginalised and their voices curtailed in the school decision-making process, the general experience was that each school encouraged inclusivity in its policy-making and in its actions. The nature of the school's staffing policies constituted one significant point of discussion. In general, it was a mix of foreign expatriate teachers, local Indonesian language teachers, Indonesian national administrative staff, unskilled Indonesian nationals, and indigenous ancillary staff. This staffing mix was hierarchical and mirrored staffing profiles in a number of other international school settings (Hayden and Thompson 2011).

Other cultural points of discussion centred on the fact that the majority of Indonesian nationals employed across the sites were Christian, in a nation where Islam makes up 86.1 % of the population. It also did not escape the notice of the participants that while female teachers were in the majority across the schools and nationalities, only one female held an administrative position. This pattern is similar to primary school profiles worldwide (Siniscalco 2002). The uneven population structure generated discussion about possible power differentials between religion and gender constructs within the three international schools and how they can have an impact on curriculum policy processes.

The multiple identities held by staff and the code switching required to navigate the political, cultural, paedagogical, language and gender landscapes at each setting, also provided points of discussion at the case study schools. Teachers were required to traverse between the diverse roles of friend, colleague, parent, practitioner, decision-maker, cultural observer, participant, a community member, and sometimes even translator. Cognizance by participants of this situation impressed upon them the difficulty of imposing, or developing, a morally homogenous society. This brings one to conclude, as with Davies (2006), that it is problematic to ignore the complex nature of identity, culture and language in a world where migration leads to complex cultural identities as an influence on curriculum policy processes.

8.2.5 Teachers' Backgrounds and Characteristics

The case studies also highlighted the global interconnectivity of political, economic, socio-cultural, paedagogical and environmental factors that have a direct impact on curriculum policy at the local level. Regarding this micro level in educational research more generally, Caffyn (2011, p. 61) warns that it is important not to overlook the diversity of experience, background and values of teachers as they "influence the decision-making, interactions, negotiations, conflict and self-interest groups that contribute to the micro-political workings of schools". Dyer (2010), in a similar vein, highlights the centrality of the teacher in the policy process, recognising that classroom dynamics and teachers' work are shaped by local, national and global realities, while Rizvi (2007) impresses that policy is enacted through the shifting subjectivity of the individual.

At the local level of international schooling, it is clear that globalization had a profound influence, especially in terms of the structure and size of the schools' teaching workforces. It seems that in the early years, American and British teachers were dominant in international schools in many settings. Increasingly, however, Southern Hemisphere native speakers of English are joining international school staff (Canterford 2003; Hardman 2001; Hayden and Thompson 2011). Global mobility has allowed them to combine their career with their desire to travel.

In the case of the specific case study schools, many staff members came from rural backgrounds, or had previous experience in either rural, or isolated, school sites. The connection between previously living in remote locations and successful living in remote international settings proved to be high. This is a matter on which one teacher expounded thus: *"I was willing to go to the middle of nowhere because I had grown up in the middle of nowhere"* (Pat, DIS). This observation suggests the addition of another 'type' to the typologies of teachers in international schools (Garton 2000; Hayden 2006; Hayden and Thompson 2011). The literature on this focuses on teachers in terms of nationality, geographical origins and contract of employment (Cambridge 2002). However, teacher characteristics and personalities have often been omitted. These, as Caffyn (2011), Dyer (2010) and Rizvi (2007) suggest in other studies, are significant influences on curriculum policy processes. On this, the findings related to the specific teaching cohort at the case study schools revealed their diversity and identity, and their characteristics, matters to which the next sub-sections now turn.

8.2.5.1 Diversity and Identity of Teachers

Although the teachers had diverse backgrounds in terms of experience and personality they can generally be classified into informal 'sub-types' based on social and paedagogical alignment. The policy processes involved in the adoption of the IBPYP at the three schools was influenced by teachers of these sub-types. They consisted of friendship groups, groups based on religious affiliations, groups based on sporting connections, groups based on cultural interests, parent groups, and company groups. Also, the identification of those who fitted into the paedagogical sub-type was informed by Payne's (2005) classification of teacher types. They mirrored his 'paedagogical powerhouses' (professionally-driven), 'capricious crusaders' (those who embraced new initiatives and ideas without critique), 'teaching technicians' (sedentary staff), and 'classroom cynics'. This classification adds to the literature on 'teacher types' in mainstream classrooms, including Payne's (2005), where he identifies 'professionals, pedestrians and procrastinators'.

Taking a different view, there was a group of teachers across the case study schools who had limited experience in either remote, or international, settings and considered the process of 'becoming' an international teacher difficult. As with those teachers identified by Britzman (2003) in a different context, they were continually shaping, and being shaped by, the dynamics of social practices and structures around them; a process that Glass (2011) refers to as the constant negotiation and shaping and the 'prickly aspect' in the process of becoming a teacher. The participants in question also acted in ways that reflect the findings in the literature indicating that teachers do not all necessarily accept, or support, change without resistance (Mansfield, et al. 2012), and have difficulty examining their own teaching practices (Glass 2011; Mansfield and Volet 2010).

8.2.5.2   Characteristics of Teachers

The research at the case study sites indicated that individual teacher characteristics provided barriers to, and filters of, change and, in certain cases, restricted their ability to fully adopt the IBPYP. For some, particularly single-subject teachers, specialist teachers and experienced teachers with limited IBPYP knowledge, huge paradigm shifts were required in their ideological, paedagogical and philosophical outlook. These findings resonate with the change management literature concerning the necessity for on-going negotiation, shared leadership, and support, to develop critical and active reflectors of change when borrowing a new curriculum, or challenging ideology, paedagogy and philosophy (Grundy 1989; Phillips and Ochs 2004). They also add to the very limited research base on teacher characteristics and attitudes within international schools which have been identified as significant influences that have had an impact on curriculum policy processes (Caffyn 2011; Dyer 2010; Rizvi 2007).

8.3   Context of Policy Text Production

The second part of the policy trajectory that framed the cross-case analysis of the study being reported here is the 'context of policy text production'. The study adopted a definition of policy text as "any vehicle or medium for carrying and transmitting a policy message" (Ozga 2001, p. 33). It also adopted a view that texts represent an element of social life dialectically interconnected in a globalized world that has constructive and transformative effects on policy production, including the ability to initiate social change (Fairclough 2006). Ball (1994, p. 19) has also made the latter point, arguing that texts are physical codes, or "cannibalized products that carry meanings representative of the struggle and conflict of their production".

The cross-case analysis related to the 'context of policy text production' was informed by the above-stated positions, along with approaches to analyses of core policy texts presented by Fairclough (2003, 2006) and Pardoe and Cook (2007). Further, use was made of the mode of interview analysis about policy put forward by Grundy (1987), which revealed how policy players make meaning of such texts. The emphasis in this latter aspect of the analysis was centred on the local level. This was in recognition of the reality that while the conditions of globalization and internationalization can have an impact at all levels of the IB's policy text production, decisions taken at the local level often have the greatest impact. This is the level at which the policy message is interpreted, produced and enacted, and where conflicts, misinterpretations and negotiations take place.

The IB policy texts analysed were the *Programme Standards and Practices* (IBO 2005a), *Strategic Plan* (IBO 2005b), the *IB Learner Profile Booklet* (IBO 2003b, 2006), *Making the PYP Happen* (IBO 2004a) and the *Programme Standards and Practices* (IBO 2004b, 2005a). Each of these texts had different purposes. The *Programme Standards and Practices* documents guided the school administration personnel on how to operationalize the IBPYP policy process. The *Making the PYP Happen* (IBO 2004a, b) guided the teachers on how to operationalize paedagogy in the classroom. The attributes identified in the *IB Learner Profile Booklet* (IBO 2003b) were used to inculcate all aspects of the IB within each school community.

Keeping in mind the theoretical lenses brought to the analysis, it was deemed consistent to view these curriculum policy texts as being socially constructed, consisting of 'what' is taught or learned, as well as 'how' it is taught and learned (Cambridge 2011). The importance of recognizing 'where' (setting) the curriculum text is taught and learned (Green 2008) and 'when' (time) it is taught and learned were also acknowledged in the study. Ion this, it was deemed important to consider curriculum to be a cultural construction concerned with the experiences people have as a consequence of the existence of the curriculum. Curriculum can also relate to a package of knowledge easily transferable to cater for students who are multi-situated, or global nomads (Pollock and Van Reken 2009; Tanu 2008). The IBPYP separates the curriculum into the written, taught and assessed curriculum. A combined view on these captures the 'what, how, where and when' of curriculum and its socio-cultural construct specific to place. The IBPYP policy texts are presented as curriculum policy that combines these elements to guide enactment.

Three key themes were generated through the analysis on this matter of the context of policy text production at the school level. These themes are 'collaboration', 'community engagement', and 'interpretation'. Each theme, while having certain interconnections, will now be considered separately.

8.3.1   Collaboration

Collaboration, the first of the three themes related to the 'context of policy text production', played a significant part in the production of the IBPYP policy texts at each of the case study schools. Collaborative practices were used to interpret central and regional policy texts and produce school based policy texts. Collaborative planning was engaged in, more because it is officially required when a school decides to adopt the IBPYP, than because there was any ground-swell desire for it. This collaboration, as with any process of curriculum policy text production, involved group engagement in planning, teaching and assessment relating to the "selection, sequencing and pacing of content" (Cambridge 2011, p. 142).

Participants were aware that they were embarking on a radically new process, as opposed to following the entrenched procedures adopted at the schools in previous years. The latter point was made as follows by one participant at SIS:

> Any [*curriculum*] policy that has existed in the past has been produced in isolation, often offsite, contextually irrelevant, forgotten or fallen between the gaps of staff transiency. We were told about the red curriculum box when we arrived but the curriculum remained in the box, teachers were literally able to do what they wanted. (Anthony, SIS)

If, as has been held for decades, curriculum policy can be viewed as a body of principles that guide action, whether implicit or explicit, then the process of examining and producing versions of the three core IBPYP policy texts can be seen as a vehicle that brought the curriculum 'out of its box' at the three case study schools. While this process of school-based curriculum production took place in slightly different ways at each school, engaging in it was unavoidable due to common requirements of the IBPYP authorization process as outlined in the *Programme Standards and Practices* (IBO 2003a) document.

Schools provided planning and assessment time for pairs and groups to collaborate in the construction of units of inquiry (UOI) for the IBPYP. They found the production of these texts, which included UOI planners, to be quite demanding. Misinterpretation and uncertainty regarding what was appropriate in terms of subject matter content and paedagogy sometimes led to tension, yet was often also overcome by further negotiation and collaboration. Many were buoyed on by a perception that the IBPYP curriculum presented them with "*a total curriculum package*" (Fay, SIS), as opposed to the trial-and-error and piecemeal approach they had been in the habit of adopting in curriculum text production prior to the adoption of IBPYP. At the same time, though, many "*found it difficult to produce texts on which there was unanimous agreement*" (Barb, DIS) because of lack of clarity and variance in interpretation on specific aspects of the IB vocabulary.

Another difficulty that presented itself was the tendency in many group settings for some people to try to dominate proceedings. Thus, while all considered the collaborative planning sessions to be valuable in the policy text production stage, the pattern observed also upheld Mosen's (2006) findings, albeit for a different context, that collaboration does not necessarily come naturally for many teachers.

Not all of the teachers who participated in the study can be deemed to have been team players during the process of policy text production. Some, indeed, considered it wise to be quiet during collaborative planning sessions when constructing the UOI, or during weekly IBPYP meetings. Thus, they allowed their dominant peers to be the main players in the construction of their school's IBPYP texts, rather than engage in extensive debating, reflecting and modifying. In other words, they chose to be compliant rather than risk upsetting colleagues.

8.3.2   *Community Engagement*

Community engagement, the second of the themes related to the 'context of policy text production', also played a significant part in the production of the IBPYP policy texts at each of the case study schools. Again, this took place, not because of any great desire on the part of the participants, but because it is a requirement of the IBO that knowledge relating to local circumstances should be infused into the locally developed interpretations of the IBPYP curriculum policy texts. There is also an IBO requirement that there be a reasonable amount of engagement with the local community. On this, there was cognizance by the participants that local content should relate to matters of culture, ecology, biology, and social and political issues. The nature of what was selected was, however, restricted. A general awareness of the national geography and history of Indonesia existed, but it was evident that there was a limited knowledge of local history that could be incorporated into the programme. Also, while outreach programmes and celebrations were identified as possible ways of making connections with the local population, they became very difficult to put into practice because of an inability to identify appropriate people with whom to liaise. As a result, most of the curriculum connections established by key players in the sites were with places rather than with people.

Community engagement in the production of the IBPYP texts at the schools studied also had a language dimension to it. The staff at the schools produced language policy texts aimed at increasing the number of language lessons for various groups of students in their mother tongue, and they also aimed at providing some of these languages to others for second-language learning. Again, however, this was a response to the requirements of the IBO and its stress on the potential of learning different languages for breaking down barriers and building respect for the local host country. Indeed, the majority of teachers across all of the schools did not lead by example, as many did not make an effort to learn the host country national language, not to mention any of the local indigenous languages. Their argument was usually that their short-term stay did not warrant investing time in language learning, or that they were too old to learn a second language. As a result, the overall experience at the three sites mirrored what Davies (2006) noted in relation to international schools more widely, when he maintained that their lack of interaction with the host country was due to the failure of staff to try to overcome language and cultural barriers.

The community development aspect of policy text production at the schools corresponded with what Zhao (2010) has termed the 'three Fs'. In other words, the focus was more on festivals, food and fashion, than it was on deep cultural understandings. This proved to be an easy and non-threatening approach to take. Similar approaches have been seen in international schools in other settings characterised as being 'cultural bubbles' (Katz 2011; Pearce 1994) and 'expatriate enclaves' (Bell and Harrison 1996; Caldwell et al. 2006). Community involvement in these settings also manifested itself as being contrived in the sense of not being based on the actual experiences of teachers, or of being superficial in content and disconnected from local circumstances.

8.3.3 Interpretation

Interpretation is the third theme related to the 'context of policy text production'. Variation in interpretation of central IB policy texts was evident along the policy trajectory in relation to the case study schools. Globally, the IB website provides the IB community of learners with an ICT reference point and a professional connection. Regionally, the IB Asia-Pacific office in Singapore provides schools with a regional professional connection. At the local level, an IBPYP coordinator supports school-based personnel. At the school level, school-based policy text production occurs, where schools connect, interpret and produce policy that is specific to place. All along this trajectory, from the macro to the micro level, the transfer of knowledge that took place was filtered through the ideology of those involved in officially interpreting the IBPYP policy messages.

Three sub-themes were generated in relation to variation in interpretation at different stages in the transfer of expectations about the nature of the IBPYP between global and local levels of the policy trajectory. The first deals with compliance with non-negotiable IBO-mandated directives. The second highlights the role of the IBPYP coordinators in facilitating interpretation. The third relates to the variation in the conceptualization of international education.

8.3.3.1 Compliance with Non-negotiable IB-Mandated Directives

The macro level IBO curriculum policy text directives were presented in the *Programme Standards and Practices* (IBO 2003a, 2005a) document and its accompanying texts. These directives were non-negotiable as the documents in question set specific parameters and demand a certain amount of accountability from schools at the micro level. Each school had to establish structural processes and systemic steps for implementing the *Programme Standards and Practices* as part of the IBPYP authorization and re-authorization process. The document outlines 9 standards (S) and 120 associated practices (P). These are grouped into four categories: A. Philosophy (2 S + 19 P); B. Organization (1 S + 23 P); C. Curriculum (4 S + 68 P); and D. Student (2 S + 15 P). All four components are intricately interlinked. The 2011 version of the *Programme Standards and Practices* (IBO 2011) document has condensed the categories into three groups, namely, philosophy, organization and curriculum.

The philosophical underpinnings offered in Standard A1 and A2 of the *Programme Standards and Practices* (IBO 2003a, b, p. 4) document, called for "an alignment of school beliefs and values with IBPYP" and the "promotion of international mindedness on the part of parents and students in the community". These standards emanated from an overall ideology embedded in the policy texts that stresses the importance of human commonalities, issues that have local, national and international significance, responsible citizenship, international mindedness, and the productive use of the diversity of cultures and perspectives that exist in the school. Officially, these broad guidelines leave much to the discretion of the school and the teacher. The reality, however, is that schools, including the three case study schools, still have to plan and work within these parameters. Thus, while participants at the three schools grappled with their interpretations of the concepts, they did not have the freedom to jettison some of them and had little freedom to embrace other concepts not listed.

8.3.3.2   The Role of the IBPYP Coordinator

The IBPYP coordinator played a significant role in supporting staff with interpreting central and regional policy texts and, subsequently, in producing texts in the case study schools. During the course of the research the majority of policy players at the school level were found to be familiar with the core IBPYP texts, namely, the *IB Learner Profile Booklet* (IBO 2003b), the *Programme Standards and Practices* (IBO 2004b), *Making the PYP Happen* (IBO 2004a), and the IB website. Within the parameters outlined in the section above, there was some room for varying interpretations of these texts. This was evidenced in the case study schools. Differences in interpretation of policy texts took place particularly in relation to curriculum, paedagogy and evaluation, with the principals playing an important role in guiding the teachers toward a common understanding of these three areas.

Significant mediators in the interpretation process were the PYP coordinators, who provided schools with IBPYP content knowledge and support. In their work they encountered the paedagogical biases and personalities of the teachers and principals in the schools. This was especially so in relation to their engagement with the *Making the PYP Happen* (IBO 2004a) document, the largest and most comprehensive IBPYP policy text available to PYP teachers. One of the participants referred to it as "*the Bible for PYP teachers*" (Pat, DIS). It provided an introduction to the IBPYP trans-disciplinary, inquiry-based and concept-driven curriculum model. Each of these components of the model, however, was still open to interpretation.

One of the roles of the IBPYP coordinators in each of the three case study schools was to support staff with interpretation and in the production of core school-based texts. Initially, participants were very dependent on these IBPYP coordinators. However, while one of the three coordinators involved was experienced in the role, those at SIS and IST were inexperienced. The outcome was that while the initial focus of the two inexperienced coordinators in their respective schools was on the area of organization and structure, the experienced coordinator focussed on paedagogy and the philosophy of the IBPYP. This meant that the process of curriculum policy text production for the local circumstances in the case study schools was slower in progressing in the schools in which the inexperienced coordinators worked, than it was in the third school. Nevertheless, participants at all three schools agreed that their particular coordinator played an important role in helping them make meaning of the IBPYP curriculum policy.

Interpretation of the *IB Learner ProfileBooklet* (IBO 2003b), marketed as being a translation of the IBO's mission statement into a set of learning outcomes for the twenty-first century, proved to be the least troublesome for participants and an area in which there was consensus. Thus, it allowed the schools to go some way towards acting along the lines advocated by Gellar (2002) in relation to international schools more generally, when he argued that they should develop a statement of universal values as an essential part of their ethos. On the other hand, various curricular and paedagogical positions embedded in the IB policy texts had to be transposed into school-based policy texts. This provided much room for debate, discussion and variation in interpretation, centred in particular on the notions of 'concept-driven curriculum', 'inquiry-based learning', 'higher order thinking skills', 'trans-disciplinary approaches to learning' and 'authentic assessment'. This is not surprising since these were key expectations for authorization in the *Programme Standards and Practices* (IBO 2004b, 2005a) document. It is also consistent with views by Apple (1993, 2004), Ball (1994) and Mosen (2006) that the reading of policy texts and the commitment to enactment is no guarantee of understanding.

8.3.3.3   Variation in the Conceptualization of 'International Education'

Much has been written about international education, including its history (Sylvester 2007), its growth (Bunnell 2011; Bates 2011b) and its relationship to the IB (Bagnall 2008; Bunnell 2011). Much has also been written about such associated notions as 'international mindedness' (Gunesch 2004; Haywood 2007; Hill 2007; Marshall 2007; Rasanen 2007; Sampatkumar 2007; Sylvester 2007), 'cosmopolitanism' (Brennan 1997; Vertovech and Cohen 2002), and 'global citizenship'. Various waves of educational reform over centuries have moved from that of 'a reasoned man' in the early 1700s to 'the educated person' (Boyer 1996) and, more recently, 'the internationally minded citizen with twenty-first century competencies' (Walker 2011; Zhao 2010).

What is now center-stage in much of the IBPYP literature is the concept of 'the international minded learner'. The IBPYP gave representation to this concept in its *IB Learner Profile Booklet* (IBO 2003b, 2006, 2009). Cause (2009), speaking beyond the specific case of the three schools in this study, states that the 'learner profile' has been successful in providing a clear framework for understanding international mindedness, yet also calls for the notion to be clearly defined rather than be represented only in the form of a set of outcomes. Such a definition, she states, is essential so that the concept can speak "for any culture from anywhere in the world" (Cause 2009, p. 18).

Given reservations like the latter by authorities in the field of international education, it is not surprising that there was much debate amongst participants in the case study schools about the conceptualization of international education, international-mindedness, and the twenty-first century global citizen. In particular, many teachers struggled with defining these concepts. Again, this should hardly be surprising given the following comment by Wylie (2011, p. 37):

> There is no static definition of international education or ideological location that exists, rather a constant struggle between ideological perspectives among constituents framed by the institutional discourse of international schools, international educational organizations and curriculum authorities.

The above position was reflected in the variety of interpretations of participants in the three schools. This, in turn, meant that no clear consensus about the key concepts emerged during the process of policy text production. Indeed, it is not going too far to say that this variety mirrored Haywood's (2007, p. 85) typology of "the diverse ways in which international mindedness [or what he terms IM] can be articulated", namely, 'diplomatic IM', 'political IM', 'economic and commercial IM', 'spiritual IM', 'multicultural IM', 'human rights IM', 'pacifist IM', 'humanitarian IM' and 'environmentalist IM'.

8.4   Context of Practices

The third context of the policy trajectory that framed the conceptualization and cross-case analysis of this study is the 'context of practices'. On this, it is important to keep in mind that the IBPYP is an example of what others have termed 'paedagogical re-contextualization' (Bernstein 2000; Cambridge 2011) and provides a foundation for curriculum policy reform for schools. Such reform, in turn, however, is often accompanied by change and challenges. This manifested itself at the three case study schools in practical changes in organizational, administrative, classroom and personal level practices. In the words of Ball (1994, p. 19), what eventuated was a "translation of the crude, abstract simplicities of policy texts into interactive and sustainable practices of some sort" through "productive thought, invention and adaptation". The nature of what happened in this regard will now be considered in the form of four themes: 'changes in policy documentation', 'changes in school practice', 'changes in teacher practice' and 'changes in interaction with the local setting'.

8.4.1   Changes in Policy Documentation

The first theme on the 'context of practices' identifies changes in policy documentation in the policy process from macro to micro levels. During the time of data collection, the IB went through an era of high growth and change. Under Director General George Walker's guidance, the number of IB schools doubled, from 1,000 to 2,000 (Bunnell 2011). During this time the central office produced policy documents for application globally. These included the *IB Learner Profile*

Booklet (IBO 2006), *Programme Standards and Practices* (IBO 2003a, 2005a), and *Making The PYP Happen* (IBO 2004a). These texts were disseminated across national and regional boundaries into IB schools, including the case study schools.

At the individual school level, the case study schools were required to develop school-based policy texts and practices to reflect the new IBPYP policy documents, with their focus on philosophy, organization, curriculum and students. School-based curriculum policy texts were also evaluated and refined by referring to the *Programme Standards and Practices* (IBO 2003a, 2005a). Each case study school developed its own strategic plans outlining intended steps for implementation. On this, different discourses were found in the documents produced by the three schools, thus reflecting the different settings and the interpretations by the schools. For example, in framing its annual plan within the parameters of available finance, time and human energy, DIS was displaying what Ball and Bowe (1992) would consider to be 'limitations'. On the other hand, IST's framing of its plan around excellence, developing image and recognition through high quality teachers and resources was displaying what they would consider to be 'marketing'.

Differences in what emerged in practice in the different schools were revealed in policy documents relating to enrolment policy, school assessment and reporting policy, staff development, school budgets, resource and property development plans, and localized health and security policies. Notwithstanding differences between the three schools in this regard, there was clear similarity in two areas, namely, in the embedding of the IB vernacular and in the attention given to the Indonesian context.

At the three schools, the IB vernacular was used extensively in curriculum policy transmission. This is similar to what Fairclough (2003) and Fitz (1994) witnessed in other policy enactment studies; teachers filter the associated terminology and concepts through their own interpretive frameworks in order to put them into practice. The schools also responded to the Indonesian setting in a common way, attempting to adapt curriculum policy to local circumstances. Each school faced particular security and health issues. Policies had to be drawn up to address concerns about possible terrorist threats, evacuation, earthquake and flood response, immunization, and hygiene. The enrolment policies were also similar for some time, as only children with foreign passports were accepted into international schools. By the mid-2000s, however, IST started to accept Indonesian nationals who had a supporting letter from the Indonesian Ministry of Education. This change in policy, led to some social, cultural and economic dissent within the school, and opened up debate about elitism, bribery and inequality. This policy change at the national level precipitated curriculum policy changes at the local level in regard to enrolment policies, language policies and cultural sensitivities.

Other developments as the three case study schools went about putting the IBPYP policy into practice also displayed similarities. For example, two of the schools sought accreditation from the Western Association of Schools and Colleges (WASC) to complement their IBPYP authorization. Having to engage in both processes, rather than just one of them, was considered over-demanding by staff. Indeed, some argued that it was an unrealistic expectation on schools to meet the demands of both. Administrators at both schools also stated that they were under pressure to meet IBPYP authorization and accreditation requirements. The overall problem was partly overcome during the mid-2000s, when discussions began between the IB Asia Pacific director and WASC representatives. As a result, a joint authorization and accreditation visit was trialled in the region to help streamline the process.

Finally, changes in the approach to documenting IBPYP school-based policy were directly linked to the authorization process. This was brought about partly through the school-based professional support offered by the principal and the PYP coordinator. Another contributing feature was the embracement of professional collaboration by teachers in order to take ownership of policy texts and become active participants within the policy process. As one participant put it, "*the policy texts provided our school with processes, targets and deadlines that we had to meet, compliance was watertight, strategic planning was imperative*" (Sophie, DIS). Such developments, as the next section indicates, also influenced changes in school practices and procedures.

8.4.2   Changes in School Practice

The second theme related to the 'context of practices' is 'changes in school practice'. Policy enactment research highlights the importance of structural processes in connecting policy to practice (Fitz 1994). Such processes were adopted in the case study schools to enact the IBPYP documents. Again, certain similarities across the three sites were evident with regard to what these entailed. In particular, the initial induction to the IBPYP vernacular in each school took place through meetings, correspondence, school signage, newsletters, school assemblies, display boards, resources, planning sheets and reports. Indeed, one participant described it as being akin to attending an IBPYP 'boot camp'. Each school also took the approach of explicitly outlining milestones for enactment of the IBPYP in its school implementation plan, and of giving the IBPYP coordinator the responsibility for managing the change.

Key structural changes brought about across the schools related to timetabling, calendar decisions, professional development and evaluation. On timetables, each school allocated time for collaborative planning sessions with classroom teachers. The specialist teachers in all three cases provided the generalist teachers with the relief time necessary for engaging in the planning. This practice was problematic because the specialist teachers were not included in regular weekly planning sessions. This caused some resentment, with specialist teachers commenting that they felt they had to 'fit in' to the planning structures, rather than contribute as equals. In turn, the specialist teachers required more time from the coordinator to help make meaning of the IBPYP, as they missed out on opportunities to collaborate.

The school calendars in the three schools also had common features that regulated school practice. The international schools each averaged 180 teaching days in a school year, structured around two semesters, or four terms. Although they all followed the northern hemisphere annual calendar, there were minor differences in the length of summer and winter breaks at each site to cater for the demands of the southern hemisphere families. All calendars included Indonesian national and religious holidays, as well as American holidays. The calendars indicated when IBPYP professional development workshops and regional conferences would take place. Major curriculum events were listed, including the dates for the summative assessment of students in their final year of the IBPYP. Community functions also featured extensively on the calendars, thus reflecting the uniqueness of teaching in a remote school. On this, it is instructive to recall White et al.'s (2008) point that teachers in such circumstances tend to organize a range of events beyond school hours for the benefit of the community.

White et al. (2008) also noted that professional development can be problematic in small schools. Each of the three case study schools, however, responded to the adoption of the IBPYP by initiating a change from their former practices. The IBPYP coordinator provided the first layer of support at the schools. This involved planning with the principal, as well as modelling recommended paedagogical practices, conducting collaborative planning sessions, attending weekly staff-meetings, and providing one-on-one support for classroom and specialist teachers. External IB personnel provided a second layer of professional development, which included IBPYP in-school workshops. A third layer of professional development was available through the provision of access to IBPYP regional conferences. In the case of two of the schools, namely SIS and DIS, all staff members attended regional conferences, but only a limited number of IST staff could attend due to budget restrictions. Not all, however, responded positively. While many were happy to engage in the various levels of professional development because of personal commitment to the IBPYP, some spoke of what they termed 'the professional development regime' as being arduous, restrictive, slow and laboured, while others considered that it moved too quickly and was overwhelming. There was also much concern expressed about the amount of paperwork and planning involved in implementing the IBPYP.

Schools also moved to incorporating mechanisms for evaluation into their whole school practices. These included evaluation of the whole-school programme, of classroom level programmes and of student attainment levels. The nature of evaluation sessions was made explicit in school calendars, in implementation plans and in collaborative planning sessions. A significant amount of time and energy were also invested in engaging in these accountability processes. All three schools rewrote and implemented new school reporting procedures during the authorization process. Also, policies related to evaluation, assessment and review were accompanied by accountability practices to meet the demands of the *Programme Standards and Practices* (IBO 2003a) policy document and external accreditation requirements.

8.4.3   Changes in Teacher Practice

The third theme related to the 'context of practices' in the adoption of the IBPYP was in regard to changes in teacher practice. Here it is instructive to consider a point made by Luke (2010, p. 2):

> Official curriculum policy documents at a level of technical abstraction are remade through the lenses and practices of teachers' substantive world, field and disciplinary knowledge, then brought to life in classrooms in relation to teachers' paedagogical content knowledge and students' cultural scripts and background schemata, which include a host of other available messages of media, institutions and community cultures.

Like Luke, many contemporary authors (Brophy 1989; Egan 2001; Hayden 2006; Hayden and Thompson 2011) believe that teachers' beliefs are central in explaining and enacting their teaching practice. Furthermore, Zhao (2010) suggests that how and where teachers interpret situations determines how they construct their practice. The findings of the study of the three case study schools support such perspectives. They also indicate that once the IBPYP was adopted, two interconnected changes in teacher practices took place, namely, teachers began to engage more actively and collaboratively in the policy process than before, while they also adopted changes in their paedagogical practices.

The collaborative involvement in, and contribution of, teachers to the planning process resulted in the development of a sense of personal ownership of the classroom 'units of inquiry' and of the whole school 'programme of inquiry'. This, in turn, as one participant stated, "*improved the accountability of the teachers*" (Anne, DIS). Although many staff members complained about the time commitments and difficulty involved in working collaboratively in the planning process, they recognized that they had greater ownership of, and responsibility to, the programme than previously.

In regard to changing their paedagogy, teachers experienced difficulty initially in interpreting such essential elements of the IBPYP as the related concepts, skills, knowledge, attitudes, and action. Defining the inquiry process and concept-based approach embedded in the programme took time and involved much debate at each school. Many teachers familiar with scientific models of inquiry, or who had some experience of engaging in inquiry, translated it into a step-by-step linear process of instruction. Also, there was evidence that they experienced difficulty translating a concept-driven curriculum into practice, a matter that Erickson (2002) considers to be a common issue for many teachers.

On the other hand, the adoption of the trans-disciplinary nature of the IBPYP proved to be less problematic. One reason for this included teacher familiarity with thematic approaches. The subject-specific teachers of Language, Mathematics and Science, however, did find the conceptual leap from thematic planning to a concept-driven trans-disciplinary approach to be very difficult. This was compounded by the fact that the Science curriculum did not have a scope and sequence laid out in order to guide the teachers. All, however, developed a positive awareness of promoting 'action' as an important outcome of learning in the teaching, learning and assessment cycle. One participant summed up the general view of staff by stating:

> That's the cool thing about IBPYP because the action is so integrated into everything that we do, kids just do things and they don't feel like they need to be praised for it or need acknowledgement, is the humbling part of PYP. (Pat, DIS)

In summary, the action component of the IBPYP was considered to be its 'point of difference' compared to other curricula.

8.4.4 Changes in Interaction with the Local Setting

The fourth theme relates to changes to interaction with the local setting as being significant in the 'context of practices'. The importance of relationship building in small school communities has been reported in previous studies (Lester 2011; White et al. 2008). In practice, this is not always easy to achieve, as evident in the findings from the three case study schools. In remote centres, when tensions occur, small issues can become enlarged and emotive.

Teachers at the three schools took on a range of roles and identities in their respective small communities. Younger staff noted a lack of professional development and a lack of preparedness to engage with local communities, whilst the more experienced staff identified relationship building as a necessary skill for successfully traversing between the different roles and identities in a small community. This corresponds with Lester's (2011) study regarding relationship-building in rural areas in Australia. Her conclusions suggest that success involves educators learning together and constructing meaning and knowledge collaboratively with community members.

The IBPYP promoted a collaborative approach at the case study schools, with its continual reference to developing a 'community of learners' in its policy documents. Again, many studies reveal that the interrelationship between teacher and community includes the school playing a leading role in the community, although Lester (2011, p. 85) did find that small communities can "hold the power and teachers can be judged by how well they become part of the community". Also, as was found by White et al. (2008) in their study concerning small schools in Australia, if a school, or individual, develops connections and invests time in building relationships with the community, the teachers become more accepted and respected. Conversely, Hayden and Thompson (2011) found that when strong connections are not made, teachers' lack of knowledge about local settings could distort the 'real' meaning of 'place' in host countries.

A common practice adopted at the three case study schools to connect them with the local setting was to include local issues within the curriculum content of the school's 'units of inquiry'. Nevertheless, connecting with local issues was fraught with difficulty. The situation was particularly problematic regarding the incorporation of environmental and economic issues surrounding mines (SIS, DIS). Pupils were able to visit the mines and discuss their history and the process of mining, but any issues surrounding social inequality, environmental responsibility, and politics, had to be promoted in a positive light, or ignored. The mining companies were extremely generous in their support for the schools. However, the power inequity that existed between them had an effect on the curriculum procedures and practices adopted within the schools. The following comment from the educational advisor for SIS outlines his perception of the impact of the uneven power differential on him:

> I require political astuteness in this position, I need to be able to identify key players, set boundaries and realize and be happy with the freedom provided knowing that the executive and their wives have the power to veto any of my suggestions or decisions. (Bo, SIS)

Also, although all policy players understood this governance process, it was not necessarily fully supported. One participant's comment reflected the sense of restriction when he stated: *"You don't bite the hand that feeds you?"* (Ken, SIS). The resultant power inequity ensured compliance.

8.5 Context of Outcomes

Thus far, the comparative analysis on the case study schools has described a complex, dynamic and evolving IBPYP policy process, shaped by an interaction of diverse influences, policy text production, and practices. The analysis now moves to those broader issues identified in Ball's (1994, 2006) policy analysis framework as 'context of outcomes' and 'political strategies'. In the study, these two contexts were combined to reflect their close interconnectedness. The consideration of them here under the single title of 'context of outcomes' provides a focus for considering the 'big picture' issues related to power differentials in the policy process by reflecting on the results of the study in the light of the works of Ball (1994, 2006), Ozga (2001), Rizvi and Lingard (2010), Vidovich (2007) and others. These authors are concerned with investigating the impact of policies on inequalities and social justice, the key focal points of critical theory. Furthermore, they emphasize how both policy processes and outcomes are complex, messy and contested.

The ensuing analysis is structured around four major themes. Each theme relates specifically to the three case study schools, while also raising wider issues connected to 'big picture' policy outcomes. The themes are as follows: 'the persistence of power inequalities', 'conceptualizing international education', 'adapting to remoteness', and 'changes following the adoption of IBPYP'. Each of these is now considered in turn.

8.5.1 The Persistence of Power Inequalities

There is a need to critically consider the impact of power relationships (Davies 2006) within international schooling in general as well as at the case studies in particular. Issues of power were embedded along the policy trajectory, at the IB headquarters, at the regional IB office, at the Indonesian national context, within the school community, and between members of the teaching cohort. Also, power inequities were revealed across the different contexts and levels of the policy trajectory.

Individual and group power-plays that featured in the micro-political environment of schools influenced the curriculum policy processes. The 'power of the individual' was evident as tensions, negotiations and power struggles in the creation and enactment of policy, while the 'power of the group' became evident in collaboration, negotiation and power inequities in economic, cultural, friendship, political and paedagogical groups. Specific examples of power inequities at the micro level were those related to self-interest groups. The groups revealed themselves at each case study site and were represented as powerful teaching couples, company couples, 'de-facto executives' and personal alliances. This supports other findings related to self interest groups found in large international schools (Caffyn 2011).

Because of the small school settings of each case study school, a strong individual voice had the capacity to become an interest group of two. If one or two joined forces, the group had the capacity to become an influential majority voice, bringing with it associated power. Furthermore, the power struggles associated with group dynamics and micro-politics involving professional and personal interrelationships in these small settings were felt in all facets of the curriculum policy process.

Social justice issues surrounding the multicultural nature of the international schools and the settings in which they were located were revealed. These related to cultural differences, religious differences, political differences, and gender of the workforce, within these settings. The findings resemble studies that describe international schools as 'cultural bubbles' (Pearce 1994), removed from the local culture that surrounds them. The hierarchical structure of mining communities within these settings also revealed issues of inequities related to position and power.

Analysis from macro or global, to micro or local, levels of the IBPYP curriculum policy process revealed political and social inequities related to power that had an impact on the curriculum policy trajectory embedded in the global IB headquarters, IB regional office, Indonesian policies and international schools. The 'power of the organization' was to be seen in economic, environmental, cultural and power differentials being balanced in company-owned and company-managed schools. The 'power of the nation' was evident in new government policy directed by the Indonesian Ministry of Education in response to the growing number of international schools in the region. The 'power of the region' was evident in negotiations with the IB Asia Pacific Office. The 'power of the global arena' was reflected in non-negotiable aspects of the IB organization's mandated policy texts. Its demands were embedded in the IBPYP authorization process and facilitated through globalization and internationalization forces such as technology and mass communication.

The *Programme Standards and Practices* (IBO 2003a) and the *IB Learner Profile* (IBO 2003b) documents were powerful curriculum policy texts and tools in promoting the IB ideology along the length of the policy trajectory. IBO texts "position the IBO as a pedagogic re-contextualising agency" (Cambridge 2011, p. 143) in that they force teachers to change paedagogy and practice by aligning to IBPYP policy demands. The re-conceptualization of paedagogy and practice through the IB revealed a dichotomy of influence and power. On the one hand, the IBPYP advocated a 'bottom-up' approach to policy development, with flexibility to meet local needs and to include local content. On the other hand, it emphasised a 'top-down' model of delivery, with little flexibility being available on such matters as the design of the UOI unit planners and the paedagogical demands of the inquiry approach and concept-based learning. These tensions reflected a global policy trend referred to as 'steering from a distance' (Mosen 2006), where organizations monitor policies and practices in schools through stringent processes of accountability that promote social change.

8.5.2   Conceptualising International Education

The social constructs of 'international mindedness' or 'global citizen', as has already been pointed out, falls within the social and cultural dimensions of globalization (Nye 2002, 2006; Bottery 2006). The desire to create a global perspective in learners is "a distinctly culture-bound exercise" (Schweisfurth 2006, p. 42) embedded with power inequities and social justice concerns. In the policy processes investigated in this study, the intent to be internationally minded was identified as a powerful reason for enacting the IB ideology in the three schools studied, yet it was difficult to conceptualize. The IBPYP policy texts were interrogated to reveal their philosophical and paedagogical biases. The investigation revealed social justice issues related to a perceived 'western viewpoint' of its content. This included a focus on such 'western paedagogical practices' as collaborative planning, inquiry-based learning and a trans-disciplinary approach to curriculum design. In a global world where the IBPYP is being enacted in a range of 'eastern' countries, this can be problematic.

Another social debate surrounding the IBPYP relates to issues of exclusiveness, or contestation over the programmes, because their complexity is seen to reinforce the existing economic and social privilege of the emerging middle class elites (Cambridge 2011; Doherty 2009; Hahn 2003). This is witnessed by the large number of middle class, English-speaking IBPYP teachers and the number of middle class, English-speaking communities that adopt the IBPYP. These patterns are challenged by the international-mindedness ideology embedded in the *Learner Profile*.

Over the last twenty years the *Learner Profile* has surfaced as the ideological core for the IBPYP programme. It embodies international mindedness and has emerged as a transferable ideal, or value, that transcends place. Indeed, it can be argued that the IBLP is more transferable than the IB programmes because it is an inclusive construct, where the discrete set of ten attributes can be readily adopted by students, parents and even non-IB teachers.

The 'expressive order values' associated with transmission of conduct, character and manner (Bernstein 2000; Cambridge 2011) is reflected in the international curriculum and curriculum policy embedded in the IBPYP and the *Learner Profile*. Yet, as Cause (2009) suggests, it needs further definition. This was found to be case in relation to the three case study schools, where international mindedness emerged as an internationally inclusive product, or ideal, that was interpreted by, and accessible to, all. Yet, it was also something over which participants continued to struggle in their efforts to form their own conceptualization of it. The struggle continued at the time this research was being completed, and was accompanied by a struggle to conceptualize two related concepts that were emerging, namely, 'rural-mindedness' for those in remote schools and 'expat-mindedness' in the case of international schooling more broadly. Each of these social constructs relate to power inequities and social justice issues imposed on 'others' in the world of international schools and they cause tension with the development of 'international mindedness'.

8.5.3   Adapting to Remoteness

Remoteness and isolation are ambiguous concepts as they can transcend place and simply refer to a sense of space and consciousness (Green 2008). Conversely, they can refer to situated geographical location. The majority of international schools are considered isolated educational entities in the first sense (Cambridge 2011). Although they are predominately located in large metropolitan, or regional, centres, they can stand as isolated enclaves removed from surrounding educational systems. Most international schools are predominately 'steered from a distance' (Mosen 2006) and managed by a large organization, religious body or national curriculum. Issues of isolation for international schools are further compounded when an international school is located in such isolated settings geographically, as are the case study schools.

International schools can experience similar issues to schools found in remote areas. Common issues experienced in each setting which are associated with the exercise of power include attraction and retention of staff, professional isolation, limited resources, lack of access to professional development and technologies, micro-political stresses related to interpersonal relationships and inequities, frac-tionalization of staff, and self-interest groups. Schools and their in-situ culture are a unique maze of power relationships, environmental pressure, personal histories and significant events (Caffyn 2011, p. 72). Such a maze can evoke power differences and compound issues related to social justice. In the case study schools they were influenced by personality and interpersonal relationship skills, knowledge about others, perspectives on others, and attitudes toward others.

These sensitivities to local settings were highlighted in Lester's (2011) findings about successful leadership in rural and remote areas. Any significant change at the school level, he argued, requires community approval and involvement. Further, in a remote setting, acceptance is often personal in focus. For example, teachers in smaller centres have a relationship role of ambassador, or leader, with the local community, unlike in urban schools where teachers can choose to engage, or not to.

Participants commented on the fact that building personal, collegial and community relationships were central to gaining acceptance and ensuring support. However, this support was unpredictable and easily removed. Participants noted that community support was based on particular events, circumstances, perspectives and relationships. This can highlight the power base of the community over that of the school.

The importance of place, the nexus between host country and expatriate community, and the relative power base of each was significant in the curriculum policy process under investigation, particularly in terms of the context of influences and the context of practices. Connections and disconnections with the local community relied on cultural understandings, technological advances and personal desire. The ability to traverse between multiple identities, hybrid cultures and interpersonal relationships in an environment that lacks confidentiality or anonymity is difficult and problematic. Add to this the changing structure, purpose and demographic pattern of remote communities worldwide and it becomes further complicated. The power inequities and social justice issues that arise from living in remote communities where space, power and communication are intermingled can also have an impact on curriculum policy processes.

8.5.4   Changes Following the Adoption of the IBPYP

In a globalized world full of technological change it is hardly surprising that the study of the three case study schools identified change and change agents as significant features of the IBPYP policy process, thus supporting Rizvi and Lingard's (2010, p. 1) belief that "policy studies as a field is inextricably linked to the processes of change". This is a study that fore-grounded the impact of globalization and internationalization influences on international education, schools, teachers and communities. Such forces of globalization include technological advances, ease of transportation and communication. These were all cited at the case study schools as catalysts for the changing face of international schools, teachers and students, including the enactment of the IBPYP. This finding reflects discourses surrounding the changing pattern of international education in general (Bagnall 2008; Bates 2011b; Cambridge 2011; Hayden and Thompson 2011). The power of globalization was recognized as forging continuous change even in isolated international schools in Indonesia.

In the study, there were many change agents along the policy trajectory. At the macro level, the Director of the IB and Head Office staff were influential in managing change. At the meso level, the regional office staff provided external support to those working at the case study sites, and the Indonesian Education

Department invoked state requirements. At the micro level, the IBPYP coordinator was identified as a significant change agent in the local world of the IBPYP. Overall, the power of significant people as change agents along the policy trajectory was evident in policy texts, policy processes and practices employed in the authorization process of enacting IBPYP.

Also, the relationship at each school between the principal and the IBPYP coordinator was a determining factor in the success of IBPYP enactment. The centrality of the teachers as change agents was highlighted and reinforced. Their personality, background experiences and paedagogical biases informed their actions and their involvement in the micro political world of schools. In general terms, their actions were related to those personal characteristics identified by Stirrat (2008), as 'missionary', 'mercenary', 'maverick', or 'misfit', and to those teacher 'types' identified by Payne (2005) as 'paedagogical powerhouse', 'capricious crusader', 'teaching technician' or 'classroom cynic'.

8.6 Conclusion

The cross-case analysis reported in this chapter has drawn together the major themes that emerged from previous chapters in which the case study schools were considered separately. This chapter has provided insight into how teachers and educators along the policy trajectory made meaning of the IBPYP. It has done so particularly by focusing the analysis on the contexts of influences, policy text production and practices. Attention has also been given to the context of outcomes to reveal 'bigger picture' issues of power and social justice along the curriculum policy trajectory.

At this point it is important to recall two points made at the beginning of the chapter. First, when undertaking the analysis, sight was not lost of the fact that, in reality, the various 'contexts' are multi-faceted, multi-dimensional and inherently interrelated. Secondly, account was taken of Vidovich's (2007) position on the importance of considering the global, national and local aspects of each context.

Overall, the 'horizontal' (cross-case) analysis of the IBPYP policy trajectory under investigation are in harmony with Gale's (1999) notion of policy as embodying ideologies, texts and discourses. In other words, they combined those aspects of the policy process identified by Kenway (1990) as 'the why', 'the what', and 'the how', with the stress Taylor et al. (1997) also place on asking 'why now?' and 'with what consequences?' The study also highlighted the important aspects of 'when' (time) and 'where' (place) to the analysis of policy processes.

Power inequities and social justice issues involved in the adoption, production and enactment of the IBPYP by the three remote international schools in Indonesia that were studied, were found along the policy trajectory. The next chapter, Chap. 9, now draws the book to a conclusion. It recalls the research aim and questions and presents the findings as a series of propositions. It then discusses implications for theory, for practice, and for further research.

References

Apple, M. W. (1993). The politics of official knowledge: Does a national curriculum make sense? *Discourse, 14*(1), 1–16.

Apple, M. W. (2004). *Ideology and curriculum*. New York: Routledge Falmer.

Azano, A. (2011). The possibility of place: One teacher's use of place-based instruction for English students in a rural high school. *Journal of Research in Rural Education, 26*(10), 1–12.

Bagnall, N. F. (2008). *International schools as agents for change*. New York: Nova Science Publishers.

Ball, S. J. (1994). *Education reform: A critical and post-structural approach*. Buckingham: Open University Press.

Ball, S. J. (2006). *Education policy and social class: The selected works of Stephen J. Ball*. Abingdon: Routledge.

Ball, S., & Bowe, R. (1992). Subject departments and the 'implementation' of national curriculum policy: An overview of the issues. *Journal of Curriculum Studies, 24*(2), 97–115.

Banks, M. (2008). Modern Ireland: Multinationals and multiculturalism. *Information, Society and Justice, 2*(1), 63–93.

Bates, R. (Ed.). (2011a). *Schooling internationally: Globalisation, internationalisation and the future for international schools*. Abingdon: Routledge.

Bates, R. (2011b, July). *Learning to teach internationally: What international teachers need to know*. Paper presented at the Australian Teacher Education Association Annual Conference Melbourne.

Beck, U. (2006). Reflexive governance: Politics in the global risk society. In J. P. Vob, D. Bauknecht, & R. Kemp (Eds.), *Reflexive governance for sustainable development* (pp. 31–56). Cheltenham: Edward Elgar.

Bell, M. P., & Harrison, D. A. (1996). Using intra-national diversity for international assignments: A model of bicultural competence and expatriate adjustment. *Human Resource Management Review, 6*(1), 47–74.

Bernstein, B. B. (2000). *Paedagogy, symbolic control, and identity: Theory, research, critique*. Lanham: Rowman & Littlefield.

Bottery, M. (2006). Education and globalization: Redefining the role of the educational professional. *Educational Review, 58*(1), 95–113.

Boyer, F. L. (1996). The commitment to character: A basic priority for every school. *Update on Law-Related Education, 20*(1), 4–8.

Brennan, T. (1997). *At home in the world: Cosmopolitanism now*. Cambridge: Harvard University Press.

Britzman, D. P. (2003). *Practice makes practice: A critical study of learning to teach*. Albany: SUNY Press.

Brophy, J. E. (1989). *Advances in research on teaching: A research annual*. Greenwich, CT: JAI Press.

Brown, C., & Lauder, H. (2011). The political economy of international schools and social class formation. In R. Bates (Ed.), *Schooling internationally: Globalisation, internationalisation and the future for international schools* (pp. 39–58). Abingdon: Routledge.

Bunnell, T. (2007). The international education industry: An introductory framework for conceptualizing the potential scale of an 'alliance'. *Journal of Research in International Education, 6*(3), 349–367.

Bunnell, T. (2011). The International Baccalaureate and 'growth scepticism': A 'social limits' framework. *International Studies in Sociology of Education, 21*(2), 161–176.

Caffyn, R. (2007). The micropolitics of international schools. *Journal of Research in International Education, 6*(3), 382.

Caffyn, R. (2011). International schools and micropolitics: Fear, vulnerability and identity in fragmented space. In R. Bates (Ed.), *Schooling internationally: Globalisation, internationalisation and the future for international schools* (pp. 59–82). Abingdon: Routledge.

Caldwell, M., Blackwell, K., & Tulloch, K. (2006). Cosmopolitanism as a consumer orientation: Replicating and extending prior research. *Qualitative Market Research: An International Journal, 9*(2), 126–139.

Cambridge, J. (2002). Recruitment and deployment of staff: A dimension of international school organization. In M. Hayden, J. Thompson, & G. Walker (Eds.), *International education in practice: Dimensions for national and international schools* (pp. 158–169). London: Kogan Page.

Cambridge, J. (2011). International curriculum. In R. Bates (Ed.), *Schooling internationally: Globalisation, internationalisation and the future for the international schools* (pp. 121–147). Abingdon, Oxford: Routledge.

Canterford, G. (2003). Segmented labour markets in international schools. *Journal of Research in International Education, 2*(1), 47–65.

Cause, L. (2009). International mindedness and 'social control'. *Asian Social Science, 5*(9), 32–46.

Davies, J. (2006). Affinities and beyond!! Developing ways of seeing in online spaces. *E-Learning, 3*(2), 217–234.

Doherty, C. (2009). The appeal of the International Baccalaureate in Australia's educational market: A curriculum of choice for mobile futures. *Discourse, 30*(1), 73–89.

Dyer, J. (2010, February). *Global education: Travel and new imaginaries for teachers' work.* Paper presented at Social Educators Association of Australia National Conference, Adelaide.

Egan, K. (2001). Why education is so difficult and contentious. *Teachers College Record, 103*(6), 923–941.

Erickson, H. L. (2002). *Concept-based curriculum and instruction: Teaching beyond the facts.* Thousand Oaks: Corwin Press.

Fail, H. (2011). Teaching and learning in international schools: A consideration of the stakeholders and their expectations. In R. Bates (Ed.), *Schooling internationally: Globalisation, internationalisation and the future for international schools* (pp. 101–120). Abingdon: Routledge.

Fairclough, N. (2003). *Analysing discourse: Textual analysis for social research.* London: Routledge.

Fairclough, N. (2006). *Language and globalization.* Abingdon: Taylor & Francis.

Fitz, J. (1994). Implementation research and education policy: Practice and prospects. *British Journal of Educational Studies, 42*(1), 53–69.

Gale, T. (1999). Trajectories: Treading the discursive path of policy analysis. *Discourse, 20*(3), 393–407.

Garton, B. (2000). Recruitment of teachers for international education. In M. Hayden & J. Thompson (Eds.), *International schools and international education: Improving teaching, management and quality* (pp. 85–95). London: Kogan Page.

Gellar, C. (2002). International education's internationalism: Inspirations from cosmopolitanism. In M. Hayden, J. Thompson, & G. Walker (Eds.), *International education in practice* (pp. 90–99). London: Kogan Page.

Giddens, A. (1994). *Beyond left and right: The future of radical politics.* Cambridge: Polity Press.

Glass, C. (2011). There's not much room for anything to go amiss: Narrative and arts-based inquiry in teacher education. *Issues in Educational Research, 21*(2), 130–144.

Green, B. (Ed.). (2008). *Spaces and places: The NSW rural (teacher) education project.* Wagga Wagga: Charles Sturt University, Centre for Information Studies.

Gruenewald, D. A. (2003). Foundations of place: A multidisciplinary framework for place-conscious education. *American Educational Research Journal, 40*(3), 619–654.

Grundy, S. (1987). *Curriculum: Product or praxis?* Abingdon: Routledge Falmer.

Grundy, S. (1989). Beyond professionalism. In W. Carr (Ed.), *Quality in teaching: Arguments for a reflective profession* (pp. 68–86). Sussex and Philadelphia: The Falmer Press.

Grundy, S. (2002). Big change questions – Is large-scale educational reform possible? *Journal of Educational Change, 3*(1), 55–62.

Gunesch, K. (2004). Education for cosmopolitanism. Cosmopolitanism as a personal cultural identity model for and within international education. *Journal of Research in International Education, 3*(3), 251–275.

Hahn, A. M. (2003). *The Intersection of language, power and international education: A critical discourse analysis of the International Baccalaureate Organization.* New York: Teachers College, Columbia University.

Hardman, J. (2001). Improving recruitment and retention of quality overseas teachers. In S. Blandford & M. Shaw (Eds.), *Managing international schools* (pp. 123–135). London: RoutledgeFalmer.

Hayden, M. (2006). *Introduction to international education.* London: Sage.

Hayden, M. C., & Thompson, J. (2011). Teachers for the international school of the future. In R. Bates (Ed.), *Schooling internationally: Globalisation, internationalisation and the future for international schools* (pp. 83–100). Abingdon: Routledge.

Haywood, T. (2007). A simple typology of international-mindedness and its implications for education. In M. Hayden, J. Thompson, & J. Levy (Eds.), *The Sage handbook of research in international education* (pp. 79–89). London/Thousand Oaks/New Delhi: Sage.

Held, D., McGrew, A., Goldblatt, D., & Perraton, J. (1999). *Global transformations: Politics, economics and culture.* Cambridge: Polity Press.

Hill, I. (2007). International education as developed by the International Baccalaureate Organization. In J. Thompson, M. Hayden, & J. Levy (Eds.), *The SAGE handbook of research in international education* (pp. 25–38). London: Sage.

IBO. (2003a). *Programme standards and practices.* Cardiff: IBO. www.ibo.org/documentlibrary/programmestandards. Accessed 30 Mar 2006.

IBO. (2003b). *IB learner profile booklet.* Cardiff. IBO. www.ibo.org/ibla/conference/.../TheLearnerProfileinActionFabian.ppt Accessed 30 March 2006

IBO. (2004a). *Making the PYP happen: A curriculum framework for international primary education.* Cardiff: IBO. www.ibo.org/documentlibrary/programmestandards/ Accessed 3 Mar 2006.

IBO. (2004b). *Programme standards and practices.* Cardiff: IBO. www.ibo.org/documentlibrary/programmestandards. Accessed 4 Sept 2006.

IBO. (2005a). *Programme standards and practices.* Cardiff: IBO. www.ibo.org/documentlibrary/programmestandards/documents/progstandards.pdf. Accessed 4 Sept 2006.

IBO. (2005b). *Strategic plan.* Cardiff: IBO. www.ibo.org/product_info.php?products_id=1626. Accessed 6 May 2007.

IBO. (2006). *IB learner profile booklet.* Cardiff. IBO. www.ibo.org/ibla/conference/.../TheLearnerProfileinActionFabian.ppt. Accessed 16 Nov 2007.

IBO. (2009). *IB learner profile booklet.* Cardiff: IBO. www.ibo.org/programmes/profile/documents/Learnerprofileguide.pdf. Accessed 14 June 2010.

IBO. (2010). *Intercultural understandings: Muslim contexts.* www.ibo.org/programmes/profile/documents/Learnerprofileguide.pdf. Accessed 9 Apr 2011.

IBO. (2011). *Programme standards and practices.* Cardiff: IBO. www.ibo.org/documentlibrary/programmestandards. Accessed 24 June 2012.

James, C. R., Connolly, M., Dunning, G., & Elliott, T. (2005). *How very successful primary schools work.* London: Sage.

Katz, M. (2011). *The price of citizenship.* Philadelphia: University of Pennsylvania Press.

Kenway, J. (1990). *Gender and education policy: A call for new directions.* Melbourne: Deakin University.

Kenway, J., Epstein, D., & Boden, R. (2005). *Building networks.* New York: Sage.

Lester, N. C. (2011). Relationship building: Understanding the extent and value. *Education in Rural Australia, 21*(1), 79–93.

Luke, A. (2010). Will the Australian curriculum up the intellectual ante in primary classrooms? *Professional Voice, 8*(1), 41–47.

MacDonald, J. (2006). The international school industry: Examining international schools through an economic lens. *Journal of Research in International Education, 5*(2), 191–213.

Mansfield, C. F., & Volet, S. E. (2010). Developing beliefs about classroom motivation: Journeys of preservice teachers. *Teaching and Teacher Education, 26*(7), 1404–1415.

Mansfield, C., Beltman, S., Price, A., & McConney, A. (2012). Don't sweat the small stuff: Understanding teacher resilience at the chalkface. *Teaching and Teacher Education, 28*(3), 357–367.

Marginson, S., & Rhoades, G. (2002). Beyond national states, markets, and systems of higher education: A glonacal agency heuristic. *Higher Education, 43*(3), 281–309.

Marshall, H. (2007). The global education terminology debate: Exploring some of the issues. In M. Hayden, J. Thompson, & J. Levy (Eds.), *The Sage handbook of research in international education* (pp. 38–50). London: Sage.

Marshall, H. (2011). Instrumentalism, ideals and imaginaries: Theorising the contested space of global citizenship education in schools. *Globalisation, Societies and Education, 9*(3–4), 411–426.

Mok, K. H., & Welch, A. (Eds.). (2003). *Globalization and educational restructuring in Asia and the Pacific region.* New York: Palgrave Macmillan.

Mosen, L. (2006). *Meeting the needs of students at educational risk: A policy process.* Perth: University of Western Australia.

Nye, J. (2002). Transnational relations, interdependence and globalization. In M. Brecher & F. P. Harvey (Eds.), *Millennial reflections on international studies* (pp. 165–175). Ann Arbor: University of Michigan Press.

Nye, J. (2006). *The hidden transcripts of ESL writers: Four longitudinal case studies on the experiences and perceptions of ESL and generation 1.5 students acquiring academic literacy at the community college.* Unpublished PhD thesis, Indiana University of Pennsylvania, Indiana, PA.

Ozga, J. (2001). Policy research in educational settings: Contested terrain. *Journal of Education Policy, 16*(1), 85–87.

Pardoe, I., & Cook, R. D. (2007). A graphical diagnostic for variance functions. *Australian and New Zealand Journal of Statistics, 49*(3), 241–250.

Payne, L. I. (2005). The discourse of development in school governance. *Issues in Educational Research, 15*(2), 156–174.

Pearce, R. (1994, November). Globalization: Learning from international schools. *Mobility,* pp. 27–29.

Pearce, R. (2011). When borders overlap: Composite identities in children in international schools. *Journal of Research in International Education, 10*(2), 154–173.

Phillips, D., & Ochs, K. (2004). Researching policy borrowing: Some methodological challenges in comparative education. *British Educational Research Journal, 30*(6), 773–784.

Pinar, W. (Ed.). (2003). *International handbook of curriculum research.* Mahwah: Taylor & Francis.

Pinar, W. (2004). *What is curriculum theory?* Mahwah: Lawrence Erlbaum.

Pollock, D. C., & Van Reken, R. E. (2009). *Third culture kids: The experience of growing up among worlds.* Boston: Nicholas Bearley.

Quist, I. (2005). The language of international education: A critique. *IB Research Notes, 5*(1), 2–6.

Rasanen, R. (2007). International education as an ethical issue. In M. Hayden, J. Thompson, & J. Levy (Eds.), *The Sage handbook of research in international education* (pp. 57–69). Thousand Oaks: Sage.

Reid, J. A., Green, B., White, S., Cooper, M., Lock, G., & Hastings, W. (2008, December). *New ground in teacher education for rural and regional Australia: Regenerating rural social space.* Paper presented at the AAREIEC Conference, Australian Association for Research in Education, Brisbane, Australia.

Rizvi, F. (2007). Internationalization of curriculum: A critical perspective. In M. Hayden, J. Thompson, & J. Levy (Eds.), *The Sage handbook of research in international education* (pp. 390–403). Thousand Oaks: Sage.

Rizvi, F., & Lingard, B. (2005). Globalization and education: Complexities and contingencies. *Educational Theory.* doi:10.1111/j.1741-5446.2000.00419.x/full

Rizvi, F., & Lingard, B. (2010). *Globalizing education policy.* London: Taylor & Francis.

Roberts, B. (2003). What should international education be? From emergent theory to practice. *International Schools Journal, 22*(2), 69–79.

Sampatkumar, R. (2007). Global citizenship and the role of human values. In M. Hayden, J. Thompson, & J. Levy (Eds.), *The Sage handbook of research in international education* (pp. 70–78). London: Sage.

Schweisfurth, M. (2006). Education for global citizenship: Teacher agency and curricular structure in Ontario schools. *Educational Review, 58*(1), 41–50.

Siniscalco, M. T. (2002). *Gender balance of the teaching workforce in publicly funded schools.* Edinburgh: Scottish Government Publications.

Sklair, L. (2001). *The transnational capitalist class.* Malden: Blackwell.

Spring, J. (2009). *Globalization of education: An introduction.* New York: Taylor and Francis.

Stake, R. E. (1995). *The art of case study research.* Thousand Oaks: Sage Publications.

Steiner-Khamsi, G. (Ed.). (2004). *The global politics of educational borrowing and lending.* New York: Teachers College Press, Columbia University.

Stirrat, R. (2008). Mercenaries, missionaries and misfits: Representations of development personnel. *Critique of Anthropology, 28*(4), 406–425.

Sylvester, R. (2007). Historical resources for research in international education. In M. Hayden, J. Thompson, & J. Levy (Eds.), *The Sage handbook of research in international education* (pp. 185–195). London: Sage.

Tanu, D. (2008, July). *Global nomads: Towards a study of Asian third culture kids.* Paper presented at 17th Biennial Conference of the Asian Studies Association of Australia, Melbourne, Australia.

Taylor, S., Rizvi, F., Lingard, B., & Henry, M. (1997). *Educational policy and the politics of change.* London: Routledge.

Vertovech, S., & Cohen, R. (2002). Introduction. In S. Vertovech & R. Cohen (Eds.), *Conceiving cosmopolitism – Theory, context and practice* (pp. 1–24). Oxford: Oxford University Print.

Vidovich, L. (2007). Removing policy from its pedestal: Some theoretical framings and practical possibilities. *Educational Review, 59*(3), 285–298.

Vidovich, L. (2013). Policy research in higher education: Theories and methods for globalising times? In J. Huisman & M. Tight (Eds.), *Theory and method in higher education research.* London: Emerald Press.

Walker, G. (2004). *To educate the nations: Reflections on an international education.* Great Glemham: Peridot Press.

Walker, G. (2011). *East is East and West is West.* Geneva: International Baccalaureate Organisation.

White, S., Green, B., Reid, J. A., Lock, G., Hastings, W., & Cooper, M. (2008, July). *Teacher education for rural communities: A focus on incentives.* Paper presented at the Australian Teacher Education Conference, Sunshine Coast, Australia.

Wylie, J. (2006). Cultural geographies in practice smoothlands: Fragments/landscapes/fragments. *Cultural Geographies, 13*(3), 458–465.

Wylie, M. (2011). Global networking and the world of international education. In R. Bates (Ed.), *Schooling internationally: Globalisation, internationalisation and the future for international schools* (pp. 21–38). Abingdon: Routledge.

Zhao, Y. (2009). *Catching up or leading the way: American education in the age of globalization.* Alexandria: Association for Supervision & Curriculum Development.

Zhao, Y. (2010). Preparing globally competent teachers: A new imperative for teacher education. *Journal of Teacher Education, 61*(5), 422–431.

Chapter 9
Conclusion

9.1 Introduction

> If we limit ourselves to examining only those policies and practices that are of direct and immediate relevance to education policy or practice, we run the real risk of neglecting the level at which the agenda for education policy is actually set (Bottery 2000, pp. 1–2).

A lesson to be learned from the above quotation is that it is essential to include a global orientation to curriculum policy analysis so as to capture the multiple and interconnecting worlds that have an impact on, surround, influence and set the agendas for, education policy. Although the study reported in this book was primarily about micro level policy actors making meaning of the IBPYP in remote international schools in Indonesia, and the micro-politics involved in how curriculum policy was enacted in these schools, cognizance was taken of the importance of accompanying meso (national and regional) and macro (global) level contexts and influences embedded in the policy processes (Marginson and Rhoades 2002; Ozga 2001; Rizvi and Lingard 2010; Winter 2012). The study findings help to fill gaps in the fields of international and remote education by identifying how different contexts drive policy processes, and highlighting the interconnectivity that can potentially exist between them.

The complexities of globalization, including the global trend towards internationalizing school curriculum (Yang 2005) and the marketization of education, are transforming twenty first century education policy agendas. The study was conceptualized against this backdrop. In doing so, it responded to concerns that critical analysis of policy is disappearing from policy work under the prevailing economic ideology associated with globalization and internationalization (Bates 2011; Ozga 2001).

This final chapter is structured in four sections following this introduction. The next section is an overview of the study. It returns to the research questions and

© Springer International Publishing Switzerland 2014   187
S. Ledger et al., *Global to Local Curriculum Policy Processes*,
Policy Implications of Research in Education 4, DOI 10.1007/978-3-319-08762-7_9

presents a total of 15 propositions generated from the findings. The following section identifies the key 'policy threads' revealed through the meta-analysis across the entire policy trajectory. The next section again section reflects on the research process undertaken and draws conclusions regarding implications for policy and practice. The final section discusses possibilities for future research.

9.2 Overview

The aim of the study which constitutes the core of this book was to explore the dynamics of curriculum policy processes involved in the adoption, production and enactment of the International Baccalaureate Primary Years Programme (IBPYP) in three remote international schools in Indonesia. The research aim was explored through a set of research questions based on the conceptualization of policy analysis as a 'trajectory study'. Vidovich's (2007) policy trajectory approach derived from Ball's (1994, 2006) policy model was used to this end. It incorporates both the macro constraints (wider policy agendas) and the micro agency of policy actors within individual educational institutions. The policy analysis examined the ongoing inter-relatedness across the differing levels and contexts of curriculum policy processes.

A qualitative research approach was adopted in undertaking the research. An interpretive methodology was used to collect data on how policy actors made meaning of policy in the case study schools. Empirical data were collected by means of semi-structured and focus group interviews and an analysis of key IBPYP documents. Critical theory offered a complementary approach to facilitate meta-analysis and examine power relationships within the curriculum policy processes investigated.

The research questions guided data collection and analysis along the policy trajectory, from the global world of the IB and globalization, to the regional and national worlds of the IB Asia Pacific regional office and the Indonesian Ministry of Education, through to the local world of remote international schools in Indonesia. Following cross-case analysis at the micro level, a meta-analysis, from macro to micro levels, revealed 'bigger picture' patterns of power flows though the curriculum policy trajectory under investigation.

In all, 15 propositions were generated in the meta-analysis. These highlight key themes in regard to the adoption, production and enactment of IBPYP curriculum policy processes in remote international schools in Indonesia. The propositions have been organized under the four policy contexts that constitute the policy trajectory framework (Ball 1994; Vidovich 2007) namely, the contexts of influences, policy text production, practices and outcomes.

9.2.1 *Context of Influences*

> Research Question One: What were the key influences that had an impact on the initiation of curriculum policy reform at the case study schools?

Five major inter-connected themes were generated in regard the 'context of influences' related to adopting the IBPYP at the case study schools. These are 'globalization', 'global branding', 'IBPYP as a unifying package', 'local politics and practices' and 'teachers' backgrounds and characteristics'. These themes informed the generation of the following propositions in relation to Research Question One:

1.1 Globalization forces such as technological advances had an impact on all contexts and levels along the IBPYP policy trajectory and helped facilitate the transmission of curriculum policy from global to school levels.
1.2 In an educational market economy, the global currency of the IBPYP and its 'recognized brand' was a powerful influence on each school's decision, which varied from school to school, to adopt curriculum reform. This process was supported by the role of the IBPYP regional office in the expansion of IBPYP schools in the region to 'franchise the brand'.
1.3 There were different rationales for adopting IBPYP, but schools were fundamentally influenced by a desire to disconnect with state or nation-based curricula and provide a unifying package for curriculum policy reform.
1.4 The schools were places of social and political complexity that resulted in different influences coming to bear on curriculum policy reform, particularly in company owned schools, which were characterized by power inequities.
1.5 The personal and professional diversity and identities of teachers had a significant impact on curriculum policy processes, particularly in small, remote international schools.

9.2.2 *Context of Policy Text Production*

> Research Question Two: What were the key features of the curriculum policy texts in the case study schools and how were they produced?

In relation to Research Question Two, three key themes were generated from the findings in relation to the 'context of policy text production'. These are 'collaboration', 'community engagement' and 'interpretation'. They, in turn, informed the generation of the following propositions:

2.1. 'Collaboration' was a significant feature in the production of the IBPYP curriculum policy texts at the school level but collaboration did not come naturally, nor was it embraced by all parties.
2.2. Socio-cultural 'power bubbles' and the 'powerful voices' within the groups in the international school communities created unequal access to participation and influence in curriculum policy production.
2.2. The IBPYP coordinators played a central role in coordinating policy text production at the school level. They had a key position moderating the interpretations and re-conceptualizations of IBPYP policy messages, pedagogies and ideologies by local policy actors to ensure essential elements and basic tenets of the programme were transferred.

9.2.3 Context of Practices

Research Question Three: What policy practices were evident in the case study schools?

The findings related to the 'context of policy practices' centred on changes that took place in the case study schools, including changes in administration and classroom practices. The nature of these changes can be considered in the form of four themes which were generated: 'changes in policy documentation', 'changes in school practice', 'changes in teacher practice' and 'changes in interaction with the local setting'. These themes, in turn, informed the generation of the following propositions in relation to Research Question Three:

3.1 The IBPYP authorization process mandates change in policy documentation and practice at the school level to align with the IB *Programme Standards and Practices* document, yet it was evident that what is mandated can be open to misinterpretation.
3.2 The *IB Learner Profile* was a powerful tool for disseminating IBPYP values, beliefs, language and practices at the school level and was used to inculcate the IBPYP vernacular into all facets of policy practice. At times, however, connections were forced and misleading.
3.3 The IBPYP authorization process required teachers to become active participants in the policy process. These processes, pedagogies and philosophies were difficult to interpret and enact.
3.4 The mandated inclusion of community engagement in the IBPYP curriculum planning documents encouraged teachers to connect with the local community. These connections, however, relied on key players and could be tenuous and ad-hoc, rather than sustainable.

9.2.4 *Context of Outcomes*

> Research Question Four: What were the longer term outcomes and implications of curriculum policy reform for the case study schools, international education and remote education?

The findings related to the 'context of outcomes' centred on four key themes; 'power inequalities', 'conceptualising of international education', 'adapting to remoteness' and 'change for schools adopting the IBPYP'. These themes informed the generation of the following propositions in relation to Research Question Four.

4.1 Power inequities and struggles persisted across all contexts and levels of the IBPYP policy trajectory, partly as a result of globalization and marketization forces, as well as issues surrounding interpersonal relationships, and philosophical and paedagogical priorities. Within this context teachers were amongst the least powerful policy actors, when, arguably, they should have been amongst the most powerful.

4.2 Conceptualizing international education is a value-laden exercise. The IB interpretation of international education for primary schools, namely the IBPYP, has emerged as a desirable commodity in the global enterprise of international education. It was recognized at the three case study schools that its global cachet can be used as a 'marketing tool' for schools to attract teachers, validate the curriculum and minimize national curriculum biases.

4.3 The three schools served to illustrate that the changing face of international schools can provide a cultural melting pot of globalized views in a localized setting, where multiple and hybrid identities co-exist. Power and social inequities were often exacerbated in the remote school settings, causing clashes of culture and magnification of difference. At the same time, there were indications that they also had the potential to empower marginalised policy actors.

4.4 The IBPYP has attempted to change perceptions of the social inequities and 'eliteness' of its policies. The indications from the case study schools, however, are that, within a globalized world, policy and policy actors can still reflect middle-class, English speaking biases at all levels of the policy trajectory.

The 15 propositions outlined above are offered to assist others in their reflections on the development of theory, policy and practices, and to assist them in future research. Regarding the global level, the propositions reflect the impact of globalization, modernization and change (Rizvi and Lingard 2010; Zhao 2010). Regarding the regional and national level, they reflect issues surrounding educational change management (Fullan 2001) and concepts of 'steering from a distance' (Mosen 2006). Regarding the local level, they are place-based (Gruenewald 2003; Van Eijk 2010), where the specific settings 'matter' in policy decisions (Reid et al. 2009) and where the need for the centrality of teachers in curriculum policy processes is highlighted (Brophy 1989; Egan 2001; Hayden 2006; Hayden and Thompson 2011).

9.3   Policy Threads

An examination of the themes and propositions explicated in the previous section reveals a number of important 'policy threads' that can act as policy change agents and can weave their way through the entire curriculum policy trajectory. These policy threads will be referred to as the 5 Ps: people, place, philosophy, processes and power. They are interconnected and interdependent, binding together the different contexts and levels of the IBPYP policy process. The following section now highlights the significance and interrelatedness of each policy thread, and links each back to the literature.

9.3.1   People

The factors presented under the policy thread of 'people' position teachers as significant players in the growing global enterprise of international education (Zhao 2010). The powerful role individual 'people' play in the policy processes was evident at all levels of the policy trajectory, from global to local. At the macro level, the IB governing board were global change agents in the policy process, while the IB Asia Pacific office personnel were regional change agents. Key people involved in supporting local level policy enactment were the principals and the IBPYP coordinator. Each policy actor plays a pivotal role in IBPYP policy adoption, production and enactment. However, the focus of this study was predominately on the school level where the centrality of teachers lies at the heart of any policy reform (Ornstein and Hunkins 2004; Sungaila 1992).

Five sub-threads related to 'people' were identified: the profile of international teachers, reasons why people enter international schooling, paedagogical alignment of educators, interpersonal relationships, and leadership roles. First, teachers' interpretation of policy and involvement in the policy process was significant. Consideration of 'who teachers are' (Dyer 2010; Hardman 2001), requires recognition of their individual attributes, character and personality. Profiling international teachers, however, is problematic given the ambiguity surrounding the term, the borderless nature of the world that currently exists, the transient nature of teachers and the lack of systems-level data.

Secondly, as teachers are cultural products related to where they were prepared as teachers, and where they were brought up (Walker 2004), their backgrounds and the reasons why they enter the international schooling arena are powerful factors that can have an impact on curriculum policy processes. Studies concerning expatriate aid and development workers (Stirrat 2008) indicate commonalities related to the teachers in the remote schools reported in this study. Stirrat (2008), in his anthropology of expatriates, classified them based on their backgrounds and reasons why they chose to work in certain locations.

Thirdly, the power of paedagogical alignment of teachers can have an impact on the micro level of curriculum policy enactment. A robust body of research confirms that teacher quality contributes to the quality of education on offer (Kaplan and Owings 2002; Glass 2011). The re-conceptualization of paedagogy and practice required by the IBPYP proved difficult for some teachers. A significant proportion of these teachers found it challenging to "piece all the IBPYP bits together" (Fay, SIS).

Fourthly, interpersonal relationship skills had a significant impact on the policy process. On this, the findings support the work of Zhao (2010), who advocates that global competence is required in order to interact with others and traverse between different worlds and identities. The suggestion is that success is dependent on personality and interpersonal relationship skills, knowledge about others, perspectives on others, and attitudes toward others (Zhao 2010).

Fifthly, the people in leadership roles were identified as powerful change agents in the curriculum reform process along the policy trajectory. This finding resonates with change management literature surrounding the adoption of curriculum reform (Caffyn 2011; Grundy 1989).

9.3.2 Place

The policy thread of 'place' can denote both context (Reid et al. 2008) and consciousness. The significance and importance of the social construct of 'place' along the whole policy trajectory was confirmed in the study. International schools in general have a unique sense of place because they are often removed from the national and local settings in which they are positioned. The situation has been described as 'cultural bubbles' (Katz 2011; Pearce 1994), 'atolls in a coral sea' (Allen 2002), and 'expatriate enclaves' (Bell and Harrison 1996; Caldwell et al. 2006). On this, the isolated world of large international schools described by the writers outlined above which gave rise to their generation of particular terminology, resembles the isolated world of small remote international schools investigated in this study, thus helping to diminish a perceived disparity between international and remote schools.

The study also revealed a range of insights into teachers' living and working conditions in remote international schools in Indonesia and their correspondence to findings by White et al. (2008) from remote school settings in Australia. Again, it forces one to cogitate the presentation of international education in a positive, global light, as opposed to the presentation of remote education through a deficit perspective (Cornish 2009; Down and Wooltorton 2004; Lock et al. 2009). The disparity that is promoted perpetuates biased assumptions about each field and reduces the possibility of cross fertilisation of ideas taking place between them.

9.3.3 Philosophy

The policy thread of 'philosophy' plays a significant role in influencing policy processes throughout the trajectory across global, regional, national and local levels. Philosophy influences the way the IBPYP is interpreted and enacted by individuals and groups. In particular, the study highlighted the power of technology and mass communication in transmitting the IBPYP philosophical underpinnings along the policy trajectory to small international schools.

The philosophical underpinnings surrounding the IBPYP educational discourses relate to 'international mindedness' and 'global citizens'. These concepts are not new in the history of international education, but the discourses have changed from the desire to develop a 'reasoned man', to that of developing a 'socially responsible person', or 'world citizen', to exploring 'the person within' and the natural curiosities of an 'educated person'. The current call is to produce a 'twenty first century global citizen' with 'twenty first century competencies'. On this, 'international mindedness' is not a new construct, but one that continues to be re-conceptualized.

The philosophical base of the IBPYP curriculum is reflected in its embedded pedagogies. The constructivist, concept-driven, inquiry-based, trans-disciplinary nature of the IBPYP has been informed by educators such as Boyer (1996) in curriculum design, by Erickson's (2002) concept-based approach, and by Wiggins and McTighe's (2005) assessment processes. How the philosophical underpinnings embedded in these discourses are interpreted along the policy trajectory, however, depends on the subjectivities of policy enactors (Marshall 2011).

9.3.4 Processes

The policy thread of 'processes' relates to managing and facilitating curriculum policy change. The processes were key factors in determining how the IBPYP policy was translated into practice at the case study schools. The study captured the filtering process involved along the IBPYP policy trajectory into local school practice. It was at the local level that formal and informal processes were developed to support the enactment of the IBPYP. The interconnectivity of processes, including the 5Ps, had an impact on the micro-political landscape of the schools.

The IBPYP authorization process provided schools with a systemic process to facilitate policy governance, accountability and enactment for schools. The process of re-contextualizing IBPYP paedagogy and practice in the case study schools revealed tensions at the micro level. This re-conceptualizing process was embedded in the global policy trend referred to as 'steering from a distance' (Mosen 2006), a process employed by bigger companies, organizations and education departments to monitor policies and practices through stringent processes of accountability.

Many teachers across the sites were new to international schooling. Eventhough they were considered experienced in their home countries, the policy processes were challenging for some of them. Furthermore, the policy processes involved in adopting the IBPYP in schools also resembles the process of 'policy borrowing' that occurs at a national level. In particular they correspond to the four-stages of 'policy borrowing' presented by Phillips and Ochs (2004), namely, policy attraction, decision-making, implementation, and internationalization, have similarities to Ball's (1994) conceptualization of the policy trajectory framework that guided the study.

9.3.5 Power

A critical examination of the policy thread of 'power' is particularly important in a world where migration is leading to the emergence of complex cultural identities (Davies 2006). Power inequities were found in the study in all facets of the IBPYP policy process involved, from the macro level organizational changes of the IB through to the employment practices in schools in relation to expatriate, local and indigenous staff. Complex connections, multiple perspectives and differences contributed to such power differentials. These reflected findings indicating that while individual and group power-plays can exist at each level of the policy process, they are heightened and more complex at the micro-political level (Caffyn 2011). When global and local cultural, social, economic and personal ideals and beliefs clash, or differ, tensions and power inequities are witnessed. Ignoring such complexity silences the interconnectedness between people and policy at the global, regional, national and local levels.

In regard to the global level of the policy trajectory, power issues are particularly associated with the marketization of education. International education is part of a global education industry driven by economic rationalization and an increasing number of mobile middle class workers (Bates 2011). This is evidenced by the exponential growth of international schools and burgeoning associated organizations linked to international schooling. The IB and its recognized global brand is well positioned within this field (Wylie 2011), as was recognized by the authorities at the case study schools.

In regard the 'regional' level, power inequities between the case study schools and regional office personnel were manifested during the authorization process. The mandated criteria and inflexibility of the authorization process at times resulted in conflict, confusion and compromise at the local level. In economic terms, the IB office could be seen as playing a role in the franchising of the IBPYP within the Asia Pacific region. The high turn-over of staff at the regional office also had an impact on relationships along the policy trajectory.

At the 'national' level, Indonesia instigated new government policy relating to employment, customs and education that had an impact on the living and working conditions of teachers from overseas at the case study schools. Policies related to customs changed after the Bali bombings of 2002 and caused angst for expatriate workers. Since then, educational policy changes have been made in response to the growing number of international schools in the region in regard to classification and enrolment (Kristiansen and Pratikno 2006). Furthermore the Indonesian Ministry of Education's push to internationalize the Indonesian national curriculum commenced during this time.

In regard to the 'local' level, power differentials and social inequities became evident at the case study schools during times of decision-making, collaboration and negotiation. Cultural, self-interest and paedagogical differences had an impact on the policy processes and on the living and working conditions of the employees. This reflects research highlighting the complexity of power struggles associated with group dynamics and micro-politics encountered in small settings (Caffyn 2011). The case studies also revealed that the power differentials and socio-cultural inequities associated with the company-owned schools occurred in all contexts and levels of the policy process.

9.4   Implications for Policy and Practice

The findings have implications for policy and practice related to the three fields that guided this study, namely policy processes, international education and remote education. While the specific implications in this regard outlined below focus on the IBPYP policy actors and their actions, they should also be of broader interest for those involved in other curriculum policy areas.

9.4.1   Implications for the IBYP at the Global Level

There are implications for IBPYP management decisions related to policy design, structures and processes for transference of policy, adequate staffing and financial accountability in a borderless changing world of migrating middle-class workers where the global marketization, modernization and commodification of education exists. Globally, the IBO faces a challenge to balance the 'educational' demands of the IBPYP and the 'economic' demands of a global educational market. The exponential growth in the number of schools adopting the IBPYP, while reflecting its global cachet, raises concerns about quality assurance methods and marketization.

The global role of the IBO is to provide organizational structures and processes to ensure that the IBPYP policy message is transmitted and policy actors have a shared vision of the IBPYP along the policy trajectory. At the macro level, decisions should focus on easing the transition of teachers into 'becoming' IBPYP teachers at the micro level. Although currently the process is facilitated by clearly articulated IBPYP policy documents, variance in interpretation is prevalent. Mandated professional development workshops are left to individual presenters to design and can result in paedagogical and philosophical discordance. Also, policy texts are only translated into three languages yet many countries have adopted the programme.

Globalization and technological advances have the capacity to intensify power inequities as well as address social reform. This also has significant implications for the IB. It is well positioned in the global education market and as such it has the capacity to address these issues. As a global leader in international education, it is important for the IBO to ensure that the IB's curriculum policy and processes are inclusive and their philosophical and paedagogical foundations are not produced to favour a particular population. The IB curriculum policy decisions need to be scrutinized for the 'good of education' in a similar way to how the 'Learner Profile' is scrutinized for the 'good of the student'.

Globalization forces such as technology and mass communication have allowed the practice of 'curriculum policy borrowing', as well as 'curriculum policy copying', to occur in international settings. International curricula have emerged that resemble many elements of the IBPYP curriculum, yet are marketed under different brands. This policy 'copying' has implications for IB management in regard to intellectual property, including issues surrounding copyright.

Globally, the IBO invests in maintaining a registry of IB Diploma students that have passed through its programme, but it has no similar method for tracking, or monitoring, IB teachers. A system-level registry of teachers would also be of assistance in informing discussions on professional development, leadership and quality assurance. Further, it would be of assistance in identifying future research possibilities.

9.4.2 Implications for the IBYP at the Regional Level

With the commodification of the IBPYP in the international education market and the increasing number of schools adopting it in the Asia Pacific region, the Asia Pacific regional office and its employees are emerging as significant actors in the IBPYP policy process. Not only is it the conduit between the IB head office and the IBPYP schools, it is influential in guiding the IBPYP authorization process for these schools. Through default, it has taken on a marketing role in the enterprise of international education in the region, by promoting professional development opportunities and resources at major educational conferences. The resulting tension between balancing economic and educational outcomes has implications for both its integrity and its future growth.

The IB regional office also plays a significant role as a catchment, or nurturing ground, for future IB leaders. Those successful in obtaining positions in the IB Asia Pacific regional office have moved on to take up senior leadership roles in international schools around the globe, or in private enterprise. However, the high rate of staff turnover can have a negative impact on the relationships developed between the regional office and the schools. The regional office should consider developing succession plans that are sustainable, transparent and inclusive. In the case of the case study schools, the role of the 'regional' context proved significant along the policy trajectory. This indicates that policy actors need to pay close attention to this regional construct when producing, planning and enacting policy.

9.4.3   Implications for the IBPYP at the Local Level

The case study schools are unique in that they are three remote international schools. Although there are many remote schools and international schools around the world, there is a limited, but growing, number of remote international schools. The findings from the case studies have implications for policy design and analysis in regard to such schools. The geography, ecology, economy, governance and population structure within these settings situate, and have an impact on, policy processes at a local level. Therefore close attention to these factors is required when producing, planning and enacting policy in such settings.

The terms 'collaboration' and 'shared responsibility' which are embedded in the IBPYP curriculum policy, have implications for leadership and management strategies in schools. Awareness of group dynamics and individual teacher traits has policy implications for management structures, leadership styles and organizational processes. Furthermore, cognisance needs to be taken of the reality that while the non-negotiable blueprint for authorized schools presented in the *Programme Standards and Practices* (IBO 2003) document directs decision-making in regard to resourcing, timetabling and management of IBPYP schools, balancing these demands at the local level, particularly in a remote setting, is a complex process.

The concept-driven, inquiry-based, trans-disciplinary approach embraced by the IBPYP curriculum policy also requires that paedagogical changes and interpretations occur at the local level. But, with paedagogical change, comes new points for debate, discussion, misinterpretation, resistance, and compromise. On this, an awareness of the paedagogical biases of teachers could help school leaders develop policy practices to guide paedagogical reforms that more accurately address the capacities and subjectivities of their unique cohort of teachers.

It is at this micro-political context of schools that individuals and group dynamics reveal strong personal barriers, filters and beliefs about the IBPYP that have implications for policy practices. Teachers in the twenty first century need to be equipped with skills that cater for the changing population in their classrooms. Policy actors along the trajectory need to ensure they address issues related to how to 'internationalize the curriculum', to an understanding of how to teach 'English as a Foreign Language', and to an increased understanding of 'socio-cultural differences and similarities'. Policy decisions that address these three factors need to be taken, with the aim of better preparing pre-service teachers for the international face of education and benefiting the IBPYP in their professional development offerings.

9.4.4   Implications for Future Research

The findings from the three case studies also raise a number of issues related to the intersection of policy processes, international education and remote settings that would benefit from further research. These relate to the profiling of international teaching cohorts, the relationship between teachers' backgrounds and remote teaching, the importance of setting, international education, and remote education.

9.4.4.1 Profiling International Teaching Cohorts

The results of the three case studies highlight the need for future research related to profiling teachers working in international schools in order to help capture and understand their background, paedagogical biases, personality traits and career trajectories. Similar findings by others have sparked interest in educational research to explore the anthropology of teachers (Anderson-Levitt 2003; Bradley and Levinson 2011; Odland and Ruzicka 2009) and the ethnography of teachers (Frank 1999; Green and Bloome 1997; Woods 2002) to help generate understanding of international teachers. The centrality of teachers in policy-making decisions is significant, yet complex. Thus, further understanding and critique in the field are required. The teachers in international schools have profiles to share and stories to tell related to enacting policy and to their involvement in the policy process. By understanding the complexities and interrelationships that international teachers bring to the world of the IBPYP, associated problems and challenges can be anticipated and addressed.

9.4.4.2 Relationship Between Teachers' Backgrounds and Remote Teaching

The findings from the study revealed a relationship between those teachers who had previous experience living in rural and remote contexts and those who were teaching in the three Indonesian international schools. The majority of teachers across all three sites had either grown up in small, rural settings, or were from transient family backgrounds. Further research is required to see if this relationship also exists in teaching cohorts in other international schools, or in schools in rural and remote settings more generally.

9.4.4.3 Importance of Setting

The findings highlighted the importance of 'setting' in the policy process, including the importance of paying attention to a 'regional' construct along the policy trajectory. It shows the significance of the integral role of place and space in the policy process, rather than its traditional role as a descriptive backdrop (Green 2009). Although Ball's (1994, 2006) conceptualization of policy identifies settings under 'context of influences', it is recommended that it be addressed separately in policy analyses in order to capture the uniqueness of place and its interconnectedness with all other policy contexts. Such closer scrutiny of 'setting' could provide insights into undiscovered power and social inequities within the policy process.

9.4.4.4 International Education

Further research on issues surrounding the socially constructed label of international education is required. Constructions of international education need to be unwrapped, re-conceptualized and rebuilt in ways that more accurately reflect the changing world around us. This includes paying attention to issues surrounding technological advances, marketization and internationalization of education, conditions related to living and working in international schools, misinterpretation of culture, and the micro-political world of international school settings, including the notion of 'international mindedness' and 'expat-mindedness'. Research on these issues could contribute to a better understanding of the living and working conditions of communities that form the micro-political world of international schooling. In particular, it could serve to highlight the complexities faced by policy actors in planning, producing and enacting policy processes in these settings.

Further investigation is also required into the impact that a borderless educational world has on 'place' and 'identity' for teachers and students. Technologies have facilitated individualized educational practices, transnational education, borderless schools and virtual classrooms. These changes could force a re-conceptualization of education and schooling for the future. Thus, more research is needed that explores the different reasons why schools engage with international education in both developed and developing countries. The study reported here revealed that the IBPYP served a purpose in minimising a connection to a national identity, developing a shared policy vision for the schools and attending to attraction and retention of teachers to 'short-term stay' locations. Future investigation of these matters might reveal recurring patterns. Finally, further research related to the conceptualization of international mindedness and global competencies would benefit schools and students in navigating through the ever-changing environment in which they exist.

9.4.4.5 Remote Education

International education in remote school communities is an under-researched area that requires further examination. The study reported here challenges the negative and deficit perspectives often portrayed in discourses surrounding rural education, in contrast to the more positive discourses surrounding international education. Research on 'rural-mindedness' in order to highlight positive elements related to living and working in remote school communities is necessary to give a more balanced view of their unique contexts. Also, the impact of globalization in such settings warrants investigation to monitor how "local histories, cultures and politics mediate the effects of globalisation discourses" (Winter 2012) in such sites.

References

Allen, K. (2002). Atolls, seas of culture and global nets. In M. C. Hayden, J. J. Thompson, & G. Walker (Eds.), *International education in practice: Dimensions for national and international schools* (pp. 112–135). London: Kogan Page.

Anderson-Levitt, K. M. (2003). *Local meanings, global schooling: Anthropology and world culture theory*. New York: Palgrave Macmillan.

Ball, S. J. (1994). *Education reform: A critical and post-structural approach*. Buckingham: Open University Press.

Ball, S. J. (2006). *Education policy and social class: The selected works of Stephen J. Ball*. Abingdon: Routledge.

Bates, R. (Ed.). (2011). *Schooling internationally: Globalisation, internationalisation and the future for international schools*. Abingdon: Routledge.

Bell, M. P., & Harrison, D. A. (1996). Using intra-national diversity for international assignments: A model of bicultural competence and expatriate adjustment. *Human Resource Management Review, 6*(1), 47–74.

Bottery, M. (2000). *Education, policy and ethics*. London: Continuum International Publishing Group.

Boyer, E. L. (1996). The commitment to character: A basic priority for every school. *Update on Law-Related Education, 20*(1), 4–8.

Bradley, A., & Levinson, M. (2011). *A companion to the anthropology of education*. London: Blackwell Publishing.

Brophy, J. E. (1989). *Advances in research on teaching: A research annual*. Greenwich: JAI Press.

Caffyn, R. (2011). International schools and micropolitics: Fear, vulnerability and identity in fragmented space. In R. Bates (Ed.), *Schooling internationally: Globalisation, internationalisation and the future for international schools* (pp. 59–82). Abingdon: Routledge.

Caldwell, M., Blackwell, K., & Tulloch, K. (2006). Cosmopolitanism as a consumer orientation: Replicating and extending prior research. *Qualitative Market Research: An International Journal, 9*(2), 126–139.

Cornish, L. (2009). Creating knowledge for action: The case for participatory communication in research. *Development in Practice, 19*(4–5), 665–677.

Davies, J. (2006). Affinities and beyond!! Developing ways of seeing in online spaces. *E-Learning, 3*(2), 217–234.

Down, B., & Wooltorton, S. (2004). Beginning teaching in rural-remote schools: Implications for critical teacher development. *Change: Transformations in Education, 7*(1), 31–46.

Dyer, J. (2010, February). *Global education: Travel and new imaginaries for teachers' work*. Paper presented at Social Educators Association of Australia National conference, Adelaide.

Egan, K. (2001). Why education is so difficult and contentious. *Teachers College Record, 103*(6), 923–941.

Erickson, H. L. (2002). *Concept-based curriculum and instruction: Teaching beyond the facts*. Thousand Oaks: Corwin Press.

Frank, C. (1999). *Ethnographic eyes: A teacher's guide to classroom observation*. Portsmouth: Heinemann.

Fullan, M. (2001). *The new meaning of educational change*. New York: Teachers College Press.

Glass, C. (2011). There's not much room for anything to go amiss: Narrative and arts-based inquiry in teacher education. *Issues in Educational Research, 21*(2), 130–144.

Green, B. (Ed.). (2009). *Understanding and researching professional practice*. Rotterdam: Sense Publishers.

Green, J., & Bloome, D. (1997). Ethnography and ethnographers of and in education: A situated perspective. In J. Flood, S. Brice Heath, & D. Lapp (Eds.), *Handbook of research on teaching literacy through the communicative and visual arts* (pp. 181–203). Mahwah: Lawrence Erlbaum Associates.

Gruenewald, D. A. (2003). Foundations of place: A multidisciplinary framework for place-conscious education. *American Educational Research Journal, 40*(3), 619–654.

Grundy, S. (1989). Beyond professionalism. In W. Carr (Ed.), *Quality in teaching: Arguments for a reflective profession* (pp. 68–86). Sussex\Philadelphia: The Falmer Press.

Hardman, J. (2001). Improving recruitment and retention of quality overseas teachers. In S. Blandford & M. Shaw (Eds.), *Managing international schools* (pp. 123–135). London: RoutledgeFalmer.

Hayden, M. (2006). *Introduction to international education*. London: Sage.

Hayden, M. C., & Thompson, J. (2011). Teachers for the international school of the future. In R. Bates (Ed.), *Schooling internationally: Globalisation, internationalisation and the future for international schools* (pp. 83–100). Abingdon: Routledge.

IBO. (2003). *Programme standards and practices*. Cardiff: IBO. www.ibo.org/documentlibrary/programmestandards/. Accessed 30 Mar 2006

Kaplan, L. S., & Owings, W. A. (2002). *Teacher quality, teaching quality, and school improvement*. Bloomington: Phi Delta Kappa International.

Katz, M. (2011). *The price of citizenship*. Philadelphia: University of Pennsylvania Press.

Kristiansen, S., & Pratikno, S. (2006). Decentralising education in Indonesia. *International Journal of Educational Development, 26*(5), 513–531.

Lock, G., Reid, J. A., Green, B., Hastings, W., Cooper, M., & White, S. (2009). Researching rural-regional (teacher) education in Australia. *Education in Rural Australia, 19*(2), 31–44.

Marginson, S., & Rhoades, G. (2002). Beyond national states, markets, and systems of higher education: A glonacal agency heuristic. *Higher Education, 43*(3), 281–309.

Marshall, H. (2011). Instrumentalism, ideals and imaginaries: Theorising the contested space of global citizenship education in schools. *Globalisation, Societies and Education, 9*(3–4), 411–426.

Mosen, L. (2006). *Meeting the needs of students at educational risk: A policy process*. Perth: University of Western Australia.

Odland, G., & Ruzicka, M. (2009). An investigation into teacher turnover in international schools. *Journal of Research in International Education, 8*(1), 5–29.

Ornstein, A. C., & Hunkins, F. P. (2004). *Curriculum foundations, principles, and issues* (4th ed.). Boston: Allyn and Bacon.

Ozga, J. (2001). Policy research in educational settings: Contested terrain. *Journal of Education Policy, 16*(1), 85–87.

Pearce, R. (1994, November). Globalization: Learning from international schools. *Mobility*, 27–29, np.

Phillips, D., & Ochs, K. (2004). Researching policy borrowing: Some methodological challenges in comparative education. *British Educational Research Journal, 30*(6), 773–784.

Reid, J. A., Green, B., White, S., Cooper, M., Lock, G., & Hastings, W. (2008, December). *New ground in teacher education for rural and regional Australia: Regenerating rural social space*. Paper presented at the AAREIEC conference. Brisbane: Australian Association for Research in Education.

Reid, J., Green, B., White, S., Cooper, M., Lock, G., & Hastings, W. (2009, May). *Understanding complex ecologies in a changing world*. Paper Presented at the AERA annual conference. Denver: American Educational Research Association.

Rizvi, F., & Lingard, B. (2010). *Globalizing education policy*. London: Taylor & Francis.

Stirrat, R. (2008). Mercenaries, missionaries and misfits: Representations of development personnel. *Critique of Anthropology, 28*(4), 406–425.

Sungaila, H. (1992). Educational reform and the new 'theory of chaos'. In F. Crowther & D. Ogilvia (Eds.), *The new political world of educational administration* (pp. 69–87). Hawthorn: Australian Council for Educational Administration.

Van Eijk, G. (2010). Exclusionary policies are not just about the 'neoliberal city.': A critique of theories of urban revanchism and the case of Rotterdam. *International Journal of Urban and Regional Research, 34*(4), 820–834.

Vidovich, L. (2007). Removing policy from its pedestal: Some theoretical framings and practical possibilities. *Educational Review, 59*(3), 285–298.

Walker, G. (2004). *To educate the nations: Reflections on an international education.* Great Glemham: Peridot Press.

White, S., Green, B., Reid, J. A., Lock, G., Hastings, W., & Cooper, M. (2008, July). *Teacher education for rural communities: A focus on "incentives."* Paper presented at the Australian Teacher Education conference, Sunshine Coast, QLD, Australia.

Wiggins, G. P., & McTighe, J. (2005). *Understanding by design.* Upper Saddle River: Pearson Education.

Winter, C. (2012). School curriculum, globalisation and the constitution of policy problems and solutions. *Journal of Education Policy, 27*(3), 295–314.

Woods, P. (2002). Teaching and learning in the new millennium. In C. Sugrue & C. Day (Eds.), *Developing teachers and teaching practice: International research perspectives* (pp. 73–91). New York: RoutledgeFalmer.

Wylie, M. (2011). Global networking and the world of international education. In R. Bates (Ed.), *Schooling internationally: Globalisation, internationalisation and the future for international schools* (pp. 21–38). Abingdon: Routledge.

Yang, R. (2005). Internationalisation, indigenisation and educational research in China. *Australian Journal of Education, 49*(1), 66–88.

Zhao, Y. (2010). Preparing globally competent teachers: A new imperative for teacher education. *Journal of Teacher Education, 61*(5), 422–431.

Index

© Springer International Publishing Switzerland 2014
S. Ledger et al., *Global to Local Curriculum Policy Processes*,
Policy Implications of Research in Education 4, DOI 10.1007/978-3-319-08762-7

Printed by Printforce, the Netherlands